Learn Azure Administration

Solve your cloud administration issues relating to networking,
storage, and identity management speedily and efficiently

Kamil Mrzygłód

BIRMINGHAM - MUMBAI

Learn Azure Administration

Commissioning Editor: Vijin Boricha
Acquisition Editor: Rohit Rajkumar
Content Development Editor: Nihar Kapadia
Senior Editor: Rahul Dsouza
Technical Editor: Cleon Baretto
Copy Editor: Safis Editing
Project Coordinator: Neil Dmello
Proofreader: Safis Editing
Indexer: Manju Arasan
Production Designer: Aparna Bhagat

First published: September 2020

Production reference: 1210820

Published by Packt Publishing Ltd.
Livery Place
35 Livery Street
Birmingham
B3 2PB, UK.

ISBN 978-1-83855-145-2

www.packt.com

To Klaudia – for being here.

– Kamil

Packt.com

Subscribe to our online digital library for full access to over 7,000 books and videos, as well as industry leading tools to help you plan your personal development and advance your career. For more information, please visit our website.

Why subscribe?

- Spend less time learning and more time coding with practical eBooks and Videos from over 4,000 industry professionals

- Improve your learning with Skill Plans built especially for you

- Get a free eBook or video every month

- Fully searchable for easy access to vital information

- Copy and paste, print, and bookmark content

Did you know that Packt offers eBook versions of every book published, with PDF and ePub files available? You can upgrade to the eBook version at www.packt.com and as a print book customer, you are entitled to a discount on the eBook copy. Get in touch with us at customercare@packtpub.com for more details.

At www.packt.com, you can also read a collection of free technical articles, sign up for a range of free newsletters, and receive exclusive discounts and offers on Packt books and eBooks.

Contributors

About the author

Kamil Mrzygłód is an independent consultant working with some of the biggest companies from several industries on their cloud architectures and technology adoption. He is an expert in Microsoft Azure and Microsoft technologies, and he has twice been recognized as a Microsoft MVP in the Microsoft Azure category; he is also a Microsoft Certified Trainer.

Writing a book is not easy, but making it something worth reading is especially difficult. Many thanks to all the editors and reviewers for hours spent fixing my mistakes, typos, and unclear sentences. As always, I want to thank Klaudia for her support and patience.

About the reviewers

Alexey Bokov is an experienced Azure architect and has been a Microsoft technical evangelist since 2011. He works closely with top-tier Microsoft customers all around the world to develop applications based on Azure. Building cloud-based applications in the most challenging circumstances is his passion, as well as helping the development community to upskill and learn new things in a hands-on way. He's a long-time contributor to many Azure books as a co-author and reviewer and speaks from time to time at Kubernetes events.

> *I'd like to thank my family – my beautiful wife, Yana, and my amazing son, Kostya, who support my efforts to help authors and publishers.*

Marcondes Alexandre is a skilled database analyst and architect in the cloud computing field. He is focused on delivering fast, reliable, and flexible cloud solutions based on Azure and the Microsoft data platform. He has spoken at multiple conferences and meetups on Microsoft technologies. He has experience in deployment, maintenance, and migration projects from SQL Server databases to on-premises and cloud scenarios, being recognized as a Microsoft MVP in the Microsoft Azure category 10 times; he is also a Microsoft Certified Trainer and Opsgility Certified Trainer - Microsoft Azure Expert.

Packt is searching for authors like you

If you're interested in becoming an author for Packt, please visit authors.packtpub.com and apply today. We have worked with thousands of developers and tech professionals, just like you, to help them share their insight with the global tech community. You can make a general application, apply for a specific hot topic that we are recruiting an author for, or submit your own idea.

Table of Contents

Preface   1

Section 1: Understanding the Basics

Chapter 1: Getting Started with Azure Subscriptions   7
   Technical requirements   8
   Getting an Azure subscription   8
      PAYG   9
      CSP   11
      Enterprise Agreement   13
      Understanding different subscription models   14
   Implementing subscription policies   16
      Getting started with Azure Policy   17
      Policy validation results   20
      Examples of Azure policies   21
   Using Azure Blueprints for repeatable deploy and update operations   22
      Getting started with Blueprint assignment   23
      Assigning an Azure blueprint   26
   Checking usage and managing quotas   33
   Cost monitoring and analysis   36
      Cost analysis   39
      Budgets   40
      Azure Advisor   43
   Implementing management automation   44
   Summary   54
   Further reading   54

Chapter 2: Managing Azure Resources   57
   Technical requirements   58
   Managing resource providers   58
   Managing resource groups   62
      Browsing resource groups   64
      Listing the available resources   66
      Moving resources   67
      Understanding resource providers   69
   Performing deployments using ARM with templates   70
      Writing a template from scratch   72
      Automation scripts   74
      Other tools   76
   Implementing resource locks   78

Subscription locks	79
Resource group locks	82
Automating resource group management with Azure Event Grid	86
Creating an event subscription	86
Analyzing the gathered data	89
Implementing proper resource naming conventions	94
Subscription	95
Resource group	96
Resources	97
Summary	99
Chapter 3: Configuring and Managing Virtual Networks	101
Technical requirements	102
Creating and configuring VNet peering	102
The Azure portal	105
The Azure CLI	108
Creating and configuring VNet-to-VNet connection	113
Single region	113
Multiple regions	114
Connecting the networks	114
The same resource group	115
Different resource groups	117
Creating and configuring subnets	119
Creating a VNet	120
Creating a subnet	121
Understanding subnet configuration	122
Securing critical Azure services with service endpoints	125
Creating a VNet and Azure Storage account	125
Creating a service endpoint	127
Configuring a service endpoint	128
Configuring a naming resolutions	132
Creating a DNS zone	132
Configuring the DNS within a VNet	134
Creating and configuring network security groups (NSGs)	136
Creating a VNet with a subnet	136
Adding an NSG to a subnet	137
Reviewing NSG rules	140
Adding an NSG rule	142
Summary	144

Section 2: Identity and Access Management

Chapter 4: Identity Management	147
Technical requirements	148
Creating users in Azure AD	148
Getting started with user creation	149

Creating a user in an Azure Active Directory tenant   150
Creating a guest user   153
Describing the user creation process   155
Assigning a role to a user   157
Registering an application in Azure AD   161
Creating a new application   162
Creating groups   165
Group creation   167
Managing groups   170
Managing directory roles   175
Monitoring and auditing users   179
Enabling MFA authentication   184
Securing an Azure Service Fabric cluster   190
Summary   196

Chapter 5: Access Management   197
Technical requirements   197
Creating a custom role   198
Configuring access to Azure resources   202
Configuring MSI   206
Securing Azure App Services   208
Using and revoking Shared Access Policies   214
Creating and managing Shared Access Policies   215
Generating SAS tokens for different services   218
Summary   227

Chapter 6: Managing Virtual Machines   229
Technical requirements   230
Adding data disks   230
Creating a data disk   231
Adding network interfaces   234
Using Desired State Configuration   236
Scaling VMs up/out   242
Scaling caveats   243
Configuring monitoring   244
Configuring guest-level monitoring   244
Extending monitoring capabilities   246
Enabling connection monitor   248
Configuring high availability   250
Deploying VMs   252
Browsing the solutions   253
Deploying resources using various tools   256
Securing access to VMs   258
Connecting to a VM   260

Connecting to a VM 261
Using RDP and SSH to connect 262
Summary 265

Section 3: Advanced Topics

Chapter 7: Advanced Networking 269
Technical requirements 270
Implementing load balancing 270
Monitoring and diagnosing networks 277
IP flow verify 280
Next hop 281
Effective security rules 281
VPN troubleshoot, Packet capture, and Connection troubleshoot 282
Configuring DDoS protection 285
Enabling VNets in AKS 289
Enabling VNets for ACI 295
Enabling VNets in Redis Cache 298
Summary 303

Chapter 8: Implementing Storage and Backup 305
Technical requirements 306
Configuring network access for Azure Storage accounts 306
Enabling monitoring and finding logs for Azure Storage accounts 310
Managing the replication of Azure Storage accounts 315
Selecting the replication mode 316
Setting up Azure file shares 318
Transferring large datasets with low or no network bandwidth 322
Understanding your case – low or no bandwidth 323
Transferring data from on-premises to Azure 324
Transferring large datasets with medium or high network bandwidth 328
Understanding your case – medium or high bandwidth 328
The available options 332
Exploring periodic data transfer 333
Enabling security for Azure Storage 336
Summary 339

Chapter 9: High Availability and Disaster Recovery Scenarios 341
Technical requirements 342
Monitoring Azure VMs 342
Creating a VM 342
Enabling monitoring 344
Understanding the details 347
Monitoring Azure Storage services 349

Monitoring Azure App Service 353
Exploring capabilities of Azure Application Insights 356
Implementing Azure SQL backup 360
Creating our SQL server and database 360
Backing up your databases 360
Implementing Azure Storage backup 364
Backing up your storage account data 364
Implementing Availability Zones for VMs and HA 366
Availability Sets versus Availability Zones 366
Implementing AZs 367
Understanding how AZs work 369
Monitoring and managing global routing for web traffic with Azure Front Door 370
Understanding Azure Front Door 370
Creating an Azure Front Door instance 372
Designing backup plans for VMs 375
Summary 379
Further reading 379

Chapter 10: Automating Administration in Azure 381
Technical requirements 382
Starting/stopping Azure VMs during off-hours 382
Getting started with a VM 382
Creating an Automation account 384
Monitoring Blob storage with Azure Event Grid 389
Extending your setup 393
Monitoring ACR with Azure Event Grid 397
Integrating ACR with Azure Event Grid 397
Integrating FTP/SFTP servers with Azure Logic Apps 402
Creating an Azure Logic App instance 403
Understanding the setup 406
Integrating Office 365 with Azure Logic Apps 408
Integrating Azure SQL Server with Azure Logic Apps 412
Getting started with Azure Logic Apps 412
Managing updates for VMs 417
Getting started with the Update Management feature 417
Enabling the feature for multiple machines 422
Tracking changes in VMs 423
Summary 427
Further reading 428

Other Books You May Enjoy 429

Index 433

Preface

The momentum of cloud technologies is approaching its peak and it is hard to overstate the value of moving your applications from on-premises to cloud environments. As Microsoft Azure is one of the top three players on the market, becoming familiar with this particular technology will definitely be a plus for any IT specialist who is seeking a better understanding of how modern applications are designed and managed. For IT administrators, moving from their previous habits and environments is especially difficult as the cloud offers a completely different level of complexity and a separate administering model. Having a quick guide like this book will assist in building new skills rapidly and allow you to compare current solutions with the new approach.

Who this book is for

This book is intended for IT pros and IT administrators who want to get started with Microsoft Azure as their cloud solution of choice. The reader is expected to have some basic administration knowledge and an understanding of basic concepts (including authentication, different levels of applications' metrics, and virtual machines). Experience in working with command-line-based tools and PowerShell will also be a plus.

What this book covers

Chapter 1, *Getting Started with Azure Subscriptions*, covers all the topics related to basic subscription management skills and overall governance.

Chapter 2, *Managing Azure Resources*, constitutes something of a guide as regards basic resource management in Azure, including resource groups, locks, and moving resources.

Chapter 3, *Configuring and Managing Virtual Networks*, covers the most important topics relating to virtual networks in Azure.

Chapter 4, *Identity Management*, includes topics related to user and application management in terms of identity.

Chapter 5, *Access Management*, covers the defining of roles and assigning identities to Azure resources.

Chapter 6, *Managing Virtual Machines*, introduces intermediary topics related to virtual machines, including scaling, monitoring, and deployment.

Chapter 7, *Advanced Networking*, introduces more advanced topics pertaining to networking, including various Azure services.

Chapter 8, *Implementing Storage and Backup*, provides information on various Azure storage solutions and ways to back them up.

Chapter 9, *High Availability and Disaster Recovery Scenarios*, explains how to ensure proper monitoring and availability of your services.

Chapter 10, *Automating Administration in Azure*, describes automation solutions in Azure.

To get the most out of this book

To perform most of the exercises contained in this book, you will need to install the Azure CLI, which is a free-to-use, open sourced project maintained by Microsoft. You may also benefit from installing Azure PowerShell (ideally PowerShell Core, which works on all operating systems).

The rest of the software listed here is optional and is not required in order to benefit from this book:

Software/hardware covered in the book	OS requirements
Azure CLI	Windows / Linux / macOS
Azure PowerShell	Windows / Linux / macOS
Microsoft Azure Storage Explorer	Windows
ArmClient	Windows

Code in Action

Code in Action videos for this book can be viewed at (http://bit.ly/2OQfDum).

Download the color images

We also provide a PDF file that has color images of the screenshots/diagrams used in this book. You can download it here: http://www.packtpub.com/sites/default/files/downloads/9781838551452_ColorImages.pdf

Conventions used

There are a number of text conventions used throughout this book.

`CodeInText`: Indicates code words in text, database table names, folder names, filenames, file extensions, pathnames, dummy URLs, user input, and Twitter handles. Here is an example: "Deploy a new Function App called `azureblueprint` inside a resource group called `blueprint-euw-rg`."

Any command-line input or output is written as follows:

```
$ az network lb probe create -g "<rg-name>" --lb-name "<lb-name>" -n
"myprobe" --protocol TCP --port 80
```

Bold: Indicates a new term, an important word, or words that you see on screen. For example, words in menus or dialog boxes appear in the text like this. Here is an example: "As you can see, you can configure additional properties such as **Session persistence** or **Floating IP**."

 Warnings or important notes appear like this.

 Tips and tricks appear like this.

Get in touch

Feedback from our readers is always welcome.

General feedback: If you have questions about any aspect of this book, mention the book title in the subject of your message and email us at `customercare@packtpub.com`.

Errata: Although we have taken every care to ensure the accuracy of our content, mistakes do happen. If you have found a mistake in this book, we would be grateful if you would report this to us. Please visit `www.packtpub.com/support/errata`, selecting your book, clicking on the Errata Submission Form link, and entering the details.

Piracy: If you come across any illegal copies of our works in any form on the internet, we would be grateful if you would provide us with the location address or website name. Please contact us at copyright@packt.com with a link to the material.

If you are interested in becoming an author: If there is a topic that you have expertise in, and you are interested in either writing or contributing to a book, please visit authors.packtpub.com.

Reviews

Please leave a review. Once you have read and used this book, why not leave a review on the site that you purchased it from? Potential readers can then see and use your unbiased opinion to make purchase decisions, we at Packt can understand what you think about our products, and our authors can see your feedback on their book. Thank you!

For more information about Packt, please visit packt.com.

Section 1: Understanding the Basics

Getting started with Azure and understanding the basics is not an easy task. In the first part of this book, we will cover all the topics you need to know about as an Azure apprentice, including the various subscription options, resource management, and networking.

This section consists of the following chapters:

- Chapter 1, *Getting Started with Azure Subscriptions*
- Chapter 2, *Managing Azure Resources*
- Chapter 3, *Configuring and Managing Virtual Networks*

Getting Started with Azure Subscriptions

1

With the recent growth of cloud usage, more and more companies are searching for skilled individuals who understand how the cloud works and how it enhances a company's processes and products. One of the roles needed is an Azure administrator (operator), who is responsible for configuring various aspects of that cloud solution and keeping an eye on users, usage, and configuration.

The first and the most important element when managing systems in Azure is a subscription. You will not be able to get started with Azure without a subscription as this is the main element of that cloud solution. In this chapter, you will learn how to get an Azure subscription and configure it. We will also cover typical management tasks such as managing cost, monitoring usage, and defining quotas for services. For the more advanced topics, we will take a look at Azure Blueprints and management automation using Azure Event Grid. This chapter should give you a better understanding of how to get started with Azure from an administrator's point of view and introduce you to the most basic concepts of this cloud solution without diving into more detailed topics (which are to be described later).

The following main topics will be covered in this chapter:

- Getting an Azure subscription
- Implementing subscription policies
- Using Azure Blueprints for repeatable deploy and update operations
- Checking usage and managing quotas
- Cost monitoring and analysis
- Implementing management automation

Technical requirements

To perform exercises from this chapter, you will need the following:

- A working Azure subscription (you can create it in the *Getting an Azure subscription* section)
- Microsoft Azure Storage Explorer, which can be found at `https://azure.microsoft.com/en-us/features/storage-explorer/`
- Read about Azure Event Grid: `https://docs.microsoft.com/en-us/azure/event-grid/overview`
- Read about Azure Logic Apps: `https://docs.microsoft.com/en-us/azure/logic-apps/logic-apps-overview`
- OPTIONAL: A Microsoft account if you want to set up a subscription in this chapter

Getting an Azure subscription

A subscription is a logical container for your resources and users, which you have to manage while using the Microsoft Azure cloud solution.

Getting a subscription differs depending on the option you choose. By default, you have two types of subscription available—open subscriptions, where you pay for usage, and prepaid ones, which guarantee a certain level of available resources and confidence when it comes to cloud costs.

In general, we have the following open subscriptions (usage-based):

- **Pay-As-You-Go (PAYG)**
- **Cloud Solution Provider (CSP)**

Then there's a subscription with an agreed minimum spend:

- **Enterprise Agreement (EA)**

Depending on the subscription type, once you reach its spending limit (if there is any), you may either end up with blocked resources or your subscription may automatically convert to PAYG. To obtain most subscriptions, all you need is access to a browser and possibly a credit card. The process may differ for more advanced subscriptions (such as CSP or EA), which will require coming to an agreement with a vendor. All of the required steps will be described in this chapter in the following sections.

There is also one more difference regarding the three mentioned subscription types when it comes to payments. In general, your choice may reflect a legal requirement or your company's business model:

- With PAYG, you are billed monthly for all of the resources you used during the billing period (which is one month). Once the billing period ends, an invoice is generated for you with a summary. This summary may help you to understand the bill and analyze the cost. Note that an invoice is usually not issued from the country you live in or where your company is registered.
- With **EA**, you are committed to spending on Azure a minimum value that you agreed upon. If you spend less, there is no way to restore lost credits.
- With **CSP**, you will be able to contact a local reseller to be charged by their company. It is a much easier way to pay for cloud resources from a financial and legal point as you are working with a company that is co-located with yours and they are responsible for charging you, not Microsoft directly.

Getting started directly relies on the option you have selected as the processes are quite different. The easiest option requires you only to provide a debit or credit card number, and the most complicated will require you to come to an agreement with Microsoft, so you have agreed on the monetary commitments and your benefits.

PAYG

This is the most simple option, where the cost is simply calculated based on your monthly usage of Azure resources. Such subscriptions can be canceled anytime and the accepted payment type is s credit or debit card attached to the subscription. The currency you will be billed in depends on the region where you are currently located—for example, for Canada, it will be in Canadian dollars while for the Netherlands, it will be in euros. The most common currencies are indeed dollars and euros, but for some particular countries (such as Norway, Brazil, or Mexico), local currencies are accepted.

Let's follow these steps to get a PAYG subscription:

1. Go to `https://azure.microsoft.com/en-us/offers/pay-as-you-go/` and click on the **Purchase now** button, as shown in the following screenshot:

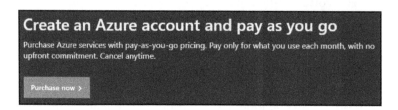

Figure 1.1 - Purchase a PAYG subscription

 If you are not currently signed in to Azure, you will be redirected to the login screen, where you have to enter your Microsoft Account credentials. If you do not have an account, you can create one from the login screen. It is not possible to get a subscription without having a Microsoft Account.

2. Sign in if you are not signed in already.
3. Fill in the form to finish the process of obtaining a subscription:

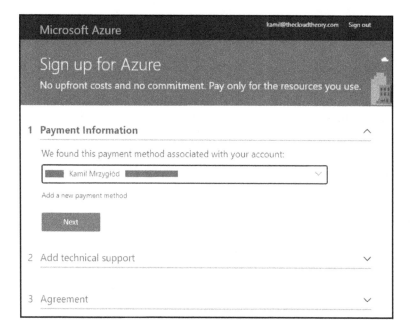

Figure 1.2 - Subscription purchase form

4. Click on the **Sign up** button to start the process of creating a subscription:

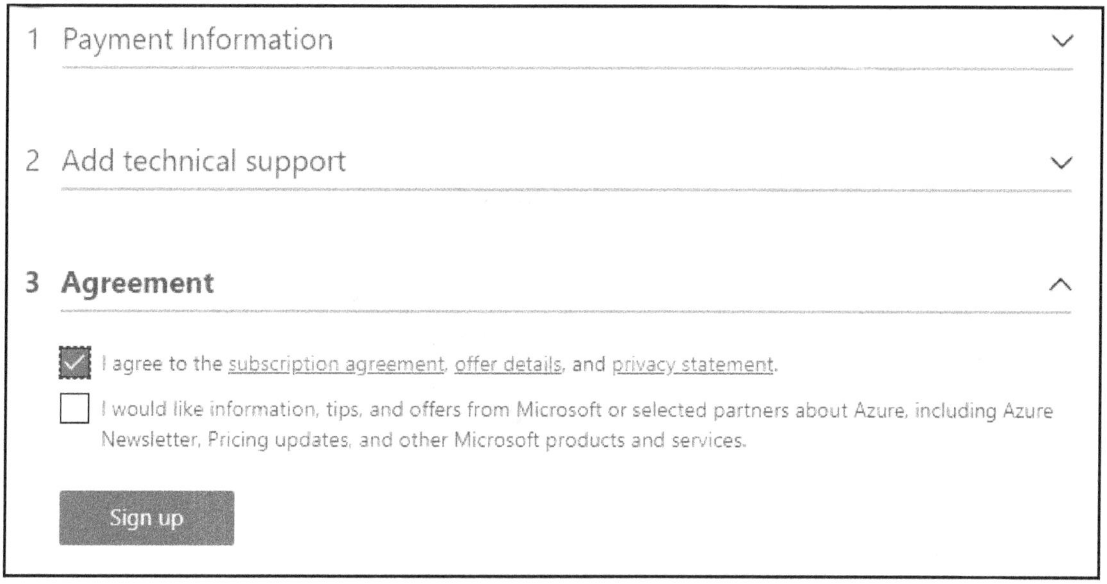

1 Payment Information ⌄

2 Add technical support ⌄

3 **Agreement** ⌃

☑ I agree to the subscription agreement, offer details, and privacy statement.

☐ I would like information, tips, and offers from Microsoft or selected partners about Azure, including Azure Newsletter, Pricing updates, and other Microsoft products and services.

Sign up

Figure 1.3 - Finishing the subscription purchase

Once all of the data and your card are validated, you are ready to go—you can sign in with your Microsoft Account at `https://portal.azure.com`, where you will be able to start provisioning resources in your brand new Azure subscription.

Now, let's look at how we can get a CSP subscription.

CSP

Another option to obtain a subscription is to collaborate with Microsoft's partner, which offers Azure indirectly and supports you in the process of obtaining access to the cloud, services, and deployments. All providers are certified by Microsoft, so you can be sure that you are working with competent specialists who will help you in case of technical issues and questions. This is the best solution when you seek expertise and do not have resources, which will take care of managing the more formal aspects of having cloud solutions in connection with your business.

Let's follow these steps to get a CSP subscription:

1. Go to `https://www.microsoft.com/en-us/solution-providers/home` and enter your city or address, as shown in the following screenshot:

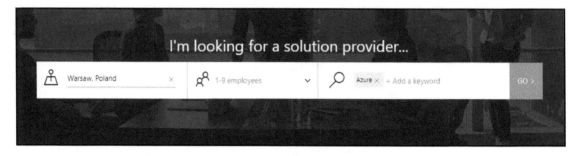

Figure 1.4 - CSP search form

1. Click the **GO >** button and you will see multiple search results categorized depending on criteria such as distance and responsiveness.
2. Click on the selected provider to get a better picture of what is offered and on what terms.
3. Click on the **SELECT PROVIDER +** button to add it to the contact form:

Figure 1.5 - Choosing a provider

4. Click on the **Contact selected providers** button to get a form that will allow you to enter everything a provider needs to know before starting cooperation:

Figure 1.6 - Contacting a selected provider

5. Wait for an answer from the provider.

Next, let's take a look at EAs.

Enterprise Agreement

This is a special type of subscription intended for big players. In general, when your monthly bill is more than only a few hundred dollars, a **PAYG** subscription does not offer anything more than simplicity. When this is the case, you can get an Azure subscription by signing an **Enterprise Agreement**. The way this particular option works is that you have to make an upfront monetary commitment. The specific use case of an EA is the possibility to create multiple subscriptions on your own—something PAYG does not offer. The benefits of this offering are really rich—you will be able to find more details in the *Further reading* section of this chapter.

The process of getting an EA is much more complicated than the other ones—you need to contact Microsoft directly to come to an understanding of aspects of the agreement such as monetary commitment, your company's requirements, and enrollments. The basic process is as follows:

1. Prepare your company's requirements regarding infrastructure and services needed.
2. Simulate the monetary commitment and how you can leverage the assigned resources.
3. Contact Microsoft to negotiate terms and sign the agreement.

Next, let's get a deeper understanding of the subscription models.

Understanding different subscription models

In general, depending on the option selected, the outcome will be a little bit different:

- If your choice was PAYG, a subscription is created immediately after your credit/debit card is validated. You can start work with it without any limits. By performing the steps from the **PAYG** section, you have connected your credit/debit card with an Azure subscription. This means that any resource that you provide from now will result in your card being charged the appropriate cost. On the other hand, your subscription has no spending limit by default—take that into account when deploying complex infrastructures containing multiple virtual machines and databases.
- If you have selected an EA, you will have to contact Microsoft and agree on specific agreement requirements and assumptions. Once you both agree on the common terms, a subscription will be created and you will able to manage it and extra subscriptions under it.
- If you decided to cooperate with a CSP, you will have to wait for an answer and then come to an agreement on payments, technical support, and your requirements. Once it is established, your CSP is your first line of support and direct contact when considering Azure. The most important thing is to select a proper provider by carefully reading their offer, which is described in *step 3* of the *CSP* section.

For a PAYG subscription, three sections need to be filled:

- **Payment Information**: As mentioned earlier, you need a credit or debit card to obtain a PAYG subscription. You will have to fill in information here such as the card number, the name on the card, and your address.
- **Add technical support**: Optionally, you can select a support service for your subscription. While this may be obsolete for a Dev/Test subscription, I strongly advise you to buy a support plan for your production subscriptions. There are three different options available: **Getting started**, **Production**, and **Business-critical**. They all are different in many aspects (such as support availability or response time) and, of course, give you a different level of confidence.

 Note that if you are covered by Microsoft Premier support, you do not have to buy a support plan here as your subscription will be covered by it.

- **Agreement**: This includes your agreements to subscription, offer details, and privacy statement.

Remember that an empty subscription is free of charge. As long as you do not have resources provisioned (or you have provisioned only free ones), your card will not be charged.

An Enterprise Agreement is quite different as you have three different kinds of enrollments:

- **Enterprise Enrollment**: This is designed for purchasing end user technologies on a per-user, per-device, or hybrid basis.

- **Server and Cloud Enrollment**: You can receive better pricing and cloud-optimized licensing options by committing to one or more cloud technologies from Microsoft.

- **Subscription Enrollment**: This allows you to subscribe to Microsoft product licenses.

As we are talking about Azure administration, the most interesting option for you will be **Server and Cloud Enrollment** (**SCE**). There are four different SCE components:

- **Core Infrastructure**: It includes products such as Windows Server and the requirement of **Core Infrastructure Suite** (**CIS**) coverage for all of them.

- **Application Platform**: It offers SQL Server with the requirement of **Full Software Assurance** coverage.

- **Developer Platform**: It contains Visual Studio Enterprise and MSDN platforms with the requirement of **Full Software Assurance** coverage.

- **Microsoft Azure**: This includes all Microsoft Azure services.

Depending on the selected option, you will have different requirements to fulfill—this is why EA is designed for bigger companies that nonetheless require hundreds of licenses and manage hundreds of subscriptions.

 It is impossible to cover all EA aspects in such a short section. If you are searching for the most flexible and advanced Azure offer for your company, take a look at the links available in the *Further reading* section to get the full picture.

Once you have your subscription, you can start managing it—setting up policies for resources, monitoring expenses, and managing access. This chapter will show you multiple ideas regarding administering subscriptions and what falls under them, so you can focus on getting the most from your subscription instead of fighting with unclear documentation and settings.

Besides the business subscriptions presented in this chapter, you may have access to slightly different subscription types:

- **Visual Studio subscriptions:** If you are a .NET platform developer, you may already have access to Azure by leveraging your free grant offered as a part of the Visual Studio subscription. Depending on the level, you may have from 50 USD to 150 USD per month to spend on Azure services.
- **Microsoft sponsorship subscriptions:** Some subscriptions are sponsored by Microsoft itself. This includes agreements on delivering proofs-of-concept of technologies, academic use, or specific individuals such as MVPs, who use those for training and various projects.

When you have your subscription ready, you can proceed to the next sections of this chapter. The next one will describe in detail how you can implement various policies, which can help to manage your account on a subscription level.

Implementing subscription policies

A subscription allows you to manage and control the cost of your Azure resources. Besides the financial aspect, it is also the main control point, where you can store policies that determine what resources can be provisioned and which features can be used. Managing such elements would be cumbersome without proper support in Azure. Fortunately, there are many built-in definitions that will help you to control things such as resource locations or proper security configuration.

 You do not have to go to the portal to get information regarding compliant/non-compliant resources—there is a detailed guide, which describes other methods (PowerShell and RESTful APIs) and that can be exceptionally helpful when automating governance over resources. To read it, check out https://docs.microsoft.com/en-us/azure/governance/policy/how-to/get-compliance-data.

Getting started with Azure Policy

To get started, we will have to actually create a policy. The process of assigning a policy is quite simple and can be covered by the following steps:

1. Search for the **Subscriptions** blade—the easiest way to do so is to use the search field at the top of the Azure portal, as shown in the following screenshot:

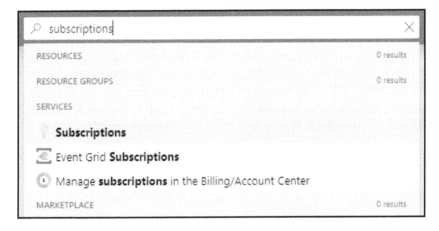

Figure 1.7 - Searching for the Subscriptions blade

2. Select the subscription you are interested in. The last thing you need to do is to click on the **Policies** blade:

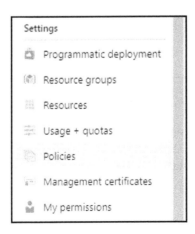

FIgure 1.8 - The Policies blade

3. Click on the **Assign policy** button, which will display a form where you can define how the policy should work:

Figure 1.9 - The Assign policy button

4. Assign a policy and configure the appropriate fields as follow: set the **Scope** of your subscription (in my case, it is **Pay-As-You-Go**) and leave the exclusions empty and the policy definition as **Not allowed resource types**. Remember that you can select either a built-in or a custom policy (if you have one).

5. Initially, the compliance state may be displayed as **Not registered** as in the following screenshot. Wait a few minutes before proceeding:

Figure 1.10 - Created policies view

6. If this status is diplayed longer than a few minutes, make sure a proper resource provider for the policies is registered. To do so, go to the **Resource providers** blade and check the status of the provider:

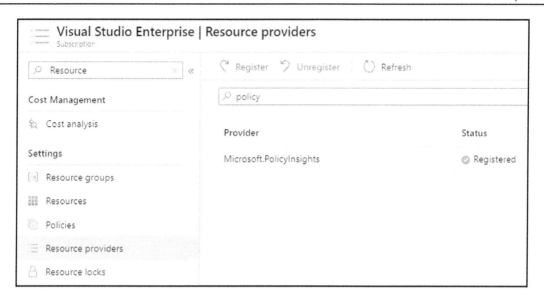

Figure 1.11 - Subscription resource providers

7. Once the status is displayed as **Registered**, you can test the results. Try to perform a forbidden action (such as creating a forbidden resource type). If you do so, you will see a result similar to the following:

Figure 1.12 - Validation error

When a policy is enabled and working, it constantly monitors your resources against configured parameters. Depending on its configuration, it may either block deploying particular services or enforce a specific naming convention. An audit policy can report on non-compliant resources and, with enforcement mode enabled, can deny the creation of resources that don't comply with the policy.

Let's now check what a policy validation result may look like.

Policy validation results

Each policy constantly monitors your resources and validates them against defined rules. When there is a validation error generated by a policy, you can click on it to reveal the details, which confirm that the action was blocked by the policy (see *Figure 1.13*):

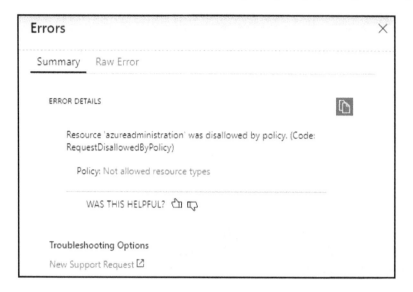

Figure 1.13 - Policy validation error details

The results of the working policy may differ depending on its type. However, they mostly focus on enforcing or forbidding an action, which will result in an error displayed in either a portal or a command line. When you want to assign a policy, you must configure it using various available options. Here, you can find the description of the fields displayed:

- **Scope**: This field defines what resources the policy is assigned to. There is a possibility to select either a subscription or a resource group.
- **Exclusions**: If you find the scope a little bit too generic, you can add excluded resources that will not be covered by a policy.
- **Policy definition**: There are two types of supported policies—built-in and custom. Unfortunately, custom policies are out of the scope of this book (but if you find this topic interesting, you can find a link in the *Further reading* section to read more about it). A policy is a definition that includes a rule and an effect and is triggered when a rule is not satisfied.

- **Assignment name**: It is the display name of an assigned policy.
- **Description** and **Assigned by**: These are optional fields that gather extra information about a policy.

Let's look at some examples of Azure policies that are available.

Examples of Azure policies

To give you a better understanding of the topic, we can take a look at various examples of policies you may use. There are many different kinds of available policies—let's try to describe the most interesting ones:

- **Audit CORS resource access restrictions for a function app**: When using Azure Functions, you may want to force developers to assign proper **Cross-Origin Resource Sharing** (**CORS**) configuration to function apps, so they are not accessible from all domains. A very simple and helpful policy that addresses a common security issue when hosting web applications.
- **Audit resource location matches resource group location**: To avoid confusion, you can ensure that resource groups and their resources are always provisioned in the same location.
- **Audit unrestricted network access to storage accounts**: If your storage accounts should not be available from the internet, you can enforce their owners to configure network rules so they are only accessible from configured networks.
- **Not allowed resource types**: Sometimes, your organization just cannot deploy some of the resources (for example, you need to audit the whole code base, so you cannot use Azure Functions). This policy is something you want when forbidding the use of a particular resource is essential.

When you assign any of the policies, it will immediately start to watch for your resources and check whether they are compliant with that policy.

 Some of the policies require you to set some parameters before they can be added. Carefully check the **Parameters** section to configure them exactly as you want.

Of course, the error displayed previously (see *Figure 1.13*) is in fact returned by an API powering Azure resources. That means that it will be returned also for other operations (such as using the command line or PowerShell).

The policy I described previously was executed during the creation of a resource, but of course, it also works for the resources created previously. Subscription policies are really powerful tools for an Azure administrator, allowing for setting strong fundamentals for further management activities such as automation and building an organization-wide mindset of what is allowed and what is not. The more resources your subscription has, the more difficult it is to manage and keep everything up to the defined rules. This is especially true for all companies for which compliance is crucial to work effectively—if you have thousands of VMs, app services, and storage accounts, you just cannot rely only on telling everyone that this one particular feature isn't allowed. For those scenarios, use properly set up policies, which can cover many different scenarios, especially if you create a custom one.

Check out the next section to learn more about ensuring proper policies are assigned to Azure resources using Azure Blueprints.

Using Azure Blueprints for repeatable deploy and update operations

Sometimes, using policies is just not enough. Reasons may vary—the number of projects is too big to govern via policies, they become obstacles because you cannot enforce a particular rule, or you find complex designs with them to be just too complicated. For all of those scenarios, Microsoft has prepared an additional tool for Azure administrators called **Azure Blueprints**. They are like sketches for buildings—you can set collect all required artifacts in one place and use it for multiple deployments. With this feature, you can orchestrate multiple deployments and shorten the time needed to achieve a coherent architecture. If you are familiar with ARM templates, you may find Azure Blueprints much easier to understand as they offer similar functionalities to Resource Manager. On the other hand, it is a great tool for preserving a connection between a blueprint and a deployment or manage multiple subscriptions at once.

 Note that, at the time of writing this chapter, Blueprints were marked as in Preview. That means that this feature has not reached **General Availability** (**GA**) and is not offered full support when used in production.

Getting started with Blueprint assignment

Blueprint definition assignment is similar to a policy assignment and is covered by the following steps:

1. Use the search box at the top of the portal and search for `Blueprints`:

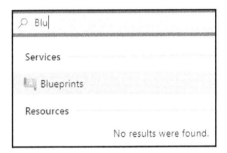

Figure 1.14 - Searching for the Blueprints blade

2. Then, you will see a welcome screen, where you can get started with the service:

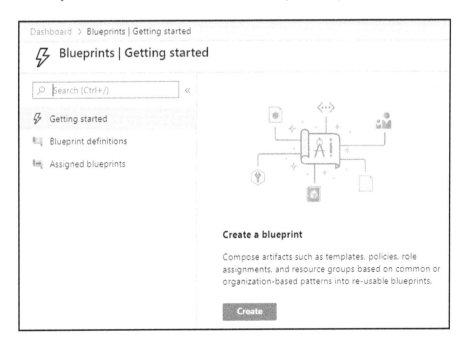

Figure 1.15 - The Blueprints blade

3. Click on the **Create** button under the **Create a blueprint** section.
4. You will see a new screen where you can see various samples. For now, click on the **Start with blank blueprint** button:

Figure 1.16 - Starting with a blank blueprint

5. Provide values for the blueprint name, description, and definition location.
6. Add artifacts (roles that will be assigned to resources and resources that will be deployed—in general, side effects of a blueprint assignment) by going to the artifacts tab.
7. Save the blueprint definition.
8. Click on **Publish blueprint**, so it will become available for assignment.
9. To assign a blueprint, you have to click on the **Assign blueprint** menu item:

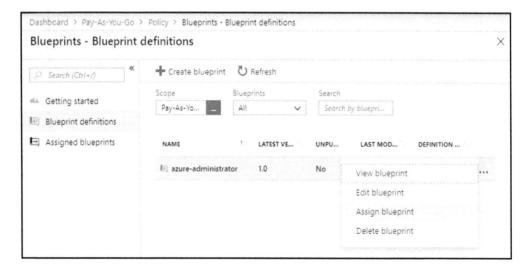

Figure 1.17 - Assigning a blueprint

10. Decide whether **Lock Assignment** should be enabled or not
11. Provide all of the mandatory parameters, such as the name of a resource group a blueprint will be assigned to or the configuration of a resource (if you did not provide them when defining the blueprint).

When creating a blueprint definition, you will see a form where you can define your blueprint. The very first thing needed is to provide the following:

- **Blueprint name**: This field is required to give a blueprint a unique name that will help you to understand what it is about.
- **Blueprint description**: If you need to add extra information, you can type it here.
- **Definition location**: This is a place for storing your blueprint.

The form described previously can be seen in the following screenshot:

Figure 1.18 - The Create blueprint form

 Under the hood, Azure Blueprints is stored with Azure Cosmos DB for resiliency, low latency, and geo-replication. This gives you the best performance, no matter where your resources are being deployed.

Once you are satisfied with the definition, you can save it. Initially, blueprint's status will be displayed as **Draft**—as long as it is not published, you can easily modify and adjust it to your needs. To assign it, you will have to click on **Publish blueprint** so it will become available for assignment:

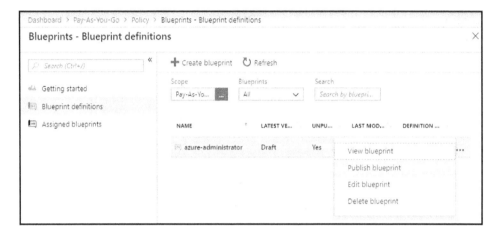

Figure 1.19 - Publishing a blueprint

 Note that publishing a blueprint requires providing a version—this is to allow the versioning of definitions so you can introduce breaking changes without breaking existing setups.

Now, we will learn how to assign an Azure blueprint.

Assigning an Azure blueprint

When making an assignment, you will see a screen where you will have to provide the following:

- **Subscription(s)**: This means which subscriptions this particular blueprint should be assigned to.
- **Assignment name**: As the same blueprint can be assigned to multiple subscriptions, you have to give the assignment a unique name to avoid confusion.
- **Location**: When deploying resources, a blueprint requires a Managed Identity to authenticate the operation. This field allows you to set the location where credentials will be stored.

- **Blueprint definition version**: If your blueprint has more than only one version, here, you can select the one you are interested in.

Besides the preceding settings, you will have to also decide whether **Lock Assignment** should be enabled or not. Locking artifacts created via Azure Blueprints makes much sense when you consider that they are governed by an administrator, not the resource owner. To make a long story short, the scenarios are as follows:

- When a lock is assigned, even a subscription owner cannot change/delete a resource. This ensures that it works exactly as assumed and planned.
- The lock cannot be removed without removing a blueprint assignment.

An example setup for a blueprint assignment could look like this:

Figure 1.20 - Assign blueprint form

As Azure Blueprints is quite a new service, it is constantly enhanced to provide functionality expected in the market. It is a great tool for ensuring a certain level of compliance and will be used mostly in heavily regulated environments. When adding artifacts to a blueprint definition, you have four different artifacts available:

- **Policy assignment**
- **Role assignment**
- **Azure Resource Manager template**
- **Resource group**

By using each artifact, you can create a complex definition that will ease the process of deployment and setting up resources. Let's think about the following scenario—I would like to make sure that both Azure App Services and Azure Functions are deployed with **HTTPS Only** enabled. Additionally, I want to assign a specific user with a specific role to each deployment. Last but not least, I want to deploy a resource group with an ARM template, which creates a storage account. My current setup looks like this:

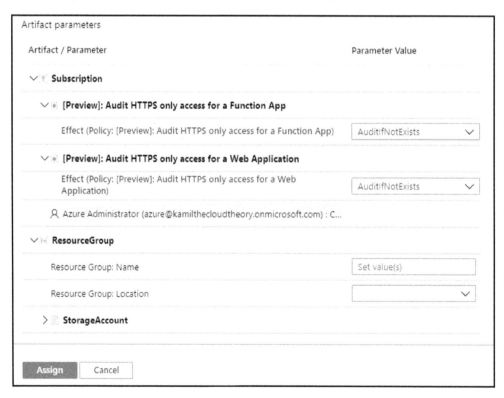

Figure 1.21 - Blueprint artifact parameters

Note the following:

- You do not have to enter all parameters during the process of creating a blueprint—they can be evaluated while creating a deployment.
- When using the resource group artifact type, each deployment covered by a blueprint will create additional resources defined by it. Using it makes the most sense when attaching an ARM template with extra resources (such as a custom monitoring solution, shared storage, or other similar elements).

To test an assigned blueprint, you can do the following:

1. Deploy a new function app called `azureblueprint` inside a resource group called `blueprint-euw-rg`. You should see a similar result to mine, shown in the following screenshot:

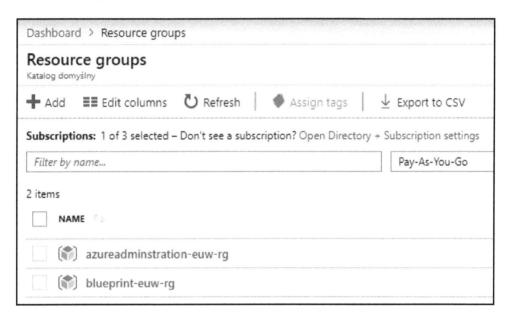

Figure 1.22 - The result of running a blueprint with an additional resource group created

2. Besides the declared resource group, Azure Blueprint created an additional group called `azureadministration-euw-rg` (the name is the result of the passed parameter to a definition, which creates a resource group). This extra resource group contains a storage account with a generated unique name, which I can use for any purpose:

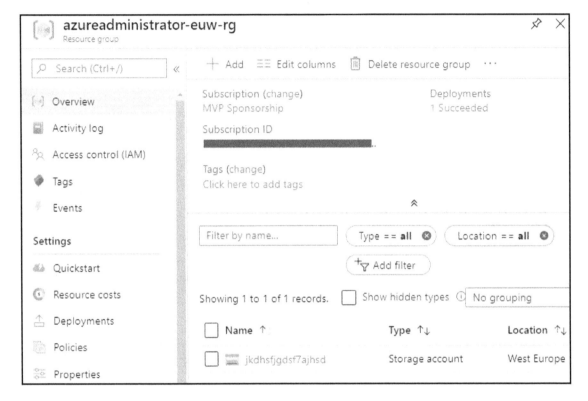

Figure 1.23 - The storage account automatically created by a blueprint

3. Let's check other resource assignments. One of the rules of my blueprint was to assign a user with a particular role (check the role assignment artifact in *Figure 1.24*). A quick look at the **IAM** blade gives the expected result:

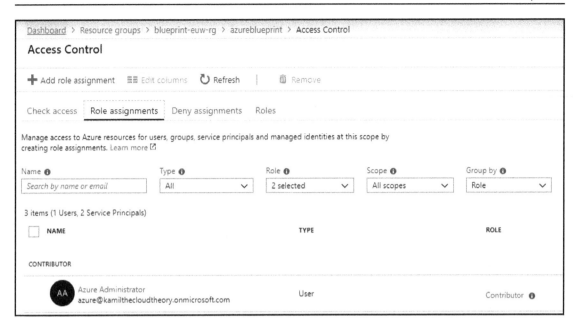

Figure 1.24 - Role assignment automatically created by a blueprint

4. The last thing to check is that the extra two policies were created. To do so, I go to the **Policies** blade in my subscription:

Figure 1.25 - Policies blade

From that, you can clearly see that I have additional policies added to the previous ones (**Audit HTTPS only access for a Function / Web App**):

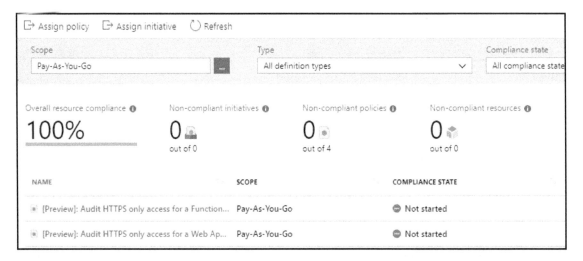

Figure 1.26 - Azure policies with compliance status

Policies allow for a certain level of inertia—even if somebody managed to create a resource, which was forbidden, very often you do not have to act immediately. The preceding screen (*Figure 1.26*), however, gives you the possibility to quickly check whether the compliance level is not below the assumed level.

With the preceding information, you should be able to enhance your current administration tasks and be able to automate many activities such as user assignments or mandatory resources provisioning. When working with Azure Blueprints, remember the following rules:

- Name the assignments uniquely to avoid collisions.
- Use the versioning feature of Azure Blueprints to introduce breaking changes without breaking current assignments.
- Use Lock Assignments to ensure that no one can mess with artifacts deployed by a blueprint. The only thing to remember is the feature inertia—Resource Manager may need up to 30 minutes to finish propagating locks for the artifacts.

Azure Blueprints is one of the best tools when it comes to managing subscriptions and resources at an enterprise level. The next topic we will cover will guide you through the process of usage and quotas management.

Checking usage and managing quotas

When working as an Azure administrator, it is crucial to effectively manage current usage for your subscription and assigned quotas for different resources. As you are probably aware, Azure offers various limits for most of the available services, with some of them being a soft limit that can be extended after contacting support.

When getting your very first subscription, you may realize that soft limits are much lower than you would expect. This is especially true for all non-commercial/test subscriptions, which are meant for educational purposes or creating a proof-of-concept solution. In fact, Microsoft aims at helping their customers to not *hurt themselves*, so some default quotas are lowered to limit spending capabilities.

Each Azure service offers different limits depending on the resource type and region availability. While, in most scenarios, it will not be the case, if you are about to deploy a complex system containing, for example, hundreds of virtual machines, you may be affected by a quota that will prevent you from completing a deployment. When in doubt, always check `https://docs.microsoft.com/en-us/azure/azure-resource-manager/ management/azure-subscription-service-limits`—it contains limits for all Azure services and storage.

 Remember that quotas are assigned to each region separately—if you change the soft limit in one region, you will not get an increase in other ones!

As you can see, the maximum request rate is set to 20,000 requests per second. However, if you read the documentation closely, you will figure out that this particular limit can be extended after contacting Azure support. Other examples of soft limits are as follows:

- Throughput units in Azure Event Hub
- IoT Hub units
- IoT Hubs in a subscription
- Container operations for Azure Container Instances
- Load balancer limits

The question is—how can you check the current usage and limits for your subscription? To check usage and manage a subscription quota, you will need to perform the following steps:

1. Go to the subscription you are interested in.
2. Click on the **Usage + quotas** blade. To do so, you can search for **Subscriptions** in the search box at the top of the Azure portal:

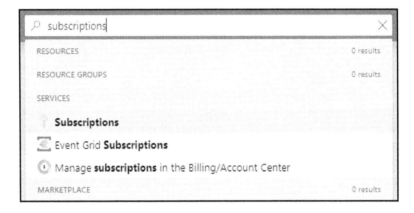

Figure 1.27 - Searching for the Subscriptions blade

3. Search for the blade in the **Settings** section:

Figure 1.28 - The Usage + quotas blade

You will see a list of the current usage depending on the provider and location.

If you do not see any usage information, make sure you have selected all providers and locations available.

4. Click on the **Request Increase** button on the upper right of the screen. This is the quickest way to request an increase for a specific quota.

You will be redirected to the support ticket, where you can provide all of the necessary details:

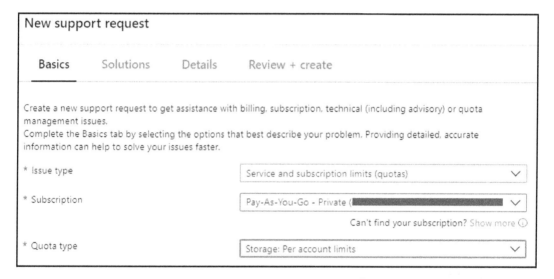

Figure 1.29 - Creating a new quota increase ticket

Once you send a ticket, you will have to wait for the support to review it and decide whether it is possible to fulfill your requirements. Here, you can find the usage data available for my subscription:

Figure 1.30 - Current quotas status

Let's assume that you are approaching the maximum number of 250 accounts—this could be the moment to send a request ticket to the support. After sending a ticket requesting changing the assigned limits, Azure support will review what is required and what your particular use case is. In fact, whether additional resources will be assigned to your subscription may rely on the business use case you provided—if you are buying many services from Microsoft, it is more likely that your request will be accepted. Depending on the type of your subscription (PAYG, CSP, or EA) it may or may not be easy—the easiest way to getting your limits changed is becoming a close partner to Microsoft with common goals. This, of course, does not mean that if you are not a Fortune 500 company, your request will be rejected—as mentioned earlier, it all depends on the use case.

Remember to actively monitor your subscription against quotas, especially if you are building a complex system with multiple resources. In some cases, you may find it especially helpful to divide your projects into multiple subscriptions—in such a setup, each project will have its own limits. This will be the easiest to achieve with EA, but of course, it is also possible for PAYG subscriptions (although it is much more complicated when it comes to managing things). Also, when having several systems under your command, make sure you are familiar with Azure resource limits, which you can find in the *Further reading* section—it will help you to govern them and plan further actions.

With proper cost and usage management, you can be certain your spending is under control. To dive into this topic further, take a look at the next section, which will describe how to monitor and analyze them.

Cost monitoring and analysis

If you are an Azure administrator, you are probably responsible for monitoring and managing the cost of all services hosted in the cloud. There are many factors related to this particular case—the types of used resources, the scale of your projects, or different discounts that you may apply, depending on the contract you have with Microsoft. Azure offers different options to make your life easier—starting from easy-to-read dashboards to cost alerts, which help you to monitor the current usage. In this section, you will learn how to use those tools and understand their outcome.

Before you really get started with hosted services, you can estimate the cost of the architecture using the following calculators:

- **Pricing calculator**: An Azure cost calculator, which can be found at `https://azure.microsoft.com/en-us/pricing/calculator/`, it is a tool that you can use to estimate how much each Azure service will cost. Of course, these calculations are only estimates as it is really hard to plan everything upfront. Nonetheless, treat it as the first step in planning funds for your architecture.
- **Total Cost of Ownership (TCO) calculator**: This is another Azure calculator, which is available at `https://azure.microsoft.com/en-us/pricing/tco/calculator/`. Using the cloud is not only about using cloud services, but also about changing the responsibilities and moving expenses from one place to another. This calculator helps you to understand the total cost of your architecture including managing server infrastructure, updates, licenses, and many more.

The preceding tools are great to understand the expected cost of the whole cloud architecture that we are about to manage. However, they require that you know how each service is configured and what features will be enabled. Doing this upfront may be tricky, so they are not always an ideal solution for managing the cost. This is why we will have to take a look at the real usage and calculated cost to be able to control it.

 To work with cost analysis, you will need a working Azure subscription. The important thing here is also correct permission assigned to your account—you have to be able to read subscription cost data (by being, for example, the owner of a subscription).

Cost management is enabled by default on all subscriptions—all you need here is to access the correct section in the Azure portal:

1. To access the cost management option, search for it in the search field at the top of the portal:

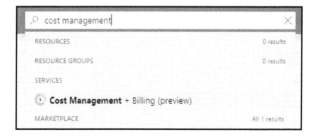

Figure 1.31 - Searching for the Cost Management blade

From this point, you can access different blades such as **Cost analysis, Budgets,** and **Cloudyn.** When you enter the subscription screen, you should be able to see a screen similar to mine:

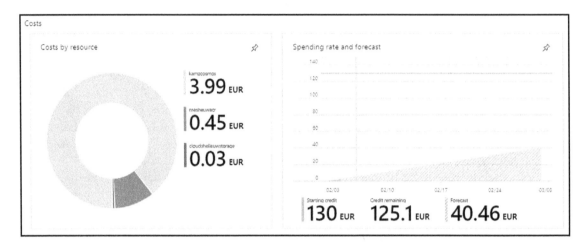

Figure 1.32 - Current cost charts

Let's focus quickly on the information displayed here. We have two categories, which inform us about the current cost of the subscription:

- **Cost by resource**: This chart displays the total cost of the subscription divided by the resources. As you can see, in my case, almost 90% of the cost is generated by a resource named `kamzcosmos` (which is probably an Azure Cosmos DB instance).
- **Spending rate and forecast**: This is an interesting chart that gives you an insight into the forecast of your spending. It also allows you to see how dynamically the cost changes.

The **Spending rate and forecast** chart may look a little bit different depending on the type of your subscription. In the preceding example, I presented a subscription that has a fixed limit of 130 EUR allowed for each month. When using, for example, a PAYG subscription, starting credit will not be displayed.

When you go to the **Cost Management**, you will see a new blade where multiple features are available:

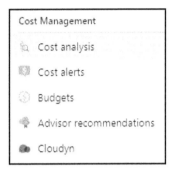

Figure 1.33 - The Cost analysis blade

The available options will be briefly described in the following.

Cost analysis

To get a better overview of how much each resource costs (or a resource group or a location), you can use **Cost analysis** to get a personalized view of different spending categories. Besides the main chart representing the accumulated view, you will have access to three additional charts, which you can alter to get a different categorization of resources:

Figure 1.34 - Cost analysis per service name, location, and resource group name

There are many interesting categories that you can use to understand the cost—you can divide services using tags, their tiers, invoice number, or even their GUIDs. If you have many resources, this becomes especially helpful as it allows you to use advanced filtering and better distinction.

Budgets

Microsoft Azure allows you to create budgets, which you can use to control the cost of the cloud services. To use this feature, you have to go to the **Budgets** blade and click on the + **Add** button. Doing so will display a form that you can use to set a budget with an alert, which will trigger if the current cost of your subscription exceeds the threshold:

Figure 1.35 - Creating a budget

In the preceding example (*Figure 1.35*), I have created a budget of 90 USD with an alert that will trigger if I spent at least 90 USD.

Note that the **Amount** field of the budget relates to the currency set for the subscription.

There is an additional feature of budgets that, from your perspective, should be very interesting. As you have probably noticed, you can divide your budget into many categories, each triggering another kind of action group. Action groups can be managed by clicking on the **Manage action groups** button:

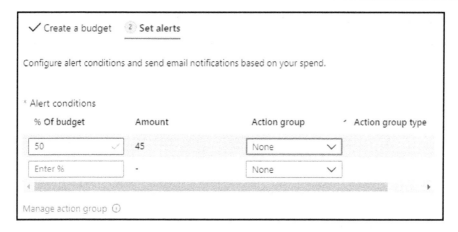

Figure 1.36 - Setting the alert of a budget

They allow you to enhance your budget with an additional level of automation using services such as Azure Functions, Azure Logic Apps, or Azure Automation to take a specific action in addition to sending an alert. Here, you can find an example with a runbook, which will stop all virtual machines in a resource group:

Figure 1.37 - Creating an action for a budget

Once a budget is created, you can see it in the main window of the feature:

Figure 1.38 - Budget status

Here, you can find an example mail triggered by defined alert rules. Note that it contains all of the necessary details you need to understand what is happening—when the budget started, what is its maximal value, and the current state:

Figure 1.39 - Budget alert email result

Such an email can be really valuable, especially when limiting expenses is crucial for a business to run smoothly. The important thing here is that you should not rely on a single channel of communication only—the email message could get lost or your mailbox might have gone down—if the budget alert is really important, always implement a backup plan for it.

Azure Advisor

In most cases, the Azure portal features should fit most of your needs. One more thing worth mentioning is Azure Advisor, which you can find in the **Cost Management** blade:

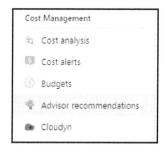

Figure 1.40 - Advisor recommendations blade

By clicking on it, you may find helpful tips related to the cost optimization for your subscription. If you have many different resources, it may be worth checking once in a while whether you have missed some occasions for saving extra money by tweaking provisioned resources.

When you set alerts via budgets in the cost management of your subscription, you will get an email each time you reach the threshold. As in most cases, you will not be the only administrator; a group of people will be notified to take a look and check which resources are utilizing the budget the most. You will find this feature really helpful, especially if you have a strict requirement when it comes to cloud cost. By adding action groups, you can plan automated saving based on the rules you define. We can think of an example here:

- When you reach 75%, you send an email to all administrators.
- When you reach 85%, you can run a script that will scale down Dev/Test environments.
- When you reach 90%, you send an SMS to all administrators, send an email to all engineers, and shut down Dev/Test environments.

With such flexibility, you can think of several scenarios that will be appropriate to your current workloads and the characteristics of your systems.

You just learned about budgets and how to configure them to monitor your resources. Let's now continue with other automation solutions that may help you to keep an eye on the Azure services and applications you manage.

Implementing management automation

Using all of the preceding knowledge should help you to better manage your subscriptions, their cost, and the policies assigned to them. There is one more thing that comes to mind when thinking about such complex tasks—automation. Fortunately, Azure offers full integration with its services, so you can build your own pipelines for handling additional tasks and monitoring actions.

Understanding the basics of the mentioned services is crucial to be able to get started with this topic. Once you are familiar with them, go to the subscription you want to automate.

To finish the integration, we need a service that will take the JSON string and push it further or trigger an action. For this example, I selected Azure Logic Apps, which seems like a better match for an administrator than Azure Event Hub and can help you to build a complex solution quickly.

 We will not cover the process of creating an Azure Logic App in this book—if you need guidance, check `https://docs.microsoft.com/en-us/azure/logic-apps/quickstart-create-first-logic-app-workflow` in the documentation.

Now we are ready to integrate the subscription with the service. To perform this exercise, you will need the following:

- A working Azure subscription
- Azure Logic Apps instance, which you can integrate with Azure Event Grid

Implementing automation will require deploying Azure Event Grid and connecting the gathered data with Azure Logic Apps. All of the steps are described here:

1. Use the search box at the top of the Azure portal and type your subscription name (or just use it to go to the **Subscriptions** blade):

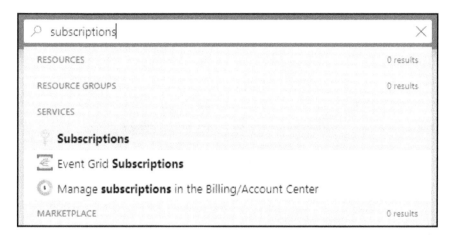

Figure 1.41 - Searching for the Subscriptions blade

2. Click on the Events blade, which is the starting point to create an Azure Event Grid subscription:

Figure 1.42 - Events blade

3. Click on the **+ Event subscription** button. You will see a new screen where you can enter details of a new subscription as shown in the following screenshot (*Figure 1.43*):

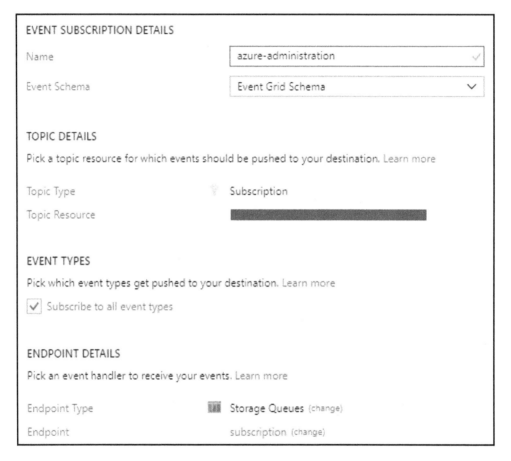

EVENT SUBSCRIPTION DETAILS

Name   azure-administration

Event Schema   Event Grid Schema

TOPIC DETAILS

Pick a topic resource for which events should be pushed to your destination. Learn more

Topic Type   Subscription

Topic Resource

EVENT TYPES

Pick which event types get pushed to your destination. Learn more

☑ Subscribe to all event types

ENDPOINT DETAILS

Pick an event handler to receive your events. Learn more

Endpoint Type   Storage Queues (change)

Endpoint   subscription (change)

Figure 1.43 - Creating an event subscription

4. When you click on the **Create** button, the process of creating a subscription will start. After a moment, you should be able to see a screen similar to mine:

Figure 1.44 - Current event subscription

5. Go to your Azure Logic Apps instance and click on the **Logic app designer** blade:

Figure 1.45 - Logic app designer blade

6. Search for Azure Queues, which is also available as a part of the recommended services:

Figure 1.46 - Recommended connectors with Azure Queues visible in the bottom-right corner

7. Click on the Azure Queues connector.
8. Provide a name for the connection and select the storage account where messages are stored.
9. Set the queue name and the check frequency.
10. Save the application.

Before a subscription is created, you have to provide additional details:

- **Name**: This is a unique name for your subscription that will help you to distinguish it from the others.
- **Event Schema**: You have three different schemas available here. As this section is not about digging deeper into Azure Event Grid, you should select the **Event Grid Schema** option. Other ones (**Cloud Event/Custom**) would also be correct here as the choice changes the schema without affecting the payload.
- **Subscribe to all event types**: By deselecting this checkbox, you will have the opportunity to explicitly select event types you are interested in. In general, it is a good idea to subscribe to all nine events, but maybe your particular case will have different requirements so feel free to choose anything you want.
- **Endpoint details**: You have four different options available here: WebHook, **Storage Queue**, **Event Hubs**, and **Hybrid Connections**. For the purpose of this exercise, I selected **Storage Queue**, but again, you can create a connection using any connector you like. The WebHooks and Storage Queues options are the most straightforward ones and suit the most needs in most of the integrations made with Azure Logic Apps.

 Note that you will have to create a new instance of a queue or Azure Event Hub if you do not have one when creating a connection.

At this moment, there is no event sent to the queue or generated by a subscription. To test the functionality, let's create a new resource, which should generate an event. For this exercise, I added an additional storage account named `azureadministratortest`.

 Monitoring events via the Azure portal may be cumbersome as the chart is refreshed only once in a while. For a better understanding of what is going on, use the connector you defined during a subscription creation.

As I used a storage account as my endpoint, I can check the queue whether there are any events related to the resources in my subscription. To do so, I used Microsoft Azure Storage Explorer (`https://azure.microsoft.com/en-us/features/storage-explorer/`), which is a free tool you can download and install on any operating system:

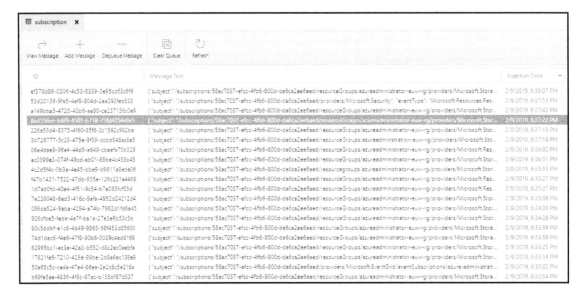

Figure 1.47 - Generated events stored within Azure Storage Queue

As you can see, I already have plenty of different messages generated by resources. Some of them are related to security events and some of them tell me details about services provisioned. One of the events is specifically related to my new storage account:

```
{
    "subject": "/subscriptions/.../resourceGroups/azureadministrator-euw-
rg/providers/Microsoft.Storage/storageAccounts/azureadministratortest",
    "eventType": "Microsoft.Resources.ResourceActionSuccess",
    "eventTime": "2019-02-09T17:36:55.8588074Z",
    "id": "c1950090-61e0-4627-9b77-776890ffb710",
    "data": {
        "correlationId": "c1950090-61e0-4627-9b77-776890ffb710",
        "httpRequest": {
        "resourceProvider": "Microsoft.Storage",
        "resourceUri": "/subscriptions/.../resourceGroups/azureadministrator-
euw-rg/providers/Microsoft.Storage/storageAccounts/azureadministratortest",
        "operationName": "Microsoft.Storage/storageAccounts/listKeys/action",
        "status": "Succeeded",
    },
    "dataVersion": "2",
```

```
    "metadataVersion": "1",
    "topic": "/subscriptions/..."
}
```

As you can see, such an event contains a massive amount of detail, such as the following:

- `data`, an object containing the event payload (all information related to an event)
- `eventType`, which may help you to decide how to react to such an event
- `subject`, a resource to which an event is related to

You, as an Azure administrator, can use this for multiple purposes:

- Building a custom monitoring solution
- Auditing changes made to resources
- Creating your own alerts based on the provided payloads

For now, we only have a complex JSON, which gives us some information—the question is how to use it in a real scenario.

We need to connect to a Storage Account—with Azure Logic Apps, it is easy; you have to either search for the service you are interested in or just use the most popular ones. In my case, I found **Azure Queues**, which happened to be available without searching for it:

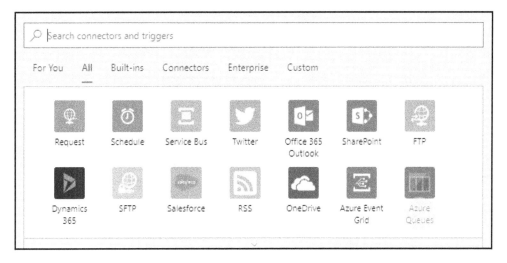

Figure 1.48 - Recommended connectors with Azure Queues visible in the bottom-right corner

When you click on the connector, you will see options available for it—for our case, we have two scenarios:

- When a specific number of messages are in a given queue
- When there are messages in a queue

I want to start my app anytime there is a message, so I use the latter. You will have to provide a name for the connection and select the storage account where messages are stored. Here, you can find my configuration:

Figure 1.49 - Available storage accounts

 If you do not see your storage account, use the **Manually enter connection information** option for the advanced configuration. You can also take a look at an in-depth article describing Azure Storage connector configuration, the link to which can be found in the *Further reading* section.

The last thing needed here will be the queue name and the check frequency. Once you are done, you can save your application. Congratulations—now events from a subscription can be read by your Logic App! Here, you can find the result of running it—as you can see, the event payload is available for further integrations by using the MessageText property of the JSON string:

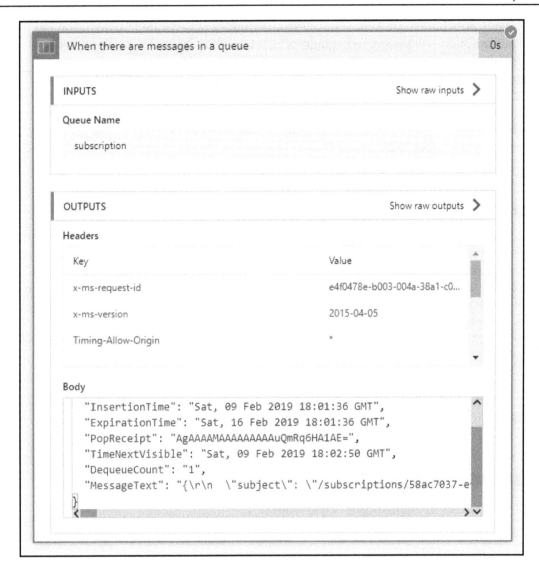

Figure 1.50 - Azure Logic App run debugging

The debug view for Azure Logic Apps is really helpful when you are in a need of investigating an issue with your application. In this particular example, you can also see what are the available fields, which you can take control of. As there is no way to attach a debugger to Azure Logic Apps, use it frequently when developing your apps, so you can be sure that everything works exactly as you designed.

Now, your possibilities are almost limitless—any message generated by the resources in your subscription will be sent to a queue, which is read by Azure Logic Apps. As this service offers over 200 different connectors that can be used in your application, you can do whatever you want with the data aggregated—starting from parsing the JSON string to advanced integrations with Office 365, Azure Functions, or even SAP or IBM MQ. The most important thing is to leverage Azure capabilities in terms of flexibility and automation—as an administrator, you will be able to quickly develop a tool that you can use for better control over resources and subscriptions.

Summary

This chapter should help you to understand the basic concepts of Azure administration regarding subscriptions and resources. We covered the most important topics such as getting a subscription and implementing the very first policies and learned about cost monitoring and usage analysis. While they seem to be simple, a good understanding of these is crucial for getting better with Azure cloud solutions. Things such as policies or blueprints are also one of the most common tasks of Azure administrators and operators—they are required to keep things consistent and compliant with your company rule set. You should now be able to control your spending limits, ensure various security rules are enforced, and analyze cloud services cost.

The next chapters will cover more detailed topics such as virtual machines, networking, or storage so you can learn different concepts related to managing cloud services.

Further reading

The following are about getting an Azure subscription:

- PAYG subscription overview: `https://azure.microsoft.com/en-us/offers/ms-azr-0003p/`
- Enterprise Agreement benefits and overview: `https://www.microsoft.com/en-us/licensing/licensing-programs/enterprise?activetab=enterprise-tab:primaryr2`
- CSP search: `https://www.microsoft.com/en-us/solution-providers/home`

For details on implementing subscription policies, see the following:

- Creating a custom policy: `https://docs.microsoft.com/en-us/azure/governance/policy/tutorials/create-and-manage`

The following is about using Azure Blueprints for repeatable deploy and update operations:

- Understanding Azure Blueprint resource locks: `https://docs.microsoft.com/en-us/azure/governance/blueprints/concepts/resource-locking`

Check out the following for more on implementing management automation:

- Managed Identities for Azure resources: `https://docs.microsoft.com/en-us/azure/active-directory/managed-identities-azure-resources/overview`
- Azure resources limits: `https://docs.microsoft.com/en-us/azure/azure-subscription-service-limits`
- Cloudyn: `https://www.cloudyn.com/`
- Azure Storage connector configuration in details - `https://docs.microsoft.com/en-us/azure/connectors/connectors-create-api-azureblobstorage`

Managing Azure Resources 2

To become a successful Azure administrator, you have to understand different concepts such as ARM, locks, and resource providers. They are the bread and butter of most Azure operations, and learning about them will help you work through more advanced topics such as automation and security and compliance. In this chapter, we will focus on the most important concepts that are used when managing Azure resources, including deployments, grouping services, and automation. We will learn how to manage resource providers and resource groups. Then, we will perform deployments using ARM with templates and also learn how to implement resource locks. The last section will cover automatic resource group management with Azure Event Grid and implementing proper resource naming conventions.

In this chapter, we will cover the following topics:

- Managing resource providers
- Managing resource groups
- Performing deployments using ARM with templates
- Implementing resource locks
- Automatic resource group management with Azure Event Grid
- Implementing proper resource naming conventions

Let's get started!

Technical requirements

To complete the exercises in this chapter, you will need the following:

- Access to an Azure subscription (you can reference `Chapter 1`, *Getting Started with Azure Subscriptions*, to learn how to create a one).
- Azure PowerShell installed on your computer: `https://docs.microsoft.com/en-us/powershell/azure/azurerm/other-install?view=azurermps-6.13.0`.
- Azure CLI: `https://docs.microsoft.com/en-us/cli/azure/install-azure-cli?view=azure-cli-latest`.

- Microsoft Azure Storage Explorer: `https://azure.microsoft.com/en-us/features/storage-explorer/`.
- Read about Azure Event Grid: `https://docs.microsoft.com/en-us/azure/event-grid/overview`.
- Read about Azure Logic Apps: `https://docs.microsoft.com/en-us/azure/logic-apps/logic-apps-overview`.
- You'll need to run the `az login` command (for Azure CLI) or `Connect-AzAccount` (for Powershell) once the appropriate tool has been installed.

Managing resource providers

In Azure, each service is managed by a separate **resource provider**. By default, most of the providers are not registered in your subscription. This is a perfectly fine scenario as you will probably never use all the RPs inside a single subscription. In most cases, a resource provider is registered immediately when provisioning a resource of a specific type for the first time. There are, however, moments when you need to do this manually. Let's learn how to do so using both the portal and PowerShell cmdlets.

Any time your subscription tries to access a non-registered resource provider, you will see a notification saying that a provider of a specific type is required before you can provision a resource of a particular type. There are two ways to check what is registered inside your subscription – you can either use the portal or a specific PowerShell command.

To check RPs in the portal, follow these steps:

1. Search for your subscription using the search field at the top of the portal, as shown in the following screenshot:

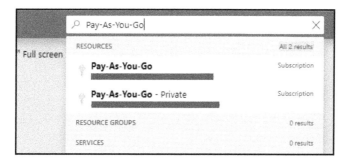

Figure 2.1: Searching for a subscription

2. The next thing to do is select the **Resource providers** blade:

Figure 2.2: Resource providers blade

3. You will see a complete list of supported RPs, along with information about whether it is available for your subscription:

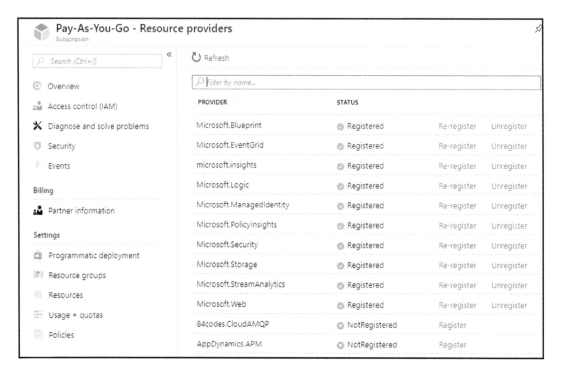

Figure 2.3: Registered subscription resource providers

The same can be done by running the following Powershell cmdlet in your Powershell environment. With the following command, we list all the providers and pipe them to the `Select-Object` function, thus filtering the fields:

```
Get-AzureRmResourceProvider -ListAvailable | Select-Object
ProviderNamespace, RegistrationState
```

 Note that you may need to connect to your subscription before calling the preceding command. To do so, use the `Connect-AzureRmAccount` cmdlet.

The following is the result of calling the command for my subscription:

```
ProviderNamespace RegistrationState
----------------- -----------------
Microsoft.Blueprint Registered
```

```
Microsoft.EventGrid Registered
microsoft.insights Registered
Microsoft.Logic Registered
Microsoft.ManagedIdentity Registered
Microsoft.PolicyInsights Registered
Microsoft.Security Registered
Microsoft.Storage Registered
Microsoft.StreamAnalytics Registered
Microsoft.Web Registered
84codes.CloudAMQP NotRegistered
AppDynamics.APM NotRegistered
Aspera.Transfers NotRegistered
Auth0.Cloud NotRegistered
Citrix.Cloud NotRegistered
. . .
```

As you can see, I got the list of providers and their registration states. Now, we will try to register/unregister a provider from a subscription.

Managing available RPs is really simple using both the Azure portal and PowerShell. To change the state of a provider in the portal, simply click on the **Register / Unregister** button above the available providers. Once you've done that, the status will be displayed as **Registering** or **Unregistering**, as shown in the following screenshot:

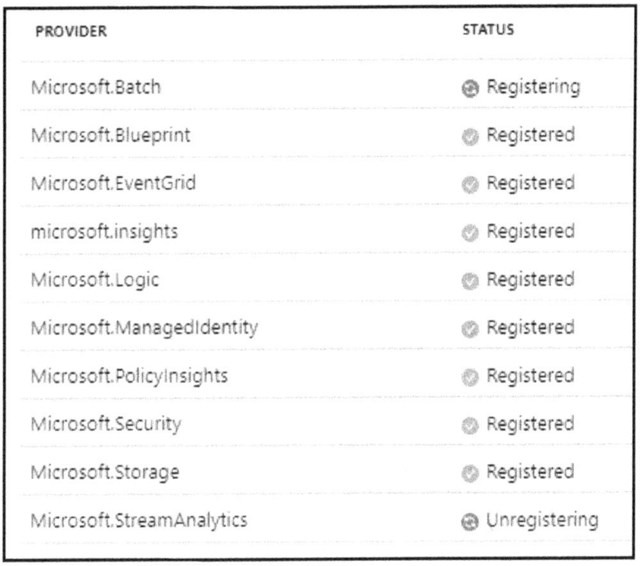

PROVIDER	STATUS
Microsoft.Batch	⊕ Registering
Microsoft.Blueprint	⊘ Registered
Microsoft.EventGrid	⊘ Registered
microsoft.insights	⊘ Registered
Microsoft.Logic	⊘ Registered
Microsoft.ManagedIdentity	⊘ Registered
Microsoft.PolicyInsights	⊘ Registered
Microsoft.Security	⊘ Registered
Microsoft.Storage	⊘ Registered
Microsoft.StreamAnalytics	⊕ Unregistering

Figure 2.4: Registering/unregistering resource providers

The same can be done in PowerShell with the following commands:

```
Register-AzResourceProvider -ProviderNamespace Microsoft.BotService

Unregister-AzResourceProvider -ProviderNamespace Microsoft.BotService
```

Under the hood, once you've initialized the process of registering a provider, a particular RP will be added to your subscription that you can manage and provision its resources. This includes registering its namespace, different types of resources (for example, if you want to deploy an Azure App Service with application settings, both the application and its configuration are managed via Azure Resource Manager separately), and the locations where it will be available.

This is also one way of limiting available services to users of your subscription – if you don't grant them the ability to register resource providers, they will not be able to provision services managed by them.

Resource providers are a simple way of separating your subscription from different kinds of resources and limiting access to them. If you are interested in how things really work, go to https://docs.microsoft.com/en-us/azure/azure-resource-manager/resource-group-overview, where you will find an overview of ARM. This is a great source of knowledge if you want to know how resources in Azure are deployed and managed behind the scenes.

In this section, you learned what resource providers are and how to use them to steer what can be used in a subscription. This will help you get started with the next section on resource groups, which are containers for Azure resources that are handled by registered RPs.

Managing resource groups

A resource group is the main logical component when it comes to governing resources provisioned in Azure. You cannot create a service without selecting one – this is why learning the basic principles of managing resource groups is crucial for becoming a better Azure administrator. We will focus on things such as performing basic actions on resource groups, moving resources, and managing them so that you can learn all the necessary operations required on a daily basis.

To get started, you'll need a resource group. Creating one is one of the easiest operations in Azure – you can use the Azure portal, PowerShell cmdlet, or Azure CLI for this. If you prefer using the graphics interface, search for the `Resource group` term in the marketplace and click on the **Create** button. You will see a really simple form where you only need to provide two things:

- Resource group name
- Resource group location

The following is an example configuration for my resource group:

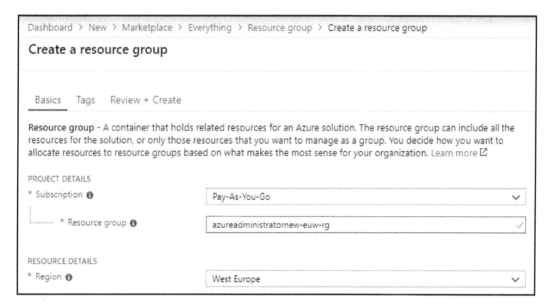

Figure 2.5: Creating a resource group

If you have more than a single subscription available, you will have to provide that value as well.

When everything is ready, you can just click the **Review + Create** button to start the process of creating an RG. Using Azure CLI or PowerShell is also just as easy. Here, you can find a command and a result when using the CLI. We will provide additional details such as its location and subscription to avoid mistakes:

```
$ az group create --name "azurecli-euw-rg" --location "West Europe" --
subscription "Pay-As-You-Go"
```

The result of creating a resource group looks like this:

```
{
  "id": "/subscriptions/.../resourceGroups/azurecli-euw-rg",
  "location": "westeurope",
  "managedBy": null,
  "name": "azurecli-euw-rg",
  "properties": {
    "provisioningState": "Succeeded"
  },
  "tags": null
}
```

As an alternative, you can use Azure PowerShell, as shown here:

```
PS C:\Users\kamz> New-AzResourceGroup -Location "West Europe" -Name
azurepowershell-euw-rg
```

PowerShell's output is quite different in terms of its structure but provides similar information to the Azure CLI:

```
ResourceGroupName : azurepowershell-euw-rg
Location : westeurope
ProvisioningState : Succeeded
Tags :
ResourceId : /subscriptions/.../resourceGroups/azurepowershell-euw-rg
```

Now, we are ready to learn about some additional management activities.

Browsing resource groups

When you have created some resource groups, they will be available in your subscription. We can quickly display them using either the Azure CLI or PowerShell window. Both commands are pretty straightforward. The result for Azure CLI is as follows:

```
$ az group list --subscription "Pay-As-You-Go"
```

The result of running the preceding command will look like this:

```
[
  {
    "id": "/subscriptions/.../resourceGroups/azureadministrator-euw-rg",
    "location": "westeurope",
    "managedBy": null,
    "name": "azureadministrator-euw-rg",
    "properties": {
      "provisioningState": "Succeeded"
    },
    "tags": {}
  }
  {
    ...
  }
]
```

You will get a similar effect for the PowerShell cmdlet, as shown here. Note that it returns a similar result containing information about the resource group's location, its tags, and its identifier:

```
PS C:\Users\kamz> Get-AzResourceGroup
```

The result of running the preceding PowerShell cmdlet should look like this:

```
ResourceGroupName : azureadministrator-euw-rg
Location : westeurope
ProvisioningState : Succeeded
Tags :
ResourceId : /subscriptions/.../resourceGroups/azureadministrator-euw-rg

(...)
```

Note that both commands provide additional parameters. The following is the result of running the Azure CLI command with an additional switch that determines the output's format (which is `--output table`):

```
$ az group list --subscription "Pay-As-You-Go" --output "table"
```

With an additional parameter, the output will change from its default JSON representation to a table:

```
Name Location Status
-------------------------- ---------- ----------
azureadministrator-euw-rg westeurope Succeeded
azureadministratornew-euw-rg westeurope Succeeded
azureadminstration-euw-rg westeurope Succeeded
azurecli-euw-rg westeurope Succeeded
azurepowershell-eue-rg westeurope Succeeded
azurepowershell-euw-rg westeurope Succeeded
```

Remember that for the Azure CLI, you can always use the -h switch to get help regarding a command.

Now that we've got some information about the available resource groups, we can dive deeper and check out the resources they contain.

Listing the available resources

As we mentioned earlier, resource groups are containers for provisioned Azure resources. If you do not want to use the Azure portal to browse and search for the available resource groups and their resources, you can use the Azure CLI for that:

```
$ az resource list --resource-group "azureadministrator-euw-rg" --
subscription "Pay-As-You-Go"
```

In the preceding command, we are using the resource group's name and a subscription name to narrow the results. The result of listing resources should look similar to the following. This should contain various pieces of information, such as the location of a resource, its name, and more:

```
[
  {
    "id": "/subscriptions/.../resourceGroups/azureadministrator-euw-
rg/providers/Microsoft.Logic/workflows/azureadministrator-euw-logicapp",
    "identity": null,
    "kind": null,
    "location": "westeurope",
    "managedBy": null,
    "name": "azureadministrator-euw-logicapp",
    "plan": null,
```

```
    "properties": null,
    "resourceGroup": "azureadministrator-euw-rg",
    "sku": null,
    "tags": {},
    "type": "Microsoft.Logic/workflows"
},
{
    ...
}
]
```

 There is no *best way* to manage resource groups and their resources – you are allowed to use any tool (the Azure portal, PowerShell, or Azure CLI) as you like. On the other hand, sometimes, some operations cannot be done from the portal – or require lots of manual work. This is why the command line is a recommended environment for Azure administrators as well.

In some cases, you may realize that a resource was placed in an invalid resource group. Fortunately, there is a solution to this, without a need to reprovision it.

Moving resources

Now, let's assume you have a resource in one resource group and want to move it to another one. There are a few possible scenarios when you would do so:

- If you simply made a mistake and provisioned a resource in an invalid resource group
- If you found resources that have a different life cycle and want to differentiate between deployments
- If you are redesigning an application and want to separate resources related to different domains
- If you do not want to perform a redeployment to place resources in a different resource group

In Azure, this operation is really simple – all you need to do is gather the following parameters:

- **Destination group**: A place where resources should be moved to
- **IDs of resources**: The identifiers of the resources you want to move

For example, I want to move an Azure Logic App named `azureadministrator-euw-logicapp` to a resource group named `azureadministratornew-euw-rg`.

The following is the full command I used to perform this operation:

```
$ az resource move --destination-group "azureadministratornew-euw-rg" --ids
"/subscriptions/.../resourceGroups/azureadministrator-euw-
rg/providers/Microsoft.Logic/workflows/azureadministrator-euw-logicapp"
```

The preceding command moves a specific resource (identified by its identifier) to a destination group inside the same subscription. Note that while moving the resource, a notification will appear in Azure portal stating that an operation is ongoing and that a certain resource may be moved in a moment, as shown in the following screenshot:

Figure 2.6: View of the resource group with resources under the Move operation

 Remember that you *cannot* rename a resource group – if you misspell a name, the only way to change it is to create a new one and move the necessary resources to it. Also, not all resources can be moved. The full list can be found at `https://docs.microsoft.com/en-us/azure/azure-resource-manager/resource-group-move-resources`.

When the operation is completed, all the resources that were moved will have new IDs attached to them. The move operation does not break anything from a service point of view. However, you will have to remember to update your CI/CD pipelines if they deploy anything to Azure – in most cases, you are providing a resource group name, which will have to be updated in that case.

 The move operation can be also used to move resources between subscriptions. This is a very helpful feature when you want to, for example, promote an environment from dev to production or use different subscriptions for different projects.

Before we sum up managing resource groups, there is one more concept worth mentioning. Each individual Azure service is managed by its API, called a resource provider. Each individual instance of a service is represented by a unique identifier called a resource ID. To understand how to build such an identifier, we must see what a resource provider identifier looks like.

Understanding resource providers

All the operations that are invoked via the command line or Azure portal are reflected with the help of Azure Resource Manager. When you look closely at resource IDs, you will see that they all have their provider provided. Take a look at the following Azure Logic App ID:

```
/subscriptions/.../resourceGroups/azureadministrator-euw-
rg/providers/Microsoft.Logic/workflows/azureadministrator-euw-logicapp
```

Here, the registered provider is `Microsoft.Logic`. The full namespace of the resource is displayed as `Microsoft.Logic/workflows`. This means that each Logic App uses that provider under the hood and all the operations that are performed on it are performed with the registered RP. If we take a look at another resource, the displayed provider will be different:

```
/subscriptions/.../resourceGroups/azureadministrator-euw-
rg/providers/Microsoft.Storage/storageAccounts/azureadministratortest
```

As you can see, here, Azure uses `Microsoft.Storage` and the `Microsoft.Storage/storageAccounts` namespace. The more you work with Azure, the more familiar you will become with the available providers. In fact, constructing such an ID will also become a piece of cake for you – the only thing hard to remember is your subscription ID.

Managing resource groups requires some practice, but once you start performing different operations on them, things will quickly become straightforward for you. Since you are just starting your journey of administrating Azure resources, I encourage you to focus on learning commands to be used in a command line as they will greatly improve your productivity when working with cloud services.

In Azure, some changes are much easier when performed with the right command than by clicking a dozen blades in the portal. The only thing required here is practice. This is why you should find other concepts from this chapter extremely interesting; they'll help you build up your knowledge when it comes to governing resources in Azure.

Using the Azure CLI or Azure PowerShell, you can perform far more operations over your resources and resource groups. Here are the most useful ones:

- The following operations can be performed on the CLI:
  - `az group exists`: Checks whether a group exists
  - `az group export`: Exports a resource group template
  - `az group update`: Updates a resource group with the desired parameters
  - `az resource create`: Creates a resource
  - `az resource invoke-action`: Invokes an action on a resource
- The following commands can be used on PowerShell:
  - `Export-AzureRmResourceGroup`: Exports a resource group template
  - `Set-AzureRmResourceGroup`: Sets the desired parameter on a resource group
  - `Move-AzureRmResource`: Moves Azure resources to another resource group
  - `Set-AzureRmResource`: Sets the desired parameter on a resource

This section helped you understand one of the most important concepts in Azure: resource groups. It is crucial that you understand how resource groups work and their capabilities so that you can work with them with no worries. In the next section, you will extend your current knowledge by learning how to perform deployments in the context of a resource group using ARM templates.

Performing deployments using ARM with templates

One of the most important features of any computer system is the ability to introduce changes to it seamlessly and in an automatic fashion. When infrastructure is considered, it is especially handy if there is a way to code it. This enables us to replicate it anywhere at any time with a single command. This approach, often abbreviated as **Infrastructure-as-Code (IaC)**, plays a major role in modern applications as it guarantees that all the components are scripted and that no manual work is required to restore them (for example, in the case of disaster recovery).

This section addresses this problem by introducing **Azure Resource Manager** (**ARM**) templates, which are JSON files that are used to describe how a service should behave and be configured.

There are multiple ways to prepare an ARM template, which can be reused and modified anytime you want. Before we get started, you have to understand how a typical template is structured. Let's take a look at the following JSON file:

```
{
    "$schema":
"https://schema.management.azure.com/schemas/2015-01-01/deploymentTemplate.
json#",
    "contentVersion": "",
    "parameters": { },
    "variables": { },
    "functions": [ ],
    "resources": [ ],
    "outputs": { }
}
```

As you can see, it contains two metadata fields (`$schema` and `contentVersion`) and five sections. Each section is used for a different purpose:

- `parameters`: Since each template can be used for different regions, tiers, or configuration settings, there has to be a way you can pass them. This section describes each parameter that can be passed to the template, including its type and the default value.
- `variables`: Sometimes, you need to evaluate a value based on the passed `parameters` (or maybe you just want to avoid duplicates and define it in one place). When using ARM templates, this section can be used for defining values that you can use for other resources. As it is parsed after `parameters`, you can leverage each value that's passed from the outside of the template.
- `functions`: A user-defined function that you can use in the template.
- `resources`: The main section in a template. It contains descriptions of the resources you want to provision in Azure. To make things more flexible, you can use values from three other sections: `parameters`, `variables`, and `functions`.
- `outputs`: This section can be used to return values from your template. Such a value could be a connection string to a storage account, resource ID, or a VM IP address.

ARM templates leverage the concept of resources managed by Azure Resource Manager. This means that with ARM templates, you can provision any element that is considered a resource in Azure. To be more specific, you can provision both an Azure App Service instance and its settings (called application settings) separately. A resource does not have to be a service, and you can find them in the Azure Marketplace.

Of course, not all sections are required – to make a template valid, it has to contain the following sections:

- `$schema`
- `contentVersion` (for versioning purposes)
- `resources`

All other sections (`parameters`, `variables`, `functions`, and `outputs`) are optional. A full description of the structure and the syntax can be found at `https://docs.microsoft.com/en-us/azure/azure-resource-manager/resource-group-authoring-templates`.

Now that you have understood the basics of ARM templates, we can try to prepare some and deploy them. As we mentioned previously, there are a few ways to generate or create such a template – we will give each one a go. To make things easier, we will assume that we want to deploy two storage accounts, with the second one related to the first one.

Now that you understand the theoretical concepts of resource groups, we will focus on writing an actual template and using it.

Writing a template from scratch

Conceptually, the easiest way to generate an ARM template is to write our very own. While, initially, it is pretty easy, you will probably reconsider your approach after a while. When your infrastructure contains tens of components, maintaining a JSON file with over 1,000 lines may be really painful. Nonetheless, this is one of the options and we should cover it so that you have the full picture of all the available options.

In the following link, you can view all the resources that are managed by ARM and their references: `https://docs.microsoft.com/en-us/azure/templates/microsoft.aad/allversions`. Each resource belongs to a particular namespace (so if you search for `Storage Account`, you will go to the **Storage** section). ARM also maintains more than one version of its API, which is why you can select from multiple available APIs.

Since we are about to create a brand-new piece of storage, it seems like a good idea to use the most recent version. The minimal (containing only required fields) version of the storage account resource for version 2019-06-01 looks like this:

```
{
    "name": "<string>",
    "type": "Microsoft.Storage/storageAccounts",
    "apiVersion": "2019-04-01",
    "sku": {
        "name": "Standard_LRS"
    },
    "kind": "Storage",
    "location": "<string>",
    "properties" {}
}
```

Now, let's check what the full template containing the aforementioned storage accounts would look like. Go and check it out at https://gist.github.com/kamil-mrzyglod/7b868e6a892cba008b7a909a1baabf43.

In the presented template, the second storage account is linked to the first one with the dependsOn property. This property is used to define identifiers of resources that have to be deployed before this particular one. This is especially helpful when deploying resources that rely on connection strings or other parameters that have to be injected into a configuration.

 There is no guarantee regarding the order of deployments performed by Azure Resource Manager. This is why you should always use the dependsOn property to avoid conflicts during deployments.

In the preceding example, we used a special function named resourceId. It takes two parameters – the namespace and the resource name. Once it has been evaluated, it returns the full resource identifier, which uniquely defines the relationship.

This section should have helped you understand some of the common concepts of writing ARM templates such as structure, syntax, and use cases. However, writing a template from scratch is not always necessary. The next section will show you how you can export a template with a single click.

Automation scripts

If you have provisioned resources manually, there is a way to generate an automation script from the whole resource group. To do so, follow these steps:

1. Go to your resource group and click on the **Export template** blade:

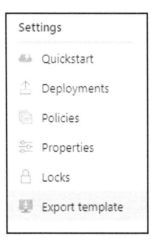

Figure 2.7: Export template blade

 In the newest version of the portal, the **Automation script** option has been renamed to **Export template**.

2. You will see a new window where you can find the whole ARM template. This can be exported. What's more, this feature generates four additional scripts that can be used if you do not like JSON templates:
    - CLI
    - PowerShell
    - .NET
    - Ruby

All are equally functional, so it is only a matter of preference.

3. In the following screenshot, we can see that the generated template is much more complex as it contains all the possible parameters that can be set for a resource:

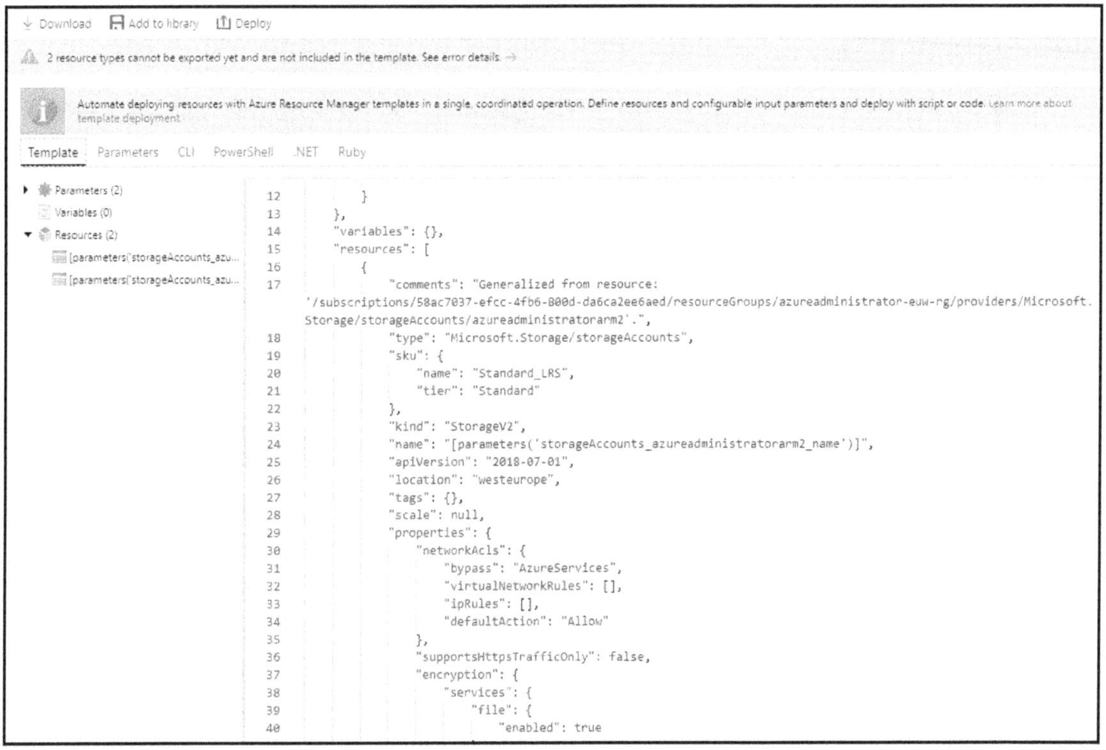

Figure 2.8: ARM template generated from the portal

From my experience, I can tell that using such a generated template is a good starting point, but unfortunately, there are situations where such templates will contain errors (because a parameter was not exported or exported partially). This is why it is a good idea to perform a quick check of it by clicking on the **Deploy** button that's available on the blade.

Exporting a template for deployed resources is a good idea, especially when starting with a proof-of-concept and proceeding to a more mature solution. In your daily work, this approach may have too many cons and you need a tool that will help you introduce logic or deploy resources in a more flexible way. This is why, in the next section, we will cover some extra tools that may suit your needs.

Other tools

ARM templates are not the only way to manage resources via ARM. There are external tools that you can consider if you find this particular feature cumbersome or counterproductive. These tools are as follows:

- **Azure Fluent**: A set of helpful SDKs that enable you to programmatically call ARM APIs to provision resources. They are written for multiple different platforms (.NET, Java, Python, or Node.js).
- **Terraform**: A tool by HashiCorp where you use a YAML file to describe your infrastructure.
- **Pulumi**: A new project where you can use TypeScript, Go, or Python to write scripts that describe your infrastructure.

Each tool has its pros and cons – your choice may be also affected by the technology stack your team is used to. I strongly encourage you to give the aforementioned tools a go as they follow the recent standards in terms of scripting infrastructure and may greatly improve your productivity.

Once you have your template prepared, you probably want to deploy it. The easiest way to do so is to use the CLI. The following is an example of the command required to deploy the template we created earlier:

```
az group deployment create --name <name-of-a-deployment> --resource-group
<name-of-rg> --template-file <name-of-your-file>.json
```

The preceding command will create a new deployment with a specific name and use a particular template file. Of course, if your template accepts parameters, you can pass them using the `--parameters` switch:

```
az group deployment create --name <name-of-a-deployment>--resource-group
<name-of-rg> --template-file <name-of-your-file>.json --parameters
storageAccountType=Standard_GRS
```

Once the deployment is finished, you should see a JSON file that represents the serialized output of the operation. Each deployment can be found in the **Deployments** blade of your resource group:

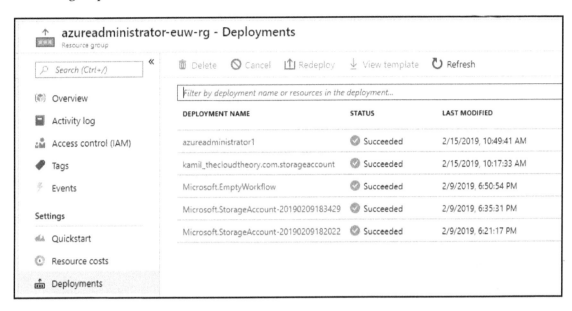

Figure 2.9: Resource group deployments list

With ARM templates, you can quickly provision your infrastructure in any region available in Azure. As it is a native way of deploying resources in Azure, it is important to understand at least the basic features of this functionality so that you can quickly multiply required services. To better understand the advanced topics (such as conditional statements, functions, and linked templates), take a look at the following link: `https://docs.microsoft.com/en-us/azure/azure-resource-manager/templates/template-syntax`. It contains a full description of the syntax and its structure.

Although JSON templates are often a recommended way of managing resources in Azure, do not forget about alternatives. Azure Fluent, Terraform, and Pulumi can be really interesting propositions, especially if you are working with IaaS architectures.

Deciding which tool is the best for you relies solely on your actual requirements. In many setups, a mix of available tools will give the best results. The next section will help you enhance your deployments by introducing locks, which help in preventing accidental deletion of resources or changes in their configuration.

Implementing resource locks

Often, there is a need to secure your deployed environment so that there is no possibility to easily change them or even remove them by a mistake. As you cannot just rely on given conventions or communication between teams, you have to implement some kind of policy that will make resources read-only. In Azure, the way to achieve that is to leverage resource locks. In this section, we'll learn how to implement resource locks and secure our workloads against accidental changes.

There are two levels of locks in Azure:

- **Subscription locks**: These are applied to all the resources inside a subscription.
- **Resource group locks**: These are applied to all the resources inside a resource group (and the resource group itself).

Also, you can choose between two different kinds of those locks:

- **Read-only**: A lock that prevents you and others from introducing changes to the resources
- **Delete**: A lock that prevents you and others from deleting resources (but allows you to change them)

In general, using locks on production resources in Azure should be one of your most important habits as an Azure administrator – it is one of the simplest features but gives you complete control over what is and what is not allowed when it comes to modifying environments.

 For more information on ARM locks, please refer to the following link: https://docs.microsoft.com/en-us/azure/templates/microsoft.authorization/allversions.

To implement a lock, you have to answer the question of whether it is a subscription lock or if you only need it for a particular resource group. The choice solely depends on the characteristics of the resources:

- If you have a subscription per project, you may need to create a production subscription that holds all the production resources and apply the subscription lock.

- If you have a mix of read-only and delete locks, you will have to implement multiple resource group locks.
- If you cannot have a separate subscription for your production workloads, you may need a resource group lock.

Let's take a look at how to implement each of them.

Subscription locks

Each lock is a separate resource and is available on either a subscription, resource group, or a resource level. In this section, we will cover working with them using Azure portal, but under the hood, locks are just Azure resources that are accessible via the ARM API. If you want to create a lock, follow these steps:

1. If you go to your subscription, you can find the **Resource locks** blade in the **Settings** section:

Figure 2.10: Resource locks blade

2. From the new screen, you can click on the **+ Add** button, where you will able to enter the lock's properties:

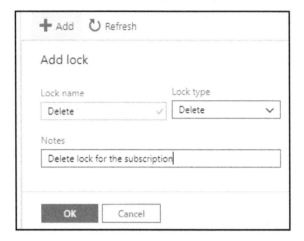

Figure 2.11: Creating a lock form

Adding a lock requires that you provide the following information:

- **Lock name**: The unique lock name across the given scope
- **Lock type**: Determines the behavior of a lock
- **Notes**: Optional notes

Once you click the **OK** button, a lock will be applied on the subscription level and a specific action (changes/deletion) will become forbidden.

3. The same can be done from the Azure CLI level. To list all the locks, you can use the following command:

```
$ az lock list
```

4. Since we are using an Azure CLI command without providing an output type, the default result representation is a JSON document. It contains information about the full identifier of the lock (`id`), its type (the `level` parameter) and additional information (such as a description and its `name`):

```
[
    {
        "id":
"/subscriptions/.../providers/Microsoft.Authorization/locks/Delete"
,
        "level": "CanNotDelete",
        "name": "Delete",
        "notes": "Delete lock for the subscription",
        "owners": null,
        "type": "Microsoft.Authorization/locks"
    }
]
```

5. Now, to create a new one, execute the following command:

```
$ az lock create -n "Read-only" -t "ReadOnly"
```

Now, you should be able to see the result of creating a read-only lock. Since we only provided the name (`-n`) and lock type (`-t`), only those fields will be filled in inside the JSON document:

```
{
    "id": "/subscriptions/.../providers/Microsoft.Authorization/locks/Read-only",
    "level": "ReadOnly",
    "name": "Read-only",
    "notes": null,
    "owners": null,
    "type": "Microsoft.Authorization/locks"
}
```

Now, let's look at resource group locks, which are more focused locks. This is because they're only applied at the resource group level.

Resource group locks

The procedure for creating a resource group lock is the same as the subscription lock – the only change is the place where the lock is applied. To add a lock from the Azure portal, follow these steps:

1. Go to your resource group and find the **Locks** blade:

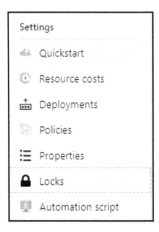

Figure 2.12: Locks blade

2. The rest is the same as in the *Subscription lock* section. When browsing a resource group lock, you will be able to also see the locks that have been applied at the subscription level:

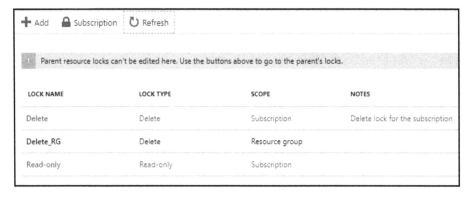

Figure 2.13: Resource group locks view

Performing the same operation from the CLI is even easier – you only need a single command where you pass the name of a lock (the -n parameter), its type (-t), and the resource group (-g) that it will be applied to:

```
$ az lock create -n "Read-only_RG" -t "ReadOnly" --resource-group
"azureadministrator-euw-rg"
```

The result of creating such a lock is a JSON representation of a created Azure resource (remember that locks are also resources in terms of Azure Resource Manager):

```
{
  "id": "/subscriptions/.../resourceGroups/azureadministrator-euw-
rg/providers/Microsoft.Authorization/locks/Read-only_RG",
  "level": "ReadOnly",
  "name": "Read-only_RG",
  "notes": null,
  "owners": null,
  "resourceGroup": "azureadministrator-euw-rg",
  "type": "Microsoft.Authorization/locks"
}
```

As you can see, the result of such a command is a little bit different than when performing it on the subscription – its identifier now contains the subscription name and the name of the resource group where the lock was applied.

Now, let's assume that we want to delete a resource group that is secured by a delete lock. To do so, we will try to delete a resource group:

```
$ az group delete -n "azureadministrator-euw-rg"
Are you sure you want to perform this operation? (y/n): y
```

As you can see, before the command runs, the CLI asks you whether you are sure about deleting the resource group. The result of running such a command will be as follows:

```
The scope '/subscriptions/.../resourcegroups/azureadministrator-euw-rg'
cannot perform delete operation because following scope(s) are locked:
'/subscriptions/.../resourceGroups/azureadministrator-euw-
rg,/subscriptions/...'. Please remove the lock and try again.
```

The result of deleting a resource group that has two delete locks (one from the subscription and one applied directly to the group) tells us that both the resource group and the subscription scopes are blocked. There is no way to remove such resources if locks are not removed beforehand.

Let's check what happens if we try to remove other resources provisioned inside a resource group:

```
PS Azure:\> az resource delete --ids /subscriptions/█████████████████████████/resourceGroups/chapter09/providers/Micros
Some resources failed to be deleted (run with `--verbose` for more information):
/subscriptions/████████████████████████████/resourceGroups/chapter09/providers/Microsoft.Network/virtualNetworks/test
Azure:/
PS Azure:\>
```

Figure 2.14: The result of deleting a resource with the "Delete" lock using Powershell

When you try to remove such a resource from the portal, you will be notified that such an operation is currently unavailable:

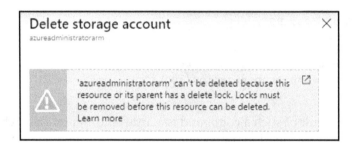

Figure 2.15: Deleting a locked resource in the portal

Additionally, if I add the read-only lock to the resource, the following message will be displayed when I try to change something:

```
Failed to update storage account 'azureadministratorarm'. Error: The scope
'azureadministrator-euw-
rg/providers/Microsoft.Storage/storageAccounts/azureadministratorarm'>azure
administratorarm' cannot perform write operation because following scope(s)
are locked:
'/subscriptions/...,/subscriptions/.../resourceGroups/azureadministrator-
euw-rg'. Please remove the lock and try again.
```

If you add a lock at the subscription/resource group level, it will be applied to all the resources provisioned there. However, there may be situations where you want to have better control over this functionality.

Fortunately, when using the Azure CLI, you can use additional switches that allow you to apply the lock to a specific resource type or even a particular resource only. To add a lock to the subscription for all storage accounts, you can use the following command:

```
az lock create --resource-type "Microsoft.Storage/storageAccounts"
```

Since the preceding command is run without additional parameters, it creates a lock at the highest level available (subscription). If you need a lock for a specific resource in a resource group, you may want to try the following snippet:

```
$ az lock create --resource
"/subscriptions/.../resourceGroups/azureadministrator-euw-
rg/providers/Microsoft.Storage/storageAccounts/azureadministratorarm" -g
"azureadministrator-euw-rg"
```

By using the whole identifier of a resource and applying the resource group's name, you can create a specific lock that is applied only at the resource level. You can also script locks using the ARM template:

```
{
  "name": "string",
  "type": "Microsoft.Authorization/locks",
  "apiVersion": "2016-09-01",
  "properties": {
    "level": "string",
    "notes": "string"
  }
}
```

Thanks to this feature, you can automatically apply it when a production environment is deployed to Azure.

For more information, you can refer to the `az lock` documentation: `https://docs.microsoft.com/en-us/cli/azure/lock?view=azure-cli-latest`.

Becoming a master in proper resource locking is especially important when managing Azure resources. With this simple feature, you can greatly enhance resource immutability and be confident that no one has changed resources without proper automation. The next section will help you understand how to audit changes and management actions on a resource group using a service called Azure Event Grid.

Automating resource group management with Azure Event Grid

Automation is one of the most important features available and is especially helpful when you're managing large workloads and have tens of systems under your control. This is especially true when the scale of your systems growths – when you have thousands of VMs under your control, doing everything manually becomes almost impossible. Fortunately, you do not have to be an Azure specialist to implement advanced workflows, which will help you understand what is happening with a particular resource group and all the resources it contains.

In this section, we'll learn how to organize a simple automation solution using Azure Event Grid and Azure Logic Apps, which will help you understand the concept and get you started with your own ideas.

Since Event Grid and Logic Apps are serverless services, infrastructure management is no longer your concern – the only thing you have to do is configure a service according to the documentation. Once you are familiar with the basics, you will understand this concept easily.

Creating an event subscription

The idea here is to leverage two Azure services that allow you to implement a complete solution without writing a single line of code. To do so, follow these instructions:

1. The gateway to automation in your resource group can be found in the **Events** blade, which can be found in every resource group:

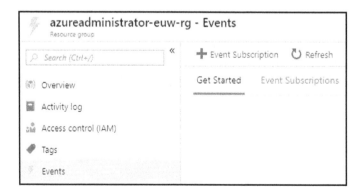

Figure 2.16: Creating an event subscription

Once you get there, we can start implementing our automation workflow.

2. When you click on the **+ Event Subscription** button, you will see a new screen where you will be able to enter all the required details for a new event subscription. Here, you can find an example of my settings:

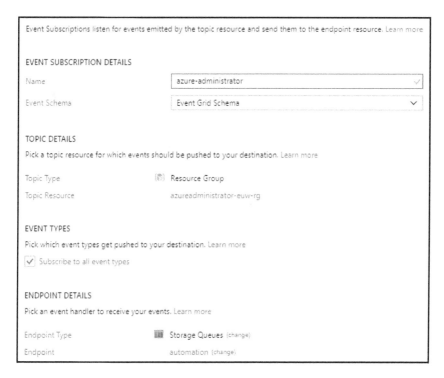

Figure 2.17: Creating an event subscription form

You will have to configure the following fields in order to add an event subscription:

- **Name**: A unique name for a subscription.
- **Event Schema**: A selected event schema supported by Azure Event Grid. Unfortunately, this topic will not be covered in this book (if you are an advanced Azure user, you can use any schema you want) – this is why I suggest you leave the default option as-is. If you are interested in the other schema, you can refer to the following link regarding the Event Grid schema: `https://docs.microsoft.com/en-us/azure/event-grid/event-schema`.

- **EVENT TYPES**: You can subscribe to all nine types or only the specific ones. Note that a resource group defines the same event types as a subscription – the difference is in the scope as here, only events from a specific resource group will be handled.
- **ENDPOINT DETAILS**: You can choose between Web Hook, Storage Queue, Event Hub, and Hybrid Connection. This example is limited to Storage Queues, but feel free to experiment on your own.

 A Storage Queue has to be configured *before* a subscription is created, so make sure you have an available Storage Account with the desired queue already created.

3. Once you are satisfied with your choices, you can click on the **Create** button. After a few seconds, a new subscription will become available for the resource group:

Figure 2.18: Event subscriptions view

The preceding view will show you the current status of the created subscription. It contains information regarding all the generated events (regardless of whether they succeeded or not). To understand the actual behavior, we will have to analyze the data.

Analyzing the gathered data

Now, we are ready to check whether everything works as expected. To do so, we can use Microsoft Azure Storage Explorer. When we access the queue we defined during the event subscription process, we can see that there are events gathered already:

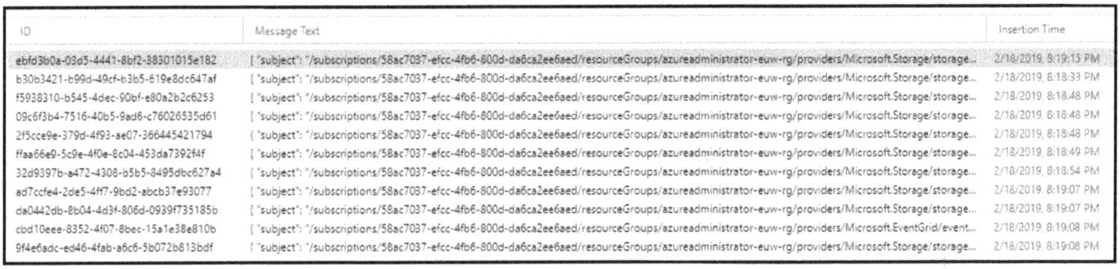

ID	Message Text	Insertion Time
ebfd3b0a-03d5-4441-8bf2-38301015e182	{ "subject": "/subscriptions/58ac7037-efcc-4fb6-800d-da6ca2ee6aed/resourceGroups/azureadministrator-euw-rg/providers/Microsoft.Storage/storage...	2/18/2019, 8:19:15 PM
b30b3421-b99d-49cf-b3b5-619e8dc647af	{ "subject": "/subscriptions/58ac7037-efcc-4fb6-800d-da6ca2ee6aed/resourceGroups/azureadministrator-euw-rg/providers/Microsoft.Storage/storage...	2/18/2019, 8:18:33 PM
f5938310-b545-4dec-90bf-e80a2b2c6253	{ "subject": "/subscriptions/58ac7037-efcc-4fb6-800d-da6ca2ee6aed/resourceGroups/azureadministrator-euw-rg/providers/Microsoft.Storage/storage...	2/18/2019, 8:18:48 PM
09c6f3b4-7516-40b5-9ad6-c76026535d61	{ "subject": "/subscriptions/58ac7037-efcc-4fb6-800d-da6ca2ee6aed/resourceGroups/azureadministrator-euw-rg/providers/Microsoft.Storage/storage...	2/18/2019, 8:18:48 PM
2f5cce9e-379d-4f93-ae07-366445421794	{ "subject": "/subscriptions/58ac7037-efcc-4fb6-800d-da6ca2ee6aed/resourceGroups/azureadministrator-euw-rg/providers/Microsoft.Storage/storage...	2/18/2019, 8:18:48 PM
ffaa66e9-5c9e-4f0e-8c04-453da7392f4f	{ "subject": "/subscriptions/58ac7037-efcc-4fb6-800d-da6ca2ee6aed/resourceGroups/azureadministrator-euw-rg/providers/Microsoft.Storage/storage...	2/18/2019, 8:18:49 PM
32d9397b-a472-4308-b5b5-8495dbc627a4	{ "subject": "/subscriptions/58ac7037-efcc-4fb6-800d-da6ca2ee6aed/resourceGroups/azureadministrator-euw-rg/providers/Microsoft.Storage/storage...	2/18/2019, 8:18:54 PM
ad7ccfe4-2de5-4ff7-9bd2-abcb37e93077	{ "subject": "/subscriptions/58ac7037-efcc-4fb6-800d-da6ca2ee6aed/resourceGroups/azureadministrator-euw-rg/providers/Microsoft.Storage/storage...	2/18/2019, 8:19:07 PM
da0442db-8b04-4d3f-806d-0939f735185b	{ "subject": "/subscriptions/58ac7037-efcc-4fb6-800d-da6ca2ee6aed/resourceGroups/azureadministrator-euw-rg/providers/Microsoft.Storage/storage...	2/18/2019, 8:19:07 PM
cbd10eee-8352-4f07-8bec-15a1e38e810b	{ "subject": "/subscriptions/58ac7037-efcc-4fb6-800d-da6ca2ee6aed/resourceGroups/azureadministrator-euw-rg/providers/Microsoft.EventGrid/event...	2/18/2019, 8:19:08 PM
9f4e6adc-ed46-4fab-a6c6-5b072b813bdf	{ "subject": "/subscriptions/58ac7037-efcc-4fb6-800d-da6ca2ee6aed/resourceGroups/azureadministrator-euw-rg/providers/Microsoft.Storage/storage...	2/18/2019, 8:19:08 PM

Figure 2.19: Generated events within Azure Storage Queue

A quick look at one of the records reveals all the data gathered here:


```
{
  "subject": "/subscriptions/.../resourceGroups/azureadministrator-euw-
rg/providers/Microsoft.Storage/storageAccounts/azureadministrator",
  "eventType": "Microsoft.Resources.ResourceActionFailure",
  "eventTime": "2019-02-18T19:17:52.7587534Z",
  "id": "407dc633-1157-46ac-97e5-92175fe78099",
  "data": {
    ...
  },
  "dataVersion": "2",
  "metadataVersion": "1",
  "topic": "/subscriptions/.../resourceGroups/azureadministrator-euw-rg"
}
```


As you can see, such a JSON document contains the following information:

- The event type (`eventType`)
- A timestamp telling us when an event occurred (`eventTime`)
- The identifier of an event (`id`)
- The origin of an event (`subject`)

You can leverage this information to implement a complete automation solution (for example, to find out when somebody changes a resource or even tries to change something). Now, let's try to extend this architecture and connect to Azure Logic Apps for an even greater set of possibilities.

As we used Storage Queues here, we can integrate events generated by our resource group with any other service that can read messages from it. For an administrator, the best choice is to use Azure Logic Apps.

 Here, we're assuming that you are familiar with the process of creating a Logic App. If you need guidance, check out https://docs.microsoft. com/en-us/azure/logic-apps/quickstart-create-first-logic-app- workflow.

Once your Azure Logic App has been provisioned, follow these steps:

1. Go to the **Logic app designer** blade to start the process of designing a new application:

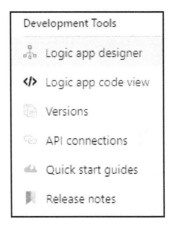

Figure 2.20: Logic app designer blade

2. In the designer window, you have multiple options to get started – there are many examples and templates that will speed up the process of creating a new app. For now, we need a custom one, so I selected **Blank Logic App**.

3. On the new screen, you will be able to search for connectors you are interested in. Since we used a queue from the Azure Storage service, this is the component we are searching for:

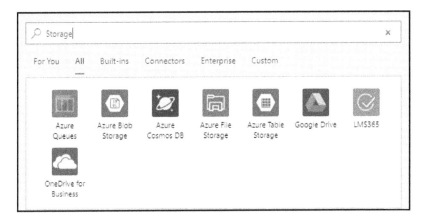

Figure 2.21: Azure Logic App connectors

Each connector has its own settings that you have to configure. For Azure Queues, the very first choice is to decide whether you do the following:

- You want to trigger an Azure Logic App when there is a specific number of messages in the queue
- See if there is a message in a queue

4. In this particular scenario, I went for the latter as I wanted to trigger it immediately when a new event is available. The second step is related to a storage account you want to use along with the connector. Obviously, you have to select a storage account you've used previously as the destination of the gathered events:

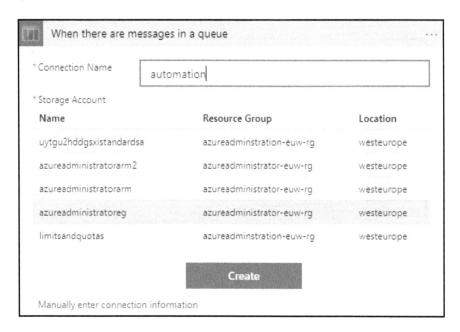

Figure 2.22: Available storage accounts for Azure Queue connector

If, for some reason, your storage account is not available, click on the **Manually enter connection information** link to switch to the advanced view.

5. The last thing needed here is to configure the interval of checks for the queue. For the purpose of this exercise, I chose 5 minutes (in a real scenario, you can select any interval that suits your needs, such as every 5 seconds):

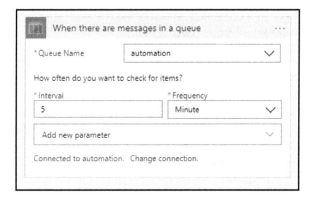

Figure 2.23: Queue connector settings

6. Now, you can save the application and test whether it works. If you followed my tutorial, you should be able to see a similar result to mine:

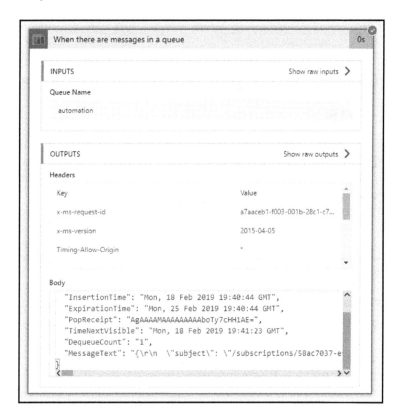

Figure 2.24: Azure Logic App run debugging

Congratulations! You have just created your very own automation pipeline that you can customize and extend to meet all your requirements.

There are over 200 different connectors available in Azure Logic Apps that you can leverage at any time to create event advanced workflows that will react to the incoming events and send emails, SMSes, raise alerts, or trigger reports. Azure Logic Apps are a great integration tool for those who do not want to develop a solution programmatically. As they rely on an intuitive and robust toolset, you can quickly implement the functionality you want. I strongly encourage you to give them a try and make them one of the common tools you are familiar with so that you can become much more productive and open many additional integration opportunities.

Using services such as Azure Event Grid and Azure Logic Apps becomes more and more important when searching for flexibility and automation in Azure administration. With proper experience, you can easily build complex pipelines that will audit resources and gather insights about their usage and configuration. The next section includes some guidance regarding naming conventions so that you can administer your resources in an even better fashion.

Implementing proper resource naming conventions

Becoming an Azure administrator means governing tens of hundreds of cloud resources. To be really productive here, you have to find a way to quickly find what you are looking for, without having to check the documentation or ask other people where a resource can be found. The real *ace in the hole* here is to find the naming convention that covers multiple projects and allows you to cover different domains of the business. In this section, we will discuss the different options that are available and what can be done to constrain them.

To get started, you have to understand why having a proper naming convention is crucial for many projects and administering them:

- You may have difficulty changing the name of a resource once it is provisioned.
- Once a naming convention is established, it is easy to find services that do not follow it.
- When a proper name is used, you can quickly understand its purpose, without the need to enter an extra command or browse the portal.

To cut a long story short, you are saving time when a convention is enforced. You should ensure that all the names are as verbose as possible. This, of course, will differ depending on the Azure service selected:

- When using Azure Storage, its name must be between 3 and 24 characters in length. You are not allowed to use anything besides letters and numbers.
- A resource group can be a maximum of 90 characters in length.
- Azure App Service offers a maximum of a little over 200 characters to be used as the service name.

Considered all these factors, you have to make sure that your naming convention does not block anybody from provisioning a resource.

There are many different levels when it comes to implementing a naming convention:

- Subscription
- Resource group
- Resources

Depending on the level, you may need a different convention to meet your requirements. Let's look at each of them.

Subscription

When governing multiple subscriptions, you will probably need to know exactly who is its owner. The recommended way of naming them can be found in the documentation (`https://docs.microsoft.com/en-us/azure/cloud-adoption-framework/ready/azure-best-practices/naming-and-tagging`):

```
<Company> <Department (optional)> <Product Line (optional)> <Environment>
```

Here, we're assuming the following parameters:

- Company: TheCloudTheory
- Department: IT
- Product Line: CRM
- Environment: Dev

You will get the following result:

```
TheCloudTheory IT CRM Dev
```

Personally, I dislike empty spaces between the names of my resources, so I would slightly modify the example and add dashes to get the following result:

```
TheCloudTheory-IT-CRM-Dev
```

Of course, this is not the only available option here. Let's prepare some other examples:

```
<Department>-<Environment>-<Product>
<Company>-<Product>-<Environment>
<Product>-<Environment>
```

Depending on the actual scenario, you may or may not need to use the department of the company here. However, it is not always possible to predict whether your company or client will need extra subscriptions. We can avoid situations where we have the following subscriptions under our command:

```
CompanyA
CompanyA-Dev
CompanyA-SuperProduct-Dev
```

To do this, always try to implement at least three different parameters in the names so that you are secure in case any modifications are made later.

The name of a subscription can be changed later. On the other hand, it is always a better option to avoid modifications instead of making them later.

Resource group

As opposed to a subscription, the name of a resource group cannot be changed once it has been created. The solution for this situation is to move the resources to a new resource group and delete the old one. To minimize the number of such situations, you should provide a proper recommendation when it comes to selecting names for groups. One extra parameter that will be useful here is called location.

Let's check out some examples of templates for resource groups names:

```
<product>-<location>-<environment>-rg
<product>-<location>-<environment>-resourcegroup
<company>-<product>-<location>-<environment>-rg
<company>-<department>-<location>-<environment>-resourcegroup
```

Whether you need to use a company name in the resource group name depends on your setup. If you govern a single subscription, it will need to know who the owner of the resource group is immediately. Let's assume that you have the following names:

```
ServiceA
CompanySuperproduct
WestEuropeCompanyC
```

In the preceding example, you are missing some key information. Let's try to answer the following questions:

- Which resource group is provisioned in West Europe?
- Which resource group belongs to CompanyB?
- Where ServiceC is deployed?
- What environments are deployed to the listed groups?

You cannot answer any of those questions with 100% confidence knowing that your answer is correct (what's more, providing an answer to the last question is impossible without checking the deployment pipelines). This is why using a proper naming convention is so important.

Resources

Resources can follow a similar naming convention to resource groups. Let's verify the following samples:

```
<service>-<location>
<product>-<location>-<environment>-<service>
<company>-<location>-<environment>-<product>-<service>
```

Depending on your needs, you may require different data to be available. In general, you can implement the following two approaches:

- Each element has to be as verbose as possible.
- A child element only has to implement the extra information that is not available for the parent.

Here are examples of those two approaches:

```
TheCloudTheory-IT-Prod -> TheCloudTheory-SomeProduct-Use-Prod-Rg ->
TheCloudTheory-SomeProduct-Use-Prod-AppServicePlan
TheCloudTheory-IT-Prod -> SomeProduct-Use-Prod-Rg -> AppServicePlan
```

The choice is yours – you have to select an approach that meets your requirements when it comes to administering resources in Azure.

Enforcing a naming convention without automating any action may be quite cumbersome. Fortunately, you can easily prepare a script that will tell you what resources do not match the rules. The following is a simple PowerShell script that displays all the resource groups that do not follow the `<product>-<location>-<service>` convention:

```
$resources = Get-AzureRmResource
foreach($resource in $resources)
{
    $resourceName = $resource.Name
    $match = $resourceName -match '[a-z]{1,}-[a-z]{1,3}-[a-z]{1,}'
    if($match -eq $false)
    {
        Write-Host $resourceName
    }
}
```

The preceding script iterates over all the resources inside a subscription and checks whether their names match the regular expression reflecting the expected naming convention. Now, let's say I have the following resource groups:

```
azure-administrator-logic
azureadministratorarm
azureadministratorarm2
azureadministratoreg
azurequeues
azureadministrator-euw-logicapp
limitsandquotas
uytgu2hddgsxistandardsa
```

The only one that follows the convention is `azureadministrator-euw-logicapp` – the rest are invalid and will be displayed.

Once you have your script ready, you can execute it any time you want. What's more is that you do not have to use PowerShell – you can leverage the Azure CLI or the REST API of the Azure Resource Manager to implement this functionality using other programming languages. Now that we've covered Azure Logic Apps, you can even implement your own pipeline integrated with Azure Event Grid, which will allow you to verify each resource once it has been provisioned.

For more information about naming conventions, refer to the following link: `https://docs.microsoft.com/en-us/azure/architecture/best-practices/naming-conventions`.

Summary

In this chapter, we learned how to manage resource providers and groups. We then learned how to perform deployments using ARM with templates and also learned how to implement resource locks. At the end of this chapter, we covered automatic resource group management with Azure Event Grid and implemented proper resource naming conventions.

Understanding the basics is really important as all the topics covered in this chapter will have their use in the following ones. Things such as resource locks, deployments with ARM templates, and moving resources are typical daily tasks of Azure administrators and operators. Remember that when it comes to cloud solutions, for most of the services you use, you are only paying for usage. When playing with a resource group, keep in mind that they are free of charge, regardless of whether they contain resources or not.

In the next chapter, we will learn how to configure and manage virtual networks, which are one of the main building blocks of Azure infrastructures.

3
Configuring and Managing Virtual Networks

One of the most important tasks for an Azure administrator is configuring the network properly. The bigger the system is, the more elements you will have to integrate. In this chapter, you will learn how to link multiple VNets and configure and secure subnets. We will also cover how to integrate virtual networks with a set of Azure services using service endpoints. We will then learn how to secure critical Azure services with service endpoints and how to configure a naming resolution. At the end of the chapter, we will create and configure a **network security group** (**NSG**). All of the topics that we will cover in this chapter are crucial for most Azure administrators as there are few systems that do not need some kind of networking attached to them. You will probably also work with internal applications that need to be enclosed inside a virtual network or placed behind a firewall.

This chapter will cover the following topics:

- Creating and configuring VNet peering
- Creating and configuring a VNet-to-VNet connection
- Creating and configuring subnets
- Securing critical Azure services with service endpoints
- Configuring a naming resolution
- Creating and configuring NSG

Technical requirements

To perform exercises from this chapter, you will need the following:

- Access to an Azure subscription (which we created in `Chapter 1`, *Getting Started with Azure Subscriptions*)
- Azure PowerShell installed on your computer (go to `https://docs.microsoft.com/en-us/powershell/azure/azurerm/other-install?view=azurermps-6.13.0` to install Azure PowerShell)
- Azure CLI installed on your computer (go to `https://docs.microsoft.com/en-us/cli/azure/install-azure-cli?view=azure-cli-latest` to install Azure CLI)

Creating and configuring VNet peering

You will often need to physically separate the different components of your system to achieve the required level of isolation for your particular components. The reason for this could be to isolate services in your company, to increase the ease of management, or to partition the system into smaller and unrelated segments. In cloud infrastructures, you do not have access to the physical layer of networking—instead, you can use software-based routers to help you segment your network. The resulting networks do not exist physically, hence the name *virtual networks*.

There are moments when you need to connect two isolated VNets. This gives you many crucial benefits—you can treat the traffic inside the networks as if it was a single ecosystem. This way, you can preserve the privacy inside the networks and achieve a low-latency and high-bandwidth connection thanks to your use of the Azure infrastructure as the backbone. Let's learn how to configure two VNets so that they are peered with each other (both locally and globally).

To get started, you will need two VNets created inside your subscription. The process of creating them is quite simple:

1. The first thing you need here is to search for a `virtual network` inside Azure Marketplace:

Figure 3.1 – Searching for VNets in Azure Marketplace

2. Once you click the **Create** button, you will see a form, where you will have to provide all the necessary details related to the new network. To create a VNet, you will have to provide the following information:

   - The actual **Name** of the network
   - Its **Address space** (the range of IP addresses from which you can select the ones for your services)
   - The **Subscription**, **Resource group**, and **Location**
   - The default **Subnet** (which can cover either the whole network or only a subset of it)

The following figure shows an example of a configuration:

Figure 3.2 – VNet configuration in the Azure portal

The parameters and settings in the preceding figure are described in the following list:

- IP addresses inside a VNet are private.
- You have to provide a valid IP range using the CIDR notation. You can refer to `https://azure.microsoft.com/en-us/resources/videos/virtual-network-vnet-peering/` for additional information.
- Basic DDoS protection is free and integrated into the Azure platform. If you feel that you need extra safety here, you can go for the Standard tier; however, you will have to pay extra for that service.

3. Once you are satisfied with the configuration, you can click on the **Create** button to initiate the process of creating a VNet. Duplicate the preceding steps so that you have two separate networks created inside your subscription:

Figure 3.3 – Two VNets created in the same resource group

We have two VNets inside the same resource group; however, they do not know anything about each other. We are also unable to make a connection from one VNet to another. Let's try to peer them so that they become a single logical unit.

The process of peering networks is quite simple. There are two ways of doing this in Azure: you can use the Azure portal or a command line. We will look at two approaches so that you can decide which one suits your needs best.

The Azure portal

VNets in Azure can be managed using various tools, including the Azure portal. The fact is that, for some people, the portal is the easiest way to use Azure, as they are used to graphic tools and the UI really helps them understand what is going on or how to use a particular feature.

To create a peering (which will allow you to access a network from another network) from the portal, you can go through the following instructions:

1. In the **Settings** section, you will find a **Peerings** blade:

Figure 3.4 – Peerings blade

2. Initially, you should not see any available peering for your network (I am assuming that you are doing this on a new VNet). To create a new connection, click on the **+ Add** button:

Figure 3.5 – Creating a peering

3. In the displayed form, you will have to enter all the required information regarding the connection. Before we dig deeper into the available options, look at my configuration:

Figure 3.6 – VNet peering configuration

Using the default options should suffice for the most common scenarios (put simply, scenarios that do not require external communication or need you to disable external communication); however, you may want to consider additional options here:

- **Allow virtual network access**: By default, two peered networks can communicate with each other. With this option, you can change the behavior so that communication will be disallowed.
- **Allow forwarded traffic**: If you want to allow external communication (not originating from the peer) to access your VNet, check this checkbox.

- **Allow gateway transit**: When you want to use VNet gateways, you can allow the peer to use another peer gateway. With this option, you have to make sure that the peer does not use a gateway already.
- **Use remote gateways**: This option is the opposite of the previous one. Use it if you want to use the gateway of the peer.

When everything is set, you can click the **OK** button and wait until the peering is created.

> Note that the selected options can be altered after the peering is created. If you want to forbid the communication between VNets later, you will have the option to do so.

Let's now try to use the CLI to do the same operation without accessing the portal.

The Azure CLI

Another tool that can be used when managing networks is the Azure CLI. With the Azure CLI, you can basically do everything you could do using the Azure portal, but this time using a more robust and automation-friendly tool that can be run on any platform.

To create a peering with the CLI, you will need to use the following command:

```
az network vnet peering create [-h] [--verbose] [--debug] [--output
{json,jsonc,table,tsv}] [--query JMESPATH] --resource-group
RESOURCE_GROUP_NAME --vnet-name NAME --name VIRTUAL_NETWORK_PEERING_NAME --
remote-vnet-id REMOTE_VIRTUAL_NETWORK [--allow-vnet-access] [--allow-
forwarded-traffic] [--allow-gateway-transit] [--use-remote-gateways] [--
subscription _SUBSCRIPTION]
```

The command is structured in a way that helps us understand its particular steps. This is why it contains the main category (`network`), service (`vnet`), feature (`peering`), and action (`create`). While it is quite rich, you will actually only need four parameters:

- Resource group
- VNet name
- Name of the peering
- The peer resource ID

For the purpose of this exercise, we will create a third VNet named `azureadministrator-euw-vnet3`. Here, you can find the full command we used to create peering between two of my networks. By providing the following parameters, Azure will connect the two VNets:

- `--vnet-name`: The VNet from which the VNet communication will originate
- `--name`: The peering name
- `--remote-vnet-id`: The destination VNet

Let's see what the command looks like:

```
$ az network vnet peering create -g "azureadministrator-euw-rg" --vnet-name
"azureadministrator-euw-vnet3" --name "SecondPeering" --remote-vnet-id
"/subscriptions/.../resourceGroups/azureadministrator-euw-
rg/providers/Microsoft.Network/virtualNetworks/azureadministrator-euw-
vnet2"
```

Once the peering is created, you will get the following output:

```
{
    ...,
    "id": "/subscriptions/.../resourceGroups/azureadministrator-euw-
rg/providers/Microsoft.Network/virtualNetworks/azureadministrator-euw-
vnet3/virtualNetworkPeerings/SecondPeering",
    ...
    },
    "remoteVirtualNetwork": {
        "id": "/subscriptions/.../resourceGroups/azureadministrator-euw-
rg/providers/Microsoft.Network/virtualNetworks/azureadministrator-euw-
vnet2",
        ...
    },
    ...
}
```

The result of running the preceding command (while not mentioned in this book) will give you the full description of the created resource. It will also contain the full identifiers of the networks connected. The only challenge here is to obtain the VNet ID, which is required to complete the operation; you can obtain it with a single Azure CLI command:

```
$ az network vnet list
```

The list of VNets should be presented in a JSON array:

```
[
    {
```

```
    "addressSpace": {
      "addressPrefixes": [
        "10.0.0.0/24"
      ]
    },
    ...,
    "id": "/subscriptions/.../resourceGroups/azureadministrator-euw-
rg/providers/Microsoft.Network/virtualNetworks/azureadministrator-euw-
vnet2",
    ...
  }
  ...
]
```

As in the previous command example, here, you will also see the full description of particular resources (VNets). This time, however, you will see a full list of them. Of course, if you are interested in the existing peerings, you can also find them with the CLI:

```
$ az network vnet peering list --resource-group "azureadministrator-euw-rg"
--vnet-name "azureadministrator-euw-vnet3"
```

Similar to a list of VNets, the list of peerings is presented as a JSON array:

```
[
  {
    ...,
    "id": "/subscriptions/.../resourceGroups/azureadministrator-euw-
rg/providers/Microsoft.Network/virtualNetworks/azureadministrator-euw-
vnet1/virtualNetworkPeerings/vnets-peering",
    ...,
    "remoteAddressSpace": {
      "addressPrefixes": [
        "10.1.0.0/28"
      ]
    },
    "remoteVirtualNetwork": {
      "id": "/subscriptions/.../resourceGroups/azureadministrator-euw-
rg/providers/Microsoft.Network/virtualNetworks/azureadministrator-euw-
vnet2",
      ...
    },
    ...
  }
]
```

With the full description, you will be able to see, for example, what the second network in the peering configuration is. To make the peering fully functional, you have to create a connection from vnet1 to vnet2 and vice versa. Once this configuration is completed, the peering status should change its value from **Initiated** to **Connected**, as shown in the following figure:

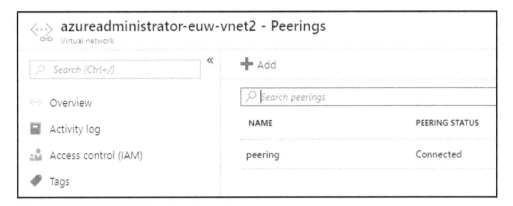

Figure 3.7 – Created VNet peering connected to another network

Once two VNets are peered, you can connect to the services provisioned inside them as if they were a single network. Peering also gives you the following benefits:

- The latency between two VMs hosted inside two peered networks (assuming they are in the same region) is the same as it would be if those two VMs were inside a single VNet.
- Traffic between peered VNets is routed through the internal Azure infrastructure. It does not reach the public internet or any kind of a gateway.
- If you want to secure access to a specific VNet or a subnet, you can use a network security group to achieve that kind of functionality (as opposed to disallowing communication between networks).
- Even if your networks are peered, you can still use the gateway to connect to the on-premises network.
- VNet peering also works for networks that are not in the same region. This, however, does not guarantee private traffic or low-latency communication.

To make sure that the connection between our networks is configured correctly, we deployed two VMs: `aa1` and `aa2`. The former has a private address of `10.0.0.4` and the latter `10.1.0.4`. To test the connection, we use the `ping` command:

```
Server Manager

Administrator: Command Prompt - ping 10.1.0.4
C:\Users\kamz>ping 10.1.0.4

Pinging 10.1.0.4 with 32 bytes of data:
Request timed out.
Request timed out.
Request timed out.
Request timed out.

Ping statistics for 10.1.0.4:
    Packets: Sent = 4, Received = 0, Lost = 4 (100% loss),

C:\Users\kamz>ping 10.1.0.4

Pinging 10.1.0.4 with 32 bytes of data:
Reply from 10.1.0.4: bytes=32 time=2ms TTL=128
Reply from 10.1.0.4: bytes=32 time=1ms TTL=128
Reply from 10.1.0.4: bytes=32 time<1ms TTL=128
Reply from 10.1.0.4: bytes=32 ti
```

Figure 3.8 – Result of running the ping with and without VNet peering

As you can see, the first VM sees the second one, even though they are not in the same VNet. With that VNet feature, you can create a global private network connecting your services and machines.

 By default, ICMP, which is used by `ping`, is disabled on Azure VMs. To enable it, use the `New-NetFirewallRule –DisplayName "Allow ICMPv4-In" –Protocol ICMPv4` command.

With the peering capability, you can create advanced topologies that contain networks from different sites and connect multiple services.

 You can refer to `https://azure.microsoft.com/en-us/resources/videos/virtual-network-vnet-peering/` for additional information.

Note that one of the most important features of the peering ability is the fact that you can connect both Azure VNet and on-premise networks. If you do this, you can leverage the bidirectional communication while still ensuring that it is kept private.

This section should help you understand what peering between different VNets involves and how it works. In the next section, you will see an alternative to peering: VNet-to-VNet connection.

Creating and configuring VNet-to-VNet connection

When building different computer systems, you often have to encapsulate them inside different networks so that they are isolated from each other and possibly from external traffic; however, there are cases when two separate VNets need to be able to connect so that they can exchange communication. In the previous section, you implemented a peering between two VNets—this time, we will show you the other option for integrating them. Knowing an alternative solution may be helpful, especially with global peering, as there are some problems with load balancers in that kind of setup; such problems include being unable to communicate with some services using the frontend IP of a load balancer if the load balancer used is a basic one.

In this section, we will consider two different options:

- VNet-to-VNet connections in the same region
- Cross-region VNet-to-VNet connections

To get started, you will have to consider two different setups:

- Two VNets in the same region
- Two VNets in different regions

We will use the commands in the following sections to prepare our own environment.

Single region

For the single-region integration method, we need to have at least two VNets in the same region. To make things simpler, we deploy them to a single resource group. The creation of all of the required resources can be done via the following commands from the Azure CLI:

```
$ az group create -l "West Europe" -n "azureadministratorvnets-euw-rg"
$ az network vnet create -g "azureadministratorvnets-euw-rg" --name "vnet1"
--address-prefixes "10.0.0.0/24"
$ az network vnet create -g "azureadministratorvnets-euw-rg" --name "vnet2"
--address-prefixes "10.1.0.0/24"
```

It is important to make sure that the IP ranges do not overlap, as this will prevent you from continuing with this section. In the preceding code block, I used two different commands:

- `az group create`: This will create a resource group in a particular region.
- `az network vnet`: This command will create a VNet with the desired parameters.

Once you have both the resource group and the networks created, you can proceed with the configuration.

Multiple regions

The process of preparing the environment is similar to the process that is used for a single region. You will have a resource group and networks that you want to connect:

```
$ az group create -l "West Europe" -n "azureadministratorvnet-euw-rg"
$ az group create -l "North Europe" -n "azureadministratorvnet-eun-rg"
$ az network vnet create -g "azureadministratorvnet-euw-rg" --name "vnet1"
--address-prefixes "10.0.0.0/24"
$ az network vnet create -g "azureadministratorvnet-eun-rg" --name "vnet2"
--address-prefixes "10.1.0.0/24"
```

In the preceding code block, I once again used two different commands:

- `az group create`: To create a resource group in separated regions
- `az network vnet`: To create VNets in separated resource groups

Now, with the two separate setups ready, we can try to implement a connection between them.

Connecting the networks

To connect two different VNets, you will have to create VPN gateways inside them with public IPs attached. As you can see, this method is completely different from using VNet peering, where you do not have to provide additional resources to make things work.

The same resource group

Here, you can find additional commands that are required to create a gateway for the VNets inside a single resource group:

1. Create subnets in both VNets. Here, we are using the `az network vnet subnet create` command to create a subnet with a specific name for our gateways:

   ```
   $ az network vnet subnet create --vnet-name "vnet1" -n
   "GatewaySubnet" -g "azureadministratorvnets-euw-rg" --address-
   prefix 10.0.0.0/28
   $ az network vnet subnet create --vnet-name "vnet2" -n
   "GatewaySubnet" -g "azureadministratorvnets-euw-rg" --address-
   prefix 10.1.0.0/28
   ```

 A gateway subnet name *has to be set* to `GatewaySubnet`—if it is set to anything else, the process of creating a VPN gateway will fail.

2. Once the subnets in both networks are created, we will need public IP addresses, which will be assigned to gateways. For this, we will use the `az network public-ip create` command to pass the VNet and resource group name and set the allocation method of the IP address to `Dynamic` so that we will not have to worry about it later:

   ```
   # Create public IP addresses
   $ az network public-ip create -n "vnet1" -g
   "azureadministratorvnets-euw-rg" --allocation-method Dynamic
   $ az network public-ip create -n "vnet2" -g
   "azureadministratorvnets-euw-rg" --allocation-method Dynamic
   ```

3. The last step is to create the actual VPN gateway with the `az network vnet-gateway create` command and pass the name of a VNet, the gateway location, the resource name of the public IP address created in the previous step, and other gateway-related parameters. Note the `--no-wait` switch at the end, which will ensure that the command is executed asynchronously:

   ```
   # Create the actual gateways in both VNets
   $ az network vnet-gateway create -n "vnet1" -l "West Europe" --
   public-ip-address "vnet1" -g "azureadministratorVNets-euw-rg" --
   VNet "VNet1" --gateway-type Vpn --sku VpnGw1 --vpn-type RouteBased
   --no-wait
   $ az network vnet-gateway create -n "vnet2" -l "West Europe" --
   ```

```
public-ip-address "vnet2" -g "azureadministratorvnets-euw-rg" --
vnet "vnet2" --gateway-type Vpn --sku VpnGw1 --vpn-type RouteBased
--no-wait
```

Once all of the preceding commands run successfully, you can check whether all the resources are provisioned correctly. In the end, you should see a similar setup to mine:

NAME	TYPE	LOCATION
vnet1	Public IP address	West Europe
vnet1	Virtual network gateway	West Europe
vnet1	Virtual network	West Europe
vnet2	Public IP address	West Europe
vnet2	Virtual network gateway	West Europe
vnet2	Virtual network	West Europe

Figure 3.9 – Resources created for establishing VPN connection

The last step is to create a `vnet1` to `vnet2` and `vnet2` to `vnet1` connection. To do this, you will need the following command:

```
$ az network vpn-connection create -n "vnet1tovnet2" -g
"azureadministratorvnets-euw-rg" --vnet-gateway1 "vnet1" -l "West Europe" -
-shared-key "qwerty" --vnet-gateway2 "vnet2"
```

The preceding command creates a connection between two gateways. This is the moment when the actual *magic* happens. Without this connection, the two gateways created during the previous steps will still be unable to process traffic. The process of creating a connection will take a while, so just be patient.

> The important thing here is to ensure that both connections use the same **shared key** (the authorization key that will be used to eventually connect both ends of the connection); if you fail to provide the same value for both of them, the connection will fail.

When both connections are ready, you can test them using the `az network vpn-connection show` command, which should give you a result similar to mine:

```
$ az network vpn-connection show --name "vnet1tovnet2" --resource-group
"azureadministratorVNets-euw-rg"
```

The result of the preceding command looks like this:

```
{
    ...,
    "id": "/subscriptions/.../resourceGroups/azureadministratorvnets-euw-
rg/providers/Microsoft.Network/connections/vnet1tovnet2",
    ...,
    "virtualNetworkGateway1": {
        "id": "/subscriptions/.../resourceGroups/azureadministratorvnets-euw-
rg/providers/Microsoft.Network/virtualNetworkGateways/vnet1",
        "resourceGroup": "azureadministratorvnets-euw-rg"
    },
    "virtualNetworkGateway2": {
        "id": "/subscriptions/...d/resourceGroups/azureadministratorvnets-euw-
rg/providers/Microsoft.Network/virtualNetworkGateways/vnet2",
        "resourceGroup": "azureadministratorvnets-euw-rg"
    }
}
```

The preceding result displays information regarding two VPN gateways that will be responsible for handling communication between VNets. Let's now try this again, but for different resource groups.

Different resource groups

Creating a connection between resources, which are not in the same resource group, will require providing additional information—a full identifier of a resource, which you will get with the `az network vnet-gateway show` command. Let's now create a connection between different regions:

1. We will start by creating two subnets in separate VNets. To do this, we will use the very same command that we used in the first step of the previous section. The only difference is that we will use a separate resource group for the second VNet:

```
$ az network vnet subnet create --vnet-name "vnet1" -n
"GatewaySubnet" -g "azureadministratorvnet-euw-rg" --address-prefix
10.0.0.0/28
$ az network vnet subnet create --vnet-name "vnet2" -n
"GatewaySubnet" -g "azureadministratorvnet-eun-rg" --address-prefix
10.1.0.0/28
```

2. The next step will be to create public IP addresses for the VNets and deploy the gateways. To learn more about the following command, consult the previous section, where we went through the same process for a single resource group:

```
$ az network public-ip create -n "vnet1" -g
"azureadministratorvnet-euw-rg" --allocation-method Dynamic
$ az network public-ip create -n "vnet2" -g
"azureadministratorvnet-eun-rg" --allocation-method Dynamic
$ az network vnet-gateway create -n "vnet1" -l "West Europe" --
public-ip-address "vnet1" -g "azureadministratorvnet-euw-rg" --vnet
"vnet1" --gateway-type Vpn --sku VpnGw1 --vpn-type RouteBased --no-
wait
$ az network vnet-gateway create -n "vnet2" -l "North Europe" --
public-ip-address "vnet2" -g "azureadministratorvnet-eun-rg" --vnet
"vnet2" --gateway-type Vpn --sku VpnGw1 --vpn-type RouteBased --no-
wait
```

3. The last thing we need to do is create a VPN connection (see the previous section) between both VNets. Note that you have to provide the `--shared-key` parameter, which has to be the same for both connections:

```
$ az network vpn-connection create -n "vnet1tovnet2" -g
"azureadministratorvnet-euw-rg" --vnet-gateway1
"/subscriptions/.../resourceGroups/azureadministratorvnet-euw-
rg/providers/Microsoft.Network/virtualNetworkGateways/VNet1" -l
"West Europe" --shared-key "qwerty" --vnet-gateway2
"/subscriptions/.../resourceGroups/azureadministratorVNet-eun-
rg/providers/Microsoft.Network/virtualNetworkGateways/VNet2"
```

4. To create the second connection, use the same command with only the parameters changed (here, we are using the full identifiers instead of the short names):

```
$ az network vpn-connection create -n "vnet2tovnet1" -g
"azureadministratorvnet-eun-rg" --vnet-gateway1
"/subscriptions/.../resourceGroups/azureadministratorvnet-eun-
rg/providers/Microsoft.Network/virtualNetworkGateways/vnet2" -l
"West Europe" --shared-key "qwerty" --vnet-gateway2
"/subscriptions/.../resourceGroups/azureadministratorvnet-euw-
rg/providers/Microsoft.Network/virtualNetworkGateways/vnet1"
```

As you can see, the only change here is the need to use the full identifier of a resource—without it, Azure will have difficulties locating the appropriate components.

Note that when connecting resources across regions, you will have to pay for the traffic between the data centers—of course, this is not the case if you are using VNets in the same location.

When you establish a VNet-to-VNet connection, you are leveraging the Azure infrastructure, so you do not have to worry about whether your communication will travel across the public internet. Another advantage is the fact that you do not need a VPN device to connect the networks, unless you are creating a connection between premises.

The fact that you have to use a gateway is related to the setup of this solution—you are connecting two VNets using VPN gateways via a VPN tunnel. This tunnel uses IPsec/IKE encryption to secure your data, so you do not have to worry about the security features of the data transmission.

A VNet-to-VNet connection is slightly different than VNet peering, mostly in terms of the configuration; you cannot, for example, block traffic that does not originate from the connected VNet (but does goes through it). One more thing to remember here is the fact that with that type of VNet connection, you must use route-based VPNs—any other type will not work in that scenario.

In the preceding examples, we did not use DNS for resolving the names of the resources hosted inside the VNets. Therefore, if you want to find a specific resource, you have to use its IP address. This documentation at `https://docs.microsoft.com/en-us/azure/virtual-network/virtual-networks-name-resolution-for-vms-and-role-instances` describes how to configure the name resolution for Azure VNets so that you can implement real names to your services so that they are easier to discover and access.

Using a VNet-to-VNet connection is another way to enhance connectivity between your services or elements of infrastructure. Until now, we have been working mostly with VNets and have not covered the more detailed features of that service. In the next section, you will learn more about subnets and service connections, which will help segment and secure your services even more.

Creating and configuring subnets

In the previous topics, we mostly handled VNets and their features. Of course, each VNet in Azure can be divided into separate subnets that leverage the address space of the whole network. Whether you use subnets is completely up to you; it is perfectly fine to use a network that does not use them to isolate the different components of your system.

However, in most cases, you will want to create an extra separation so that you can clearly know which subsystem a particular component belongs to. These scenarios often involve several web applications that have to be segmented inside the same VNet so that they can connect to each other while remaining in isolated parts of the network. Such subnets may include additional resources so that you have an architecture of a network inside a network. We will now learn how you can use subnetworks in Azure VNets for your needs.

To get started, you will need a VNet that can be divided into subnets.

Creating a VNet

Creating a VNet using the Azure CLI is really simple, as it only requires you to provide its name and resource group:

```
$ az network vnet create -g "azureadministrator-euw-rg" -n "vnetforsubnets"
```

Once you are ready, we can start adding new subnets to it. Of course, it is possible to create a subnet during the creation of a VNet. All you need to do is use additional parameters:

```
$ az network vnet create -g "azureadministrator-euw-rg" -n
"vnetforsubnetswithsubnet" --subnet-name "FirstSubnet" --subnet-prefix
"10.0.0.0/29"
```

In the preceding command, we used the following parameters:

- −g: Resource group name
- −n: VNet name
- −−subnet−name: Name of the subnet created
- −−subnet−prefix: Available address space for a subnet

 Remember that in Azure, all the subnets use CIDR to declare the available address space. In the preceding example, we declared that our subnet will contain eight available addresses using the 10.0.0.0/29 prefix.

In the preceding example, I will have a new VNet created with a subnet named FirstSubnet already added to it.

Creating a subnet

When you have created your VNet, you can manage and create its subnets with the following command:

```
az network vnet subnet
```

 When using the Azure portal, you can also create a specific type of a VNet called a gateway subnet. This kind of subnet is designed particularly for VPN gateways, which you used in the *Creating and configuring a VNet-to-VNet connection* section.

To create a new subnet, use the following command:

```
$ az network vnet subnet create -g "azureadministrator-euw-rg" --vnet-name
"vnetforsubnets" -n "Subnet1" --address-prefix "10.0.0.1/29"
```

The preceding command contains two important parameters:

- `--vnet-name`: Identifies the VNet in which a subnet will be created.
- `--address-prefix`: The address space of a subnet presented as CIDR block.

In the case that any errors are found, Azure will tell you what needs to be fixed before attempting to create it again. The preceding command is quite simple, but of course, it has much wider capabilities—you can see all the possible parameters at https://docs. microsoft.com/en-us/cli/azure/network/vnet/subnet?view=azure-cli-latest.

Here, we are using the Azure CLI to create our VNet subnet, but no matter what tool you use, you will get access to the same functionality. The following list contains descriptions of several additional features that can be configured via additional parameters:

- **NSGs**: Network security groups, which you can treat as firewalls (see the `--network-security-group` parameters in the Azure CLI).
- **Route tables**: These describe exactly how particular requests are routed (see the `--route-table` parameters in the Azure CLI).
- **Service endpoints**: These help to secure various Azure services by providing secure tunnels for their connections (see the `--service-endpoints` parameters in the Azure CLI).
- **Subnet delegation**: Allows you to designate this particular subnet to one or a set of Azure services for better network policies or routes filtering.

Some of the preceding features will be described in the following sections of this chapter. For now, I would like you to focus on one specific element—the address range. As you can see, the portal displays the available range of addresses, which you will be able to use once a subnet is created. The important thing here is the fact that Azure reserves five addresses for itself. This means that you will be unable to use the following blocks:

- /32
- /31
- /30

The reason for this is the fact that you need at least six addresses available in your address space to make a subnet functional. In the preceding list, you will be able to use at least four addresses (using the /30 suffix), which cannot work when Azure needs at least five of them for its resources and services. Let's now learn about the configuration of a subnet.

Understanding subnet configuration

When you are done with dividing your VNets, you can list all the subnets using the following Azure CLI command. You will have to use two particular parameters to get the result, the resource group name and the VNet name:

```
$ az network vnet subnet list --resource-group "azureadministrator-euw-rg"
--vnet-name "vnetforsubnets"
```

The result of listing the available subnets should look similar to the following output:

```
[
  {
    "addressPrefix": "10.0.0.0/29",
    "etag": "W/\"52664431-6d97-4098-9baa-f085738b1425\"",
    "id": "/subscriptions/.../resourceGroups/azureadministrator-euw-
rg/providers/Microsoft.Network/virtualNetworks/vnetforsubnets/subnets/Subne
t1",
    "ipConfigurations": null,
    "name": "Subnet1",
    "networkSecurityGroup": null,
    "provisioningState": "Succeeded",
    "resourceGroup": "azureadministrator-euw-rg",
    "resourceNavigationLinks": null,
    "routeTable": null,
    "serviceEndpoints": null,
    "type": "Microsoft.Network/virtualNetworks/subnets"
  }
]
```

The preceding output includes a list of subnets containing information such as its current state, the route table that is attached to it, or service endpoints, which are described later. When a subnet is created, it is not yet in use. This means that you are allowed to change its address range. For example, I can modify the available range for the previously created subnet by using the `az network subnet update` command with the following parameters:

```
$ az network vnet subnet update --resource-group "azureadministrator-euw-
rg" --vnet-name "vnetforsubnets" --name "Subnet1" --address-prefix
"10.0.0.0/28"
```

The result of running the preceding command will be as follows. Note the change in the `addressPrefix` field:

```
{
    "addressPrefix": "10.0.0.0/28",
    "etag": "W/\"a2b885de-840f-4a45-8b23-be8be7619d07\"",
    "id": "/subscriptions/.../resourceGroups/azureadministrator-euw-
rg/providers/Microsoft.Network/virtualNetworks/vnetforsubnets/subnets/Subne
t1",
    "ipConfigurations": null,
    "name": "Subnet1",
    "networkSecurityGroup": null,
    "provisioningState": "Succeeded",
    "resourceGroup": "azureadministrator-euw-rg",
    "resourceNavigationLinks": null,
    "routeTable": null,
    "serviceEndpoints": null,
    "type": "Microsoft.Network/virtualNetworks/subnets"
}
```

On the other hand, if you have a subnet that is in use (one of the cases is the use of a VPN gateway), you will not be allowed to change it:

Figure 3.10 – Subnet blocked from being modified

Another thing to remember is the fact that subnets cannot overlap (in terms of address spaces). Let's assume that you want to create a new subnet with another one already created. The current subnet has an address range that is declared as `10.0.0.0/28` and you want to create a new one with an address range defined as `10.0.0.0/29`:

```
$ az network vnet subnet create -g "azureadministrator-euw-rg" --vnet-name
"vnetforsubnets" -n "Subnet2" --address-prefix "10.0.0.0/29"
Subnet 'Subnet2' is not valid in virtual network 'vnetforsubnets'.
```

Of course, such an action is not allowed in Azure, as this would mean that it would be impossible to decide where a particular IP address belongs. In this case, you would have to modify the address range like this:

```
$ az network vnet subnet create -g "azureadministrator-euw-rg" --vnet-name
"vnetforsubnets" -n "Subnet2" --address-prefix "10.0.1.0/29"
```

Note that you can modify an addess range of a subnet by using the `az network vnet subnet create` command.

The result of running the preceding command is as follows (see the previous paragraphs for an explanation):

```
{
    "addressPrefix": "10.0.1.0/29",
    "etag": "W/\"91d591c7-0cd0-4f08-99c3-77f8e43e8d11\"",
    "id": "/subscriptions/.../resourceGroups/azureadministrator-euw-
rg/providers/Microsoft.Network/virtualNetworks/vnetforsubnets/subnets/Subne
t2",
    "ipConfigurations": null,
    "name": "Subnet2",
    "networkSecurityGroup": null,
    "provisioningState": "Succeeded",
    "resourceGroup": "azureadministrator-euw-rg",
    "resourceNavigationLinks": null,
    "routeTable": null,
    "serviceEndpoints": null,
    "type": "Microsoft.Network/virtualNetworks/subnets"
}
```

The rule of a thumb here is to configure as much as you can during the creation of the subnet. Once it is defined, things such as the address range of NSGs will be blocked, and we will have to recreate it to introduce the changes.

If you want to find out more details regarding subnets in Azure VNets, you can refer to https://docs.microsoft.com/en-us/azure/virtual-network/virtual-network-vnet-plan-design-arm to plan your VNet design. The important thing to understand here is the CIDR notation and how it reflects the underlying address range.

 You can refer to https://docs.microsoft.com/en-us/azure/virtual-network/virtual-network-manage-subnet#create-subnet for more information on how to manage the subnets.

Subnets are another important feature in networking as they allow you to divide a particular naming address space into more granular logical components that can hide various services. As the features that we have discussed cover mainly infrastructure, and Azure contains many platform components that are not managed by you, the next topic we will discuss will be service endpoints. This feature grants better security in terms of connection by closing the public endpoint of a PaaS.

Securing critical Azure services with service endpoints

In Azure, most PaaS services are accessible using their public IPv4 addresses. This works perfectly well for all systems that are intended to be public, but of course, that is not always the case. Fortunately, Azure VNets give you the option to configure a service endpoint, a special kind of endpoint that switches an IP address that is used by a service from a public to a private one.

In this section, you will learn how to configure those endpoints in your VNets so that you can encapsulate your services and protect them from unauthorized access.

Creating a VNet and Azure Storage account

To get started, we will need a resource group with a VNet created inside it. To do this, you can use the following PowerShell or CLI command:

- **PowerShell**: `New-AzureRmVirtualNetwork -ResourceGroupName myResourceGroup -Location location -Name myVirtualNetwork -AddressPrefix 10.0.0.0/16`
- **CLI**: `az network vnet create -g myResourceGroup -n vnetName`

The next thing that we need here is a subnet, which will contain an endpoint. To create it, you can once again use a PowerShell or CLI command:

- **PowerShell**: `New-AzureRmVirtualNetworkSubnetConfig`
- **CLI**: `az network subnet create`

In this section, we will try to configure an endpoint for Azure Storage. To create a new account, you will need the following PowerShell command (if you do not have Azure PowerShell installed, go to `https://docs.microsoft.com/en-us/powershell/azure/install-az-ps-msi?view=azps-3.0.0`):

```
PS C:\> New-AzStorageAccount
cmdlet New-AzureRmStorageAccount at command pipeline position 1
Supply values for the following parameters:
(Type !? for Help.)
ResourceGroupName: myResourceGroup
Name: accountName
SkuName: Standard_LRS|Standard_ZRS|Standard_GRS|Standard_RAGRS|Premium_LRS
Location: location
```

Note that passing no parameters results in PowerShell asking you to provide them. The same can be done with the Azure CLI using a slightly different syntax:

```
az storage account create -g myResourceGroup -n accountName
```

Let's assume that I created an account with the name `serviceendpoint123`. Its primary endpoints will be as follows:

```
"primaryEndpoints": {
    "blob": "https://serviceendpoint123.blob.core.windows.net/",
    "file": "https://serviceendpoint123.file.core.windows.net/",
    "queue": "https://serviceendpoint123.queue.core.windows.net/",
    "table": "https://serviceendpoint123.table.core.windows.net/"
}
```

As you can see, each endpoint is an address that is available via `HTTPS`, which can be used to connect with a specific service. They are all available via the public internet (you can try to `ping` any of them so you can see whether they respond). Now we will try to hide them inside a VNet.

Creating a service endpoint

To add an endpoint in the Azure portal, you can go through the following steps:

1. Go to your VNet and search for the **Service endpoints** blade:

Figure 3.11 – Service endpoints blade

2. You will see an empty list of available endpoints added to this particular VNet. Now, when you click on the **+ Add** button, you will see a new window, where you can provide the following parameters:

   - A **Service**, which you would like to create an endpoint for
   - **Subnets**, which you would like to use here:

Figure 3.12 – Creating a service endpoint

3. Let's now click the **Add** button at the bottom of the window. After a moment, you will see an endpoint created, which we can further configure:

Figure 3.13 – Service endpoint created within a VNet

Now, when an endpoint is created, we can try to configure it.

Configuring a service endpoint

When you click on the three dots to the right of the created endpoint, you will see an option to configure VNet with a storage account (**Configure virtual networ...**):

Figure 3.14 – Integrating a storage account with VNet

When you click on it, you will see a list of available storage accounts, which you can integrate with this particular VNet:

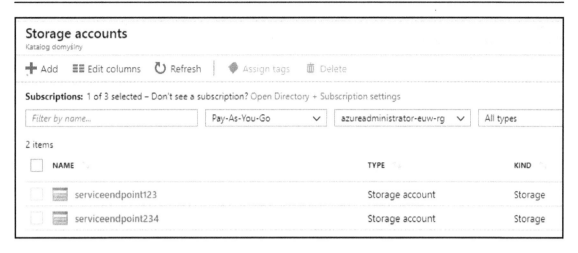

Figure 3.15 – Available storage accounts

What you need to do now is click on the account of your choice and search for the **Firewalls and virtual networks** blade:

Figure 3.16 – Firewalls and VNets blade

By default, a storage account will accept all incoming traffic; however, if you change the **Allow access from** radio button value to **Selected networks**, you will be able to configure a VNet, which can use it and communicate with it. You can see my configuration in the following figure:

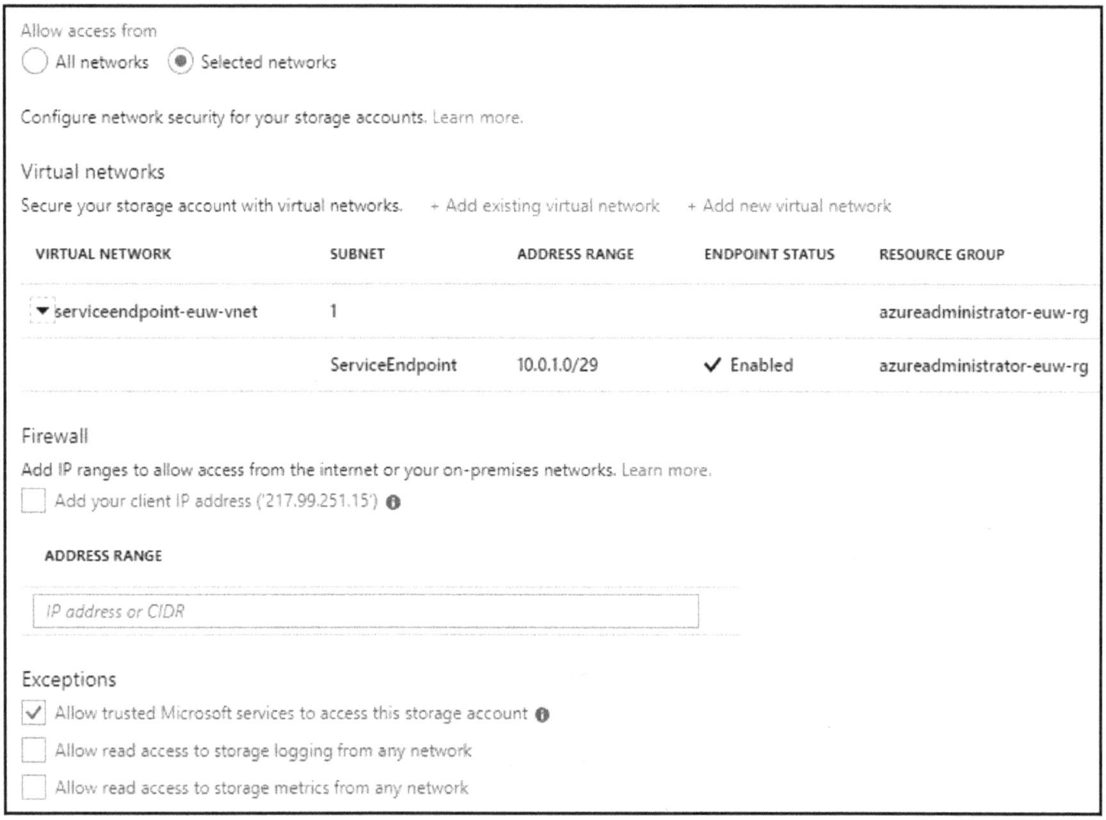

Figure 3.17 – Configuring a service connection for the storage account

Once the changes are saved, the service endpoint configuration is finished. We can now compare the results of our security measures; if we either disable the endpoint or allow our IP address to access it, we will get the following result when listing all the tables inside an account:

```
$ az storage table list --account-name serviceendpoint123
```

When security is disabled, you should see no errors displayed:

```
[]
```

Now, with endpoint security enabled, the result is completely different:

```
$ az storage table list --account-name serviceendpoint123
Forbidden
{"odata.error":{"code":"AuthorizationFailure","message":{"lang":"en-
US","value":"This request is not authorized to perform this
operation.\nRequestId:5381bd05-1002-00a7-3115-
d5e87a000000\nTime:2019-03-07T18:45:10.1293559Z"}}}
```

As you can see, the traffic from the public internet is completely shut down. The same will be true for the machines and services inside a configured VNet—if you allow them, they will be able to access this particular storage account (or any other service that supports service endpoints in VNets).

Service endpoints are a must-have if your system cannot access the public internet; otherwise, your services will not be accessible outside of a network. When using IaaS components, such functionality is much easier to achieve (thanks to load balancers and security groups); when using only PaaS components, things are much more difficult without using the endpoints.

The important thing to remember here is the fact that while enabling a service endpoint, any existing TCP connections are disconnected—this is especially important if you are running a critical job during the switch. Even if a service endpoint is enabled, the DNS entries of Azure service are intact—you will still be able to ping the service, but you will not be allowed to access it.

The last thing to mention here is the service endpoint policies—this is an extra feature (currently only available for Azure Storage) that gives you the option to filter the outbound traffic from a VNet to only *particular* Azure services. This was not possible when only using service endpoints (as they allow you to connect to an Azure service) and was addressed with the policies. You can refer to `https://docs.microsoft.com/en-us/azure/virtual-network/virtual-network-service-endpoint-policies-overview` for more information on service endpoints policies.

In many environments, having a PaaS component exposed to the public internet is a violation of compliance rules, and so you will not be allowed to use many managed services. With service endpoints, you can overcome this problem by excluding public IP addresses and communicating with services securely. The next section covers DNS zones in Azure, which help in improving discoverability and ease service management by providing human-friendly addresses to your applications.

Configuring a naming resolutions

In Azure, you are able to create your own hosting service for DNS domains. With Azure DNS, you will able to host your domains for record management and integrate them with your VNets. In this section, we will cover two things: creating an instance of Azure DNS and configuring a VNet to use it for resolving names.

Azure DNS is a service that is based on the Azure Resource Manager. This gives you benefits such as **role-based access control** (**RBAC**), the ability to audit all activities, and the ability to lock it so that no one can remove it without permission. This also means that you can create it using standard tools such as the Azure portal or the Azure CLI. When it comes to the CLI, the command you will be looking for will be as follows:

```
az network dns zone
```

The same can be achieved with Azure PowerShell, as shown in the following code:

```
New-AzDnsZone
```

As you can see from the preceding code, what you need here is a DNS zone, which is used to host DNS records. Without it, you will not be able to configure the service. Zones, however, have some limitations:

- They must be unique within the resource group.
- If you want to delegate a domain to Azure DNS, you have to own it.
- If you have multiple DNS zones that share the same name, they will be assigned differently named server addresses.

Let's try to create the service and configure it with our VNet.

Creating a DNS zone

Creating a DNS zone is quite a simple process that you can learn by going through the following steps:

1. To create a DNS zone, run the following command. It is a pretty simple one as it only requires you to pass the resource group name and the zone name:

```
$ az network dns zone create -g myResourceGroup -n zoneName
```

2. The result will be similar to the following output. Besides the common fields, it will contain the name servers, which is important if you want to register a specific domain for that zone:

```
{
  "id": "...",
  "location": "global",
  "maxNumberOfRecordSets": 5000,
  "name": "azureadministrator.com",
  "nameServers": [
  "ns1-06.azure-dns.com.",
  ...
  ],
  "resourceGroup": "azureadministrator-euw-rg",
  "type": "Microsoft.Network/dnszones",
  "zoneType": "Public"
}
```

3. In my particular case, I used `azureadministrator.com` as my domain name (which is reflected in the `name` property in the result). As you can see, there are four different named servers assigned that you can use for your purposes:

```
"nameServers": [
    "ns1-06.azure-dns.com.",
    "ns2-06.azure-dns.net.",
    "ns3-06.azure-dns.org.",
    "ns4-06.azure-dns.info."
  ]
```

4. Once a DNS service is created, you can create a new record that will point to an IP address. Here, you have an example of a record configuration in the portal. By using `az network dns record-set a add-record`, you will create a new DNS A record, which is an address record and maps a domain to an IP address:

```
az network dns record-set a add-record --resource-group <your-
resource-group> --zone-name my-domain.com --record-set-name www --
ipv4-address 10.0.01
```

5. Once the record is set, you can see it on the list of available DNS records in your Azure DNS instance, which is accessible, for example, via the following command:

```
$ az network dns record-set list -g myResourceGroup -z zoneName
```

As you can see, you are allowed to configure a DNS record that points to a specific IP address. This is, of course, a way to configure a naming resolution for a particular VNet, as you can add names that can be resolved, for example, to specific VM addresses.

Configuring the DNS within a VNet

When you have domains configured inside your DNS service, you can reconfigure VNet to leverage its configuration. When you go to your VNet in the portal, you will see a **DNS servers** blade:

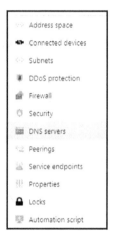

Figure 3.18 – DNS servers blade

Initially, a VNet uses the Azure-provide servers to translate names. Here, you can change this setting so that you will be able to provide your very own server with a custom configuration.

> You do not need to use Azure DNS here—in fact, you can use any kind of DNS server that is available over the internet.

To obtain the IP address of your Azure DNS instance, you can simply ping it. Look at the following output for the `az network dns zone create` command from the previous section for the name server address:

```
$ ping ns1-06.azure-dns.com
```

The result of running the `ping` command for the given DNS address is as follows:

```
Pinging ns1-06.azure-dns.com [40.90.4.6] with 32 bytes of data:
Request timed out.
Request timed out.
Request timed out.
Request timed out.

Ping statistics for 40.90.4.6:
    Packets: Sent = 4, Received = 0, Lost = 4 (100% loss),
```

The final configuration looks like this:

Figure 3.19 – Configured DNS server

 Remember that if you change the DNS for the VNet, all the VMs inside it will have to be restarted to fetch the new configuration.

In the preceding example, we set only a single DNS server. Make sure that you have different servers configured in your production environments so that the names can be still resolved if there are any problems.

In this section, we only covered a simple scenario of integrating the Azure DNS service with your VNet; however, the service itself has much greater capabilities—you can implement name resolution across multiple VNets, use the split-horizon functionality, or delegate domains. The following are links to the full documentation of the service, which you can use to extend your knowledge and implement more advanced scenarios:

- **Name resolution for resources in Azure VNets:** `https://docs.microsoft.com/en-us/azure/virtual-network/virtual-networks-name-resolution-for-vms-and-role-instances`
- **Azure DNS:** `https://docs.microsoft.com/en-us/azure/dns/`

With a naming resolution configured, you can much more easily route traffic without the need to keep the IP tables. Azure DNS zones are also a great way to automate domain assignment; this is especially valuable in a microservices ecosystem where you dynamically deploy and configure various services. In the next section, you will learn how you can configure a software firewall called a network security group.

Creating and configuring network security groups (NSGs)

In a typical computer system, you always want to create rules that determine who (or what) is allowed to access them. When using VMs, you will often leverage the capabilities of firewall software, which is provided with the system (or bought from an external vendor). Such a solution applies to a VM only—it does not forbid access to the whole network.

In Azure, you can use the concept of network security groups. They allow you to filter both the inbound and outbound traffic using custom rules, including protocols or the port range. In this section, you will learn how to extend the security of your VNets with NSGs and combine them to achieve an advanced filter.

Creating a VNet with a subnet

To get started, we will need a VNet with a subnet created. You need a subnet because NSGs are applied on the subnet level. To create a VNet with a subnet, you can use the following Azure CLI or PowerShell commands.

You can use the following commands in the CLI (see the *Creating and configuring VNet-to-VNet connection* section for reference):

```
$ az network vnet create -g myResourceGroup -n vnetName
$ az network vnet subnet create -g myResourceGroup --vnet-name vnetName -n
subnetName --address-prefixes 10.0.0.0/16
```

Alternatively, you can use the following commands in PowerShell. They use the same parameters as the Azure CLI command—the only difference is the syntax:

```
$vnet = New-AzVirtualNetwork -AddressPrefix 10.0.0.0/16 -Location location
-Name vnetName -ResourceGroupName myResourceGroup
Add-AzVirtualNetworkSubnetConfig -AddressPrefix 10.0.0.0/16 -Name
subnetname-VirtualNetwork $vnet
```

 Remember that you are not allowed to create a network security group if a subnet is a gateway subnet.

Once both the VNet and subnet are created, we are ready to create an NSG for them.

Adding an NSG to a subnet

Let's now learn how we can add an NSG to a subnet. To do so, go through the following steps:

1. Go to your VNet and click on the **Subnets** blade. You should be able to see the subnet that you have just created:

Figure 3.20 – List of created subnets

2. When you click on it, you will see its current configuration. From this screen, you can either change the address range or add a service endpoint; however, we are interested in one particular feature here: the **Network Security Group** section. When you click on it, you will be able to select an existing NSG. Because there are currently none available, we have to create one:

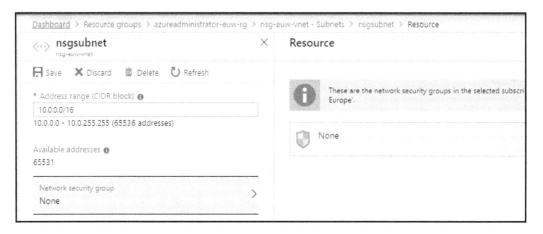

Figure 3.21 – Blank network security group configuration

3. To add an NSG to the Azure portal, you have to go to the marketplace and search for **network security group**:

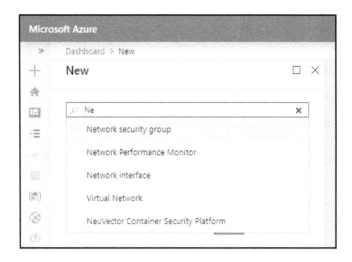

Figure 3.22 – Adding a network security group

4. The form to configure the service is really simple—you are only required to provide basic information, such as the name of the group, the resource group, and the resource's location. Once you are satisfied with your configuration, click on the **Create** button:

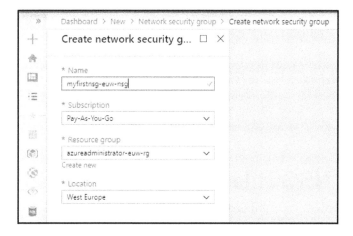

Figure 3.23 – Configuring an NSG

5. To add an NSG to a subnet, you have to go back to the previous screen with a subnet configuration and select the group you have just created:

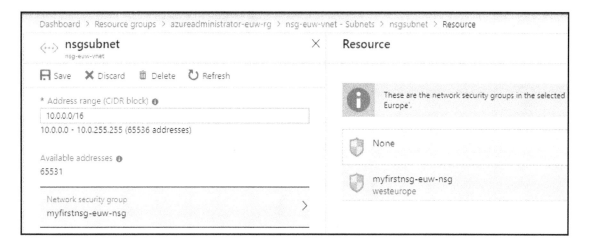

Figure 3.24 – Selecting a created network security group

Of course, the same result can be achieved with the Azure CLI. To create a network security group, you have to run the following command:

```
$ az network nsg create -g myResourceGroup -n nsgName
```

The last alternative is Azure PowerShell. Like the previous examples, all you need is a single command. Here, we are creating an empty NSG with a specific location and resource name inside a particular resource group:

```
New-AzureRmNetworkSecurityGroup -Location westeurope -Name powershellnsg-euw-nsg -ResourceGroupName azureadministrator-euw-rg
```

Now we have an NSG created and attached to a subnet. How about some security rules that will make our network more secure?

Reviewing NSG rules

When an NSG is created, it contains a set of default rules that completely shut down the inbound and outbound traffic:

Inbound security rules

PRIORITY	NAME	PORT	PROTOCOL	SOURCE	DESTINATION	ACTION
65000	AllowVnetInBound	Any	Any	VirtualNetwork	VirtualNetwork	☺ Allow
65001	AllowAzureLoadBalancerInBound	Any	Any	AzureLoadBalancer	Any	☺ Allow
65500	DenyAllInBound	Any	Any	Any	Any	☺ Deny

Outbound security rules

PRIORITY	NAME	PORT	PROTOCOL	SOURCE	DESTINATION	ACTION
65000	AllowVnetOutBound	Any	Any	VirtualNetwork	VirtualNetwork	☺ Allow
65001	AllowInternetOutBound	Any	Any	Any	Internet	☺ Allow
65500	DenyAllOutBound	Any	Any	Any	Any	☺ Deny

Figure 3.25 – Default security rules

The current setup can be read as follows:

- It allows for any inbound traffic that originates in the VNet and ends in the VNet (see the **SOURCE** and **DESTINATION** columns).
- It allows for any inbound traffic that accesses a load balancer first (see the **SOURCE** column).

- It denies any traffic that does not fulfill the preceding inbound rules (the lowest priority rule—**65500**).
- It allows for outbound traffic inside the network.
- It allows any resource in the VNet to access the internet (see **DESTINATION** column).
- It denies any outbound traffic that does not meet the preceding outbound rules (the lowest priority rule—**65500**).

You should see the preceding result when you access your NSG in the portal. In fact, a similar result is displayed when creating a security group via the CLI:

```
$ az network nsg create -g azureadministrator-euw-rg -n clinsg-euw-nsg
{
  "NewNSG": {
    "defaultSecurityRules": [
      {
        "access": "Allow",
        "description": "Allow inbound traffic from all VMs in VNet",
        "destinationAddressPrefix": "VirtualNetwork",
        ...
        "name": "AllowVNetInBound",
        "priority": 65000,
        "protocol": "*",
        "provisioningState": "Succeeded",
        "sourceAddressPrefix": "VirtualNetwork",
        "sourceAddressPrefixes": [],
        "sourceApplicationSecurityGroups": null,
        "sourcePortRange": "*",
        "sourcePortRanges": [],
        "type":
"Microsoft.Network/networkSecurityGroups/defaultSecurityRules"
      },
      ...
    ]
  }
}
```

As you can see, each rule is built from the following parameters:

- `priority`: Describes in what order the rules are applied
- `name`: The name of the rule
- `port`: To what port the rule applies
- `protocol`: To what protocol the rule applies

- `source`: What source of traffic to apply this rule to
- `destination`: What traffic destination will be covered by this rule
- `action`: What action should be taken

 TIP
Always try to leave some space between particular priorities. Doing so will make the management activities much easier, as you will be able to easily add a new rule in between them later.

As you can see, an NSG is a set of rules that are executed in a particular order. To be more specific, the higher number is assigned to the `Priority` field value, decreasing in value as the rules' priorities decrease. With this in mind, let's look at the following rules:

- **Rule 1:** Priority `1000`
- **Rule 2:** Priority `2000`

From this, we can tell that Rule 1 is more important than Rule 2. Now that you are familiar with the basics, we can now proceed to learn how to create new rules for NSGs.

Adding an NSG rule

To add an inbound or an outbound rule, you can use either the portal, CLI, or PowerShell. In the portal, the configuration is available via the following blade:

Figure 3.26 – Inbound security rules blade

For the Azure CLI, you can use the following command (in the following example, we opened port `3389` for the RDP activities on Windows):

```
$ az network nsg rule create -g azureadministrator-euw-rg --nsg-name
myfirstnsg-euw-nsg -n AllowRDP --priority 1000 --access Allow --direction
Inbound --source-port-ranges 3389 --destination-port-ranges 3389
```

The preceding command creates a new rule with priority `1000`, allowing inbound access on port `3389` to port `3389`. For Azure PowerShell, you will have to use the `New-AzureRmNetworkSecurityRuleConfig` command:

Figure 3.27 – Cmdlet details shown in the PowerShell ISE

As you can see, there are many different parameters available to be set—you can prepare very detailed rules that combine different protocols, port ranges, and directions (see `https://docs.microsoft.com/en-us/powershell/module/az.nctwork/new-aznetworksecurityruleconfig?view=azps-3.7.0` for more information). This is where NSGs really shine—you can easily steer your VNet and decide what is and what is not allowed.

 A single NSG can be associated with different subnets. This enables you to reuse functionality among different parts of your network.

In this section, we have covered the basic configuration of NSGs and their association with subnets; however, the whole concept of security groups is much more complex; for example, you can use **service tags**, which group a set of IP addresses managed by Microsoft to ease the creation of an NSG (so you can use the SQL term instead of an IP range to allow only outbound traffic to use Azure SQL services). You can also leverage **network interfaces** to enable security on particular VMs.

You can refer to `https://docs.microsoft.com/en-us/azure/virtual-network/security-overview` for additional information about NSGs, which will help you understand the feature in great detail, enabling you to implement more advanced scenarios.

Summary

In this chapter, we learned about how to create and configure VNet peering, VNet-to-VNet connections, and subnets. We then learned about how to secure critical Azure services with service endpoints. We also learned how to configure a naming resolution. At the end of the chapter, we learned how to create and configure network security groups. You should now be able to create basic and intermediate setups, including separate VNets, which have to connect with each other. With NSGs, you will able to decide what type of connection and ports are available for communication (in the same way that you would configure a firewall in an operating system).

In the next chapter, we will cover identity management, which is another important topic when training to be an Azure administrator. As the cloud contains resources, applications, and identities, you will have to understand how to manage users, handle permissions, and secure your catalog so that everything is authenticated and authorized according to business and technical requirements.

Section 2: Identity and Access Management

2

This section will help you manage Azure identities and configure access for users – the bread and butter of all Azure administrators. In this section, we will cover the basics regarding users, groups, and roles.

This section consists of the following chapters:

- Chapter 4, *Identity Management*
- Chapter 5, *Access Management*
- Chapter 6, *Managing Virtual Machines*

Identity Management 4

To easily and correctly manage resources in Azure, you have to find a way to provide proper identity management in the cloud. By using Azure Active Directory, you can handle the identity and security for your users with ease. This chapter is designed to allow you to find solutions to many common problems, such as managing groups and registering service principals for applications. In this chapter, we will begin by creating users in Azure AD. We will also learn how to assign a user to a role and register an application in Azure AD. Then, we will learn how to create and manage groups, followed by managing directory roles, along with monitoring and auditing users. Finally, we will learn how to enable MFA authentication.

In this chapter, we will cover the following topics:

- Creating users in Azure AD
- Assigning a user to a role
- Registering an application in Azure AD
- Creating groups
- Managing groups
- Managing directory roles
- Monitoring and auditing users
- Enabling MFA authentication
- Securing an Azure Service Fabric cluster

Let's get started!

Technical requirements

To complete the exercises in this chapter, you will need the following:

- Access to an Azure subscription (created in `Chapter 1`, *Getting Started with Azure Subscriptions*)
- Azure PowerShell installed: `https://docs.microsoft.com/en-us/powershell/azure/?view=azps-4.3.0`
- The Azure CLI installed: `https://docs.microsoft.com/en-us/cli/azure/install-azure-cli?view=azure-cli-latest`

Creating users in Azure AD

When using Azure subscriptions, you need a way to let other people access them and work with them. When a subscription is created, you automatically have access to an Azure AD directory, which handles identity functionalities such as authentication, access management, and security features (including MFA, conditional access, and service principals). In this section, you will learn the basics of user management, including the differences between the directory and guest users.

Before we get started, there is one topic that is really important from a user management perspective – **tenants**. When you create an Azure subscription, an Azure AD tenant is created along with it, with your account attached as the global administrator. You can think of a tenant as a catalogue of users inside an organization. Each Azure subscription is linked to a single tenant. This is a one-to-many relationship (one tenant, multiple subscriptions).

The confusion often comes with personal and work/school accounts being used for authentication. Note that you can have two accounts (one that's personal and one that's for work/school) identified by the same email address, but pointing to different tenants (and, by extension, different subscriptions). Some people accidentally create their personal account inside the company's tenant or vice versa. This may impact what is available to them, including prepaid subscriptions, which may be linked to their work accounts only.

Getting started with user creation

To get started, you will have to access the Azure AD service in the portal. Once you're logged in, follow these steps:

1. Log into your subscription and search for `Azure Active Directory` using the search box at the top of the page:

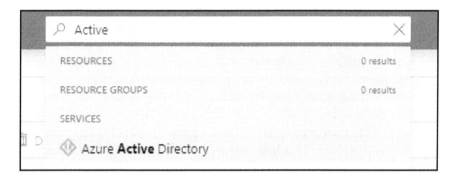

Figure 4.1 - Searching for the Azure Active Directory blade

2. You will see an Azure AD blade, from where you have access to multiple different features of the service. As this section focuses on managing users, let's go directly to the **Users** blade, which can be found in the **Manage** section. When you access it, you will see a new screen, where you will be able to manage users inside your directory:

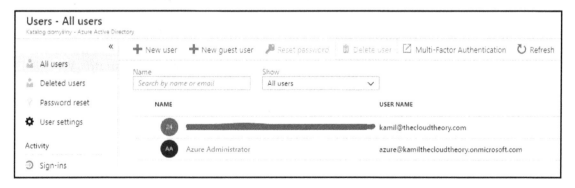

Figure 4.2 - Users within a directory

3. Before we proceed, I would like you to take note of two available buttons:

- **+ New user**
- **+ New guest user**

As you can see, when creating a new user, you will have to choose whether you want to create a directory or a guest user. There are some major differences between these two types of users:

- A directory user is configured using the provided parameters during its creation. This includes its profile, properties, groups, or a directory role. As the user's username has to be in the `something@domain.com` format, you cannot use any username you want. You are forced to use a verified domain for your directory. On the other hand, by creating a directory user, you can assign it any role you want.
- A guest user (sometimes referred to as a partner user) is a user that comes from an external directory. This includes an external Azure AD tenant or, for example, a Microsoft Account. When a guest user is created, an invitation is sent to an email address provided during user creation. Once the invitation is accepted, a user is created inside your directory.

Now that you are familiar with the differences between the different types of users, we can try to create them.

Creating a user in an Azure Active Directory tenant

While users can be created in a number of ways, we will focus on using the Azure portal to do so so that we can focus on things that are available to an Azure administrator. We will start by creating a directory user. To do so, follow these steps:

1. Click on the **+ New user** button:

Figure 4.3 - The + New user button

You will see a form where you can provide user information. A filled-in form may look like this:

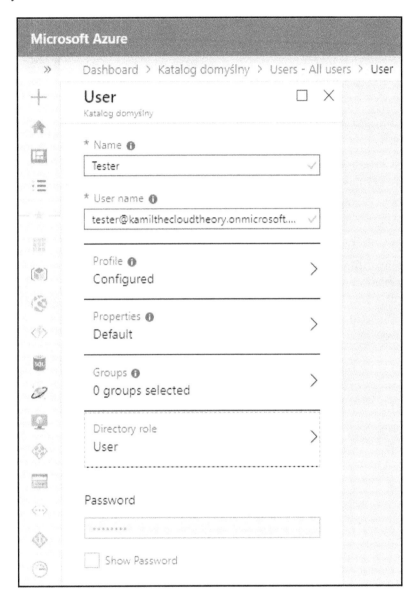

What you can see in the preceding screenshot is the most basic configuration you can create. Let's talk about these in more detail:

- **Name**: The name and surname of the user.
- **User name**: By using this value, a user will be able to sign into the directory.
- **Profile**: By filling in these fields, you can add some more information about the user, such as their department or role.

- **Groups**: If you have created a group, you can assign a user to it. We will cover groups in the upcoming section as they are the easiest way to effectively manage access to resources.
- **Directory role**: By default, you can create a typical user. By changing the value of this field, you can create users with different roles (global and limited administrators) who have much more control over the directory.

2. The next thing here is the password, which is generated automatically. Once a user has been created, they will have to change the password. When you are ready, you can click on the **Create** button to initiate this process. After a few seconds, you should be able to see the user on the list:

Figure 4.5 - Created user within a tenant

Now, anyone can sign into the directory using the username and password that was generated. With that, we have succeeded in creating a directory user. Now, we will try to compare this with the process of creating a guest user.

Creating a guest user

In this section, we will learn how to create a guest user. Follow these steps:

1. To get started, you will need to click on the **+ New guest user** button. You will see a screen that's quite different from the one for creating an Azure Active Directory tenant:

Figure 4.6 - Creating a new guest user

As you can see, now, you only have two fields to provide – an email address, where an invitation will be sent, and the optional message to a user. Here is what an invitation will look like:

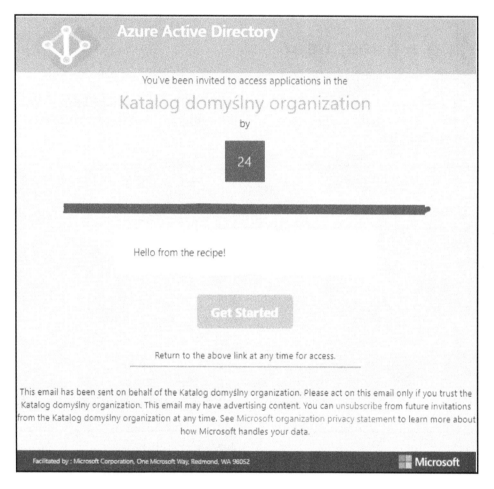

Figure 4.7 - Invitation email for Azure AD

2. When you click on the **Get Started** button, you will be asked to sign into your Microsoft Account (or an external Azure AD).

With a guest user, you can send an invitation to any email address provider (such as Gmail), but still, you will have to use a limited set of identity providers to sign into the directory.

Describing the user creation process

Since, internally, the process of user creation is quite complicated, let's stop for a moment and describe it. We can separate the process of creating it into the following steps:

1. A user is created by an administrator or is invited if it is a guest user.
2. A user record is created inside a tenant containing all the information that was configured in the previous step.
3. Optionally, if a user comes from another tenant, an invitation email is sent containing a link for account activation.

Even if a user has not logged in yet, you still will be able to alter its record and assign different directory roles. The important distinction here is the concept of local and guest accounts – they offer a completely different feeling from an administrator perspective as they are covered by a different set of rules (for example, guest accounts are limited when it comes to giving access to a directory in terms of possible permissions).

 Note that, by default, all local usernames have to follow the following naming convention: `;username;@;tenantname;.onmicrosoft.com`. To use a custom domain, you will have to register a domain you own and verify it against your tenant. Instructions for doing so can be found here: `https://docs.microsoft.com/en-us/azure/active-directory/fundamentals/add-custom-domain`.

When a user is created in your tenant, a variety of actions are performed under the hood, including the following:

- User records are created inside Azure Active Directory databases.
- Its accounts are synchronized with additional services such as Office 365 or your on-premises environments.
- Its account is linked with groups or roles so that the appropriate access is given to it.

The important thing here is the optional possibility to synchronize an account that's been created in Azure Active Directory with your on-premises Active Directory controllers. With this feature, you can automatically create users in the cloud and vice versa, thus saving your management tasks.

Depending on your needs, you will have to use either a directory user or a guest user. Guest users are often used in B2B scenarios where you have external collaborators or partners who would like to access your directory, but they have to be treated differently. Of course, there is still a possibility to turn off the guest user limitations (if, for any reason, you want to give a user full access to the directory).

When these limitations are on, guest users cannot, for example, create application registrations. If you are an Azure administrator, you will often use the Azure AD service for additional things such as automating user provisioning between the cloud and on-premises environments or to meet any security requirements (such as two-factor authentication).

Azure Active Directory is quite an advanced service and is crucial for your subscription to work. It gives you the ability to configure access for your users and determine how they can use Azure services. In the following sections, you will learn about more advanced scenarios such as managing groups and roles or enabling MFA. Don't forget to check the following links:

- `https://docs.microsoft.com/en-us/azure/active-directory/b2b/`: For more information about Azure AD B2B
- `https://docs.microsoft.com/en-us/azure/active-directory/b2b/add-users-administrator`: Guest user features

This section should help you understand the basics of user creation in Azure Active Directory and how to manage a user account at various levels. The next section will cover role management, which is crucial for proper identity and access implementation.

Assigning a role to a user

Once a user has been created, you will often need to assign them a role so that a particular set of permissions is immediately assigned to them. In Azure AD, you have multiple roles available that can be used to set things such as a directory administrator or a billing administrator (so that a user is limited to subscription billing tasks only). In this section, we will focus on understanding the different functionalities that are available for a user and learn how to perform the basic management operations.

To get started, you will need to either select an existing user or create a new one. To do so, either use one you created in the previous section or create a brand new one that will serve our test purposes.

 Note that Azure AD tenant and Azure subscriptions are separate topics that have a specific connection. You can have a tenant without a subscription attached, but the opposite is not possible. When it comes to users, you can add a user to a tenant that does not have access to a subscription. You can even add a user's Microsoft Account using its ID so that you don't have to create a new user.

Once a user has been created, you will need to click on them on the user list:

Figure 4.8 - Searching for a created user

As you can see, we have selected a user called `Tester`. Once we click on this name, we will be able to see their full profile, as shown in the following screenshot:

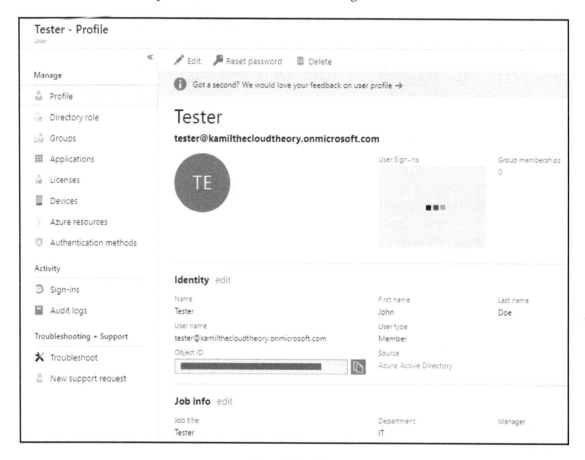

Figure 4.9 - User details

By accessing the user profile, you can also manage things such as **Applications**, **Licenses**, and **Devices**. These are out of the scope of this chapter, but you can read more about them by going to `https://docs.microsoft.com/en-us/azure/active-directory/devices/overview` and `https://docs.microsoft.com/en-us/azure/active-directory/fundamentals/license-users-groups`.

Now, let's assign a user to a role. Follow these steps to do so:

1. To change the user's directory role, click on the **Directory role** blade. Once you've done this, you will see a screen that, initially, will be empty:

Figure 4.10 - User directory role screen

2. From here, click on the **+ Add role** button. You will see a list of different roles that can be assigned to the user:

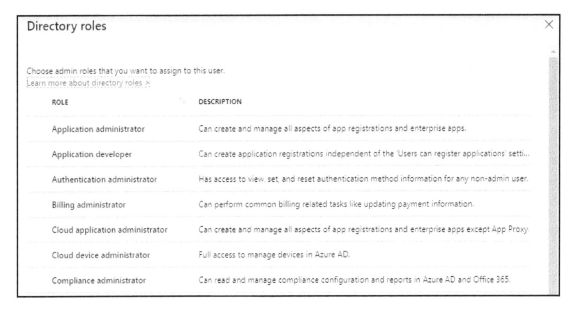

Fig.ure 4.11 - Available directory roles

Depending on the chosen role, a user will have a different set of permissions assigned to them, thereby granting them access to different features.

 There is one special role available here that is called **Global administrator**. By assigning it to a user, you are giving it full access to the Azure AD directory and its identities.

The other features of user management will be covered in later sections.

To assign a role to a user, you have to find the user you are looking for and decide what role you are supposed to assign to them. Since each directory has multiple roles assigned (including billing administrator, application developer, and global administrator), you have to know how to structure it to ensure there's a smooth flow of permissions between users.

Once a role has been assigned, a particular set of permissions is granted. This implies what a user can do. Under the hood, the user's record is updated to reflect these changes. Although they are applied immediately, sometimes, we have to wait several seconds as they propagate.

Assigning a user to a proper directory role is important if you want to give it more advanced access to your tenant features. This includes things such as licenses, user management, billing, compliance features, and so on. Before you assign a role to a user, make sure you have considered the following things:

- You are aware of the implications of your choice. If you make another user an administrator, many advanced features in Azure AD will be unblocked for it.
- Enforce (if possible) MFA authentication so that even if an administrator loses its password, logging in still requires an additional device to proceed.

Nonetheless, always try to leverage directory roles whenever possible – they can save you time that's normally spent on configuring different levels of access.

With multiple roles assigned to a user, you can easily decide what application and feature a user can access. Remember that role management happens at different levels, which means you can configure it globally (for example, at a subscription level) or on a particular resource. The next section will show you how to leverage applications in Azure so that you can introduce automation and impersonate services so that they act like users.

Registering an application in Azure AD

Azure AD enables you to govern not only users but also applications. An application in Azure AD is a special type of entity that acts like a user. However, in reality, it is an artificial being inside your directory. With applications, you can, for example, leverage RBAC and allow them to read other services settings or data. In this section, you will learn how to register an application and configure its parameters so that you can control it.

To get started, you will need to go to your Azure AD directory in the Azure portal and click on the **App registrations** blade:

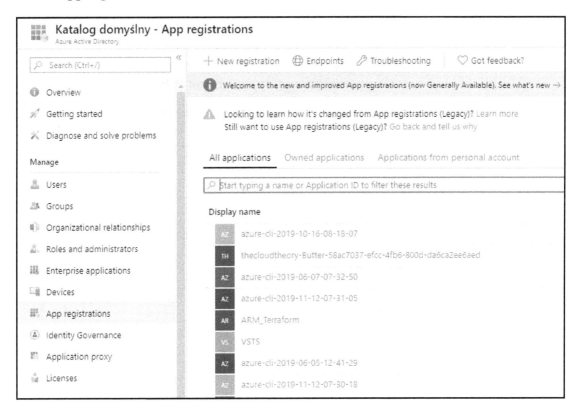

Figure 4.12 - Application registrations within a tenant

In the displayed list, you will be able to see all the created registrations (it is quite possible that, in your case, the list is currently empty). Now, we are ready to create a new app registration.

Creating a new application

To get started, follow these steps:

1. Click on the **+ New registration** button in the top-left corner of the page, as shown in the following screenshot:

Figure 4.13 - The + New registration button

2. You will see the following form, where you will have to provide three fields – an application **Name**, **Supported account types**, and an optional **Redirect URI**:

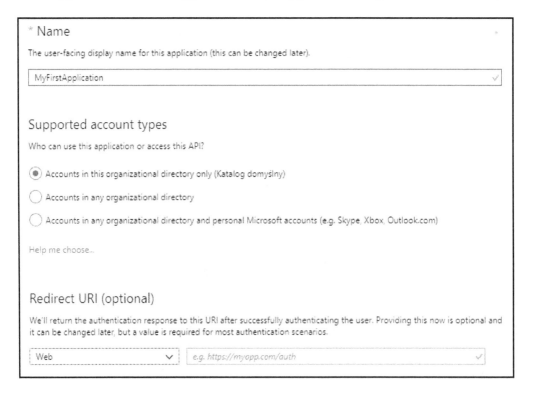

Figure 4.14 - Creating an application

While the name is self-explanatory, you are probably wondering what the account types are for, as well as the redirect URI:

- The account type field defines the audience of your application. The most limited one is the first option (**Accounts in the organizational directory only**), while the least limited one is the third one (as it includes other accounts such as Skype or Xbox). The choice is, of course, dependent on the requirements of the application you are creating.
- Redirect URI is an optional field that is required for many authentication scenarios. In general, when you are creating an API or a native application, you will have to set this field to an appropriate value so that the authenticated user will be redirected to the given web page.

3. Once you are done with configuring everything, you can click on the **Register** button at the bottom of the page. After a few seconds, you will see a screen displaying information about the created application:

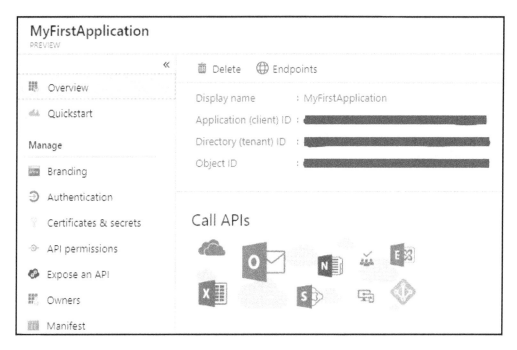

Figure 4.15 - Application overview screen

Congratulations – you have created your very first application in your Azure AD directory! Now, we can focus on its settings and decide how to configure it.

A created application gives you access to various features, as shown in the following screenshot:

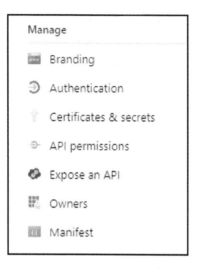

Figure 4.16 - Various features of an Azure AD application

Each available blade has its own set of settings:

- **Branding** gives you access to basic identity configuration such as the name of an application, its logo, and informational URLs.
- **Authentications** lets you decide how authentication works in the application (for example, whether an implicit grant is enabled) and what audience is allowed to access it.
- **Certificates & secrets** enable you to manage the credentials of the application.
- **API permissions** is a place where you define what permissions are requested by the application.
- **Expose an API** describes what is required from anyone requesting access to the application (for example, define proper scopes).
- **Owners** show you who can see, edit, and manage the application.
- **Manifest** is a JSON representation of the application that you can edit and download.

By using all these blades, you can configure the basic and advanced features of the application, all of which can be used to secure it on different levels and explicitly define who can access it.

 It is important to avoid granting applications too much access to other resources (if you do so, pay attention to its keys and certificates). When somebody controls an application, there is a risk that it will be allowed to control or even provision new resources in your subscription.

By using applications in Azure AD, you can impersonate a service or an API inside your directory so that you can manage its access as if it was a real user (so that you can add it to a group or assign it a role). Using applications will become really important when you have multiple services under your control that you have to authorize to use Azure services. You will be allowed to leverage the built-in functionalities of Azure instead of implementing your very own authentication logic using things such as tokens or passwords.

Using applications will be required by many different scenarios as, often, you'll need an impersonated application to interact with other services or your users. By assigning an identity to your app, you can give it access to particular resources and decide which permissions it has. The next section will help you find a way to simplify identity management by using groups.

Creating groups

When assigning roles or permissions to users, there are two basic setups that can work – either you treat each user as an individual and manage them one by one, or you can create a group that encapsulates security logic and allows you to handle different scenarios in your ecosystem in a more robust fashion.

In this section, we will cover using groups in Azure AD so that you can use them to quickly decide who is allowed to access or modify a resource (or its particular functionality).

To get started, you will need to access your instance of Azure AD. Once you're logged in, follow these steps:

1. Search for `Azure Active Directory` in the search box at the top of the Azure portal:

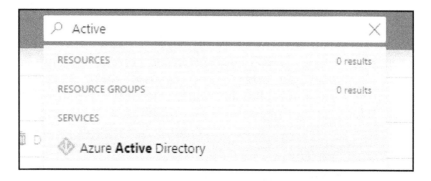

Figure 4.17 - Searching for the Azure Active Directory blade

2. Now, you will need to search for the **Groups** blade on the left:

Figure 4.18 - Groups blade

3. When you click on it, you will see a new screen, where you will be able to manage all the groups inside your directory:

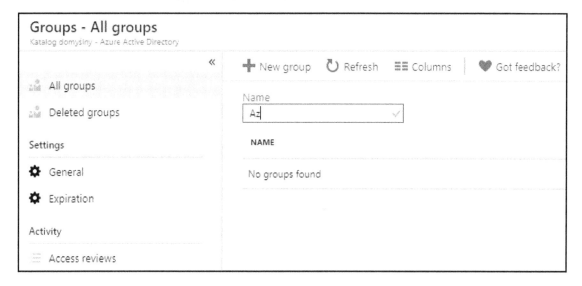

Figure 4.19 - All groups screen

Now, we are ready to look at the functionality of group creation. To proceed, move on to the next section.

Group creation

Now, we will look at how to create a group. Let's get started:

1. Click on the **+ New group** button:

Figure 4.20 - The + New group button

2. You will see a simple form where you have to enter the following information:

- **Group type**: You can choose whether you want to create a security group or an Office 365 group here.
- **Group name**: A unique name for identifying a group.
- **Group description**: If you have many different groups, it will be easier to understand which group is which by providing a proper description here.
- **Membership type**: You can decide whether your group has a dynamic or assigned membership. Dynamic membership allows you to automatically add or remove users based on their attributes. For the purpose of this example, I chose the latter type.

The following screenshot shows what my form looks like:

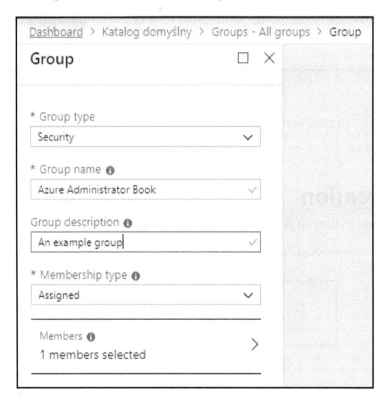

Figure 4.21 - Creating a group

3. Now, when you click on the **Create** button, a new group will be created and should be visible within the groups list:

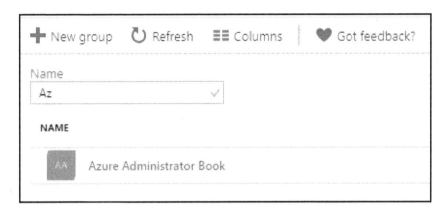

Figure 4.22 - The new group created and available within the groups list

Now, we are able to manage the group and assign it to other resources. From this point, a group acts like a normal element in your Azure AD directory – you can assign it roles, access, and decide which Azure resources it can manage.

 Remember that you can assign applications to the groups you have created. For example, if you have a set of jobs that perform some administration tasks inside your subscription, it may be a good idea to create identities for all of them and use a group to make security tasks easier for you.

Group creation is a simple process as it includes selecting a group type and its name only. While a group name does not mean anything special from the tenant perspective, group type gives you a glimpse of what its purpose is. As you have two types available (security and Office 365), you can select between a plain access management group or a group for things such as mailbox sharing or team collaboration.

When it comes to the membership type, most groups will be based on a simple assignment that's performed by an administrator. For more advanced scenarios (or automation purposes), dynamic assignment (based on the attributes evaluated by your tenant) will be a better choice. You can read more about this here: https://docs.microsoft.com/en-us/ azure/active-directory/users-groups-roles/groups-dynamic-membership.

While selecting members is optional, you will often finish the process of creating a group with a proper user selection. This will link members of your directory to a group, thereby giving them immediate access to resources that this particular group has access to.

While the concept of groups is pretty simple (as is the process of creating them), they are really important from the security point of view of your resources. While managing identities in your tenant, you do not want to operate at the user level – instead, you should focus on scopes such as teams, roles, or positions so that you can quickly alter things or revoke access.

To get a better insight into this topic, take a look at the next section, which shows how easy it is to assign a role to a group.

It is important to implement groups as quickly as you can as postponing that decision may affect your tenant by making access to various resources too granular, hence making management more difficult. To learn more about groups, proceed to the next section, where we will cover access assignment for groups.

Managing groups

In Azure AD, groups are meant to act as simple containers for multiple identities so that you can easily assign them to resources instead of giving access to individual objects in your tenant. Once a group has been created, you often want to decide which services it should have access to and what permissions should be assigned to it. In this section, we will cover the process of managing them by giving a group a role assignment.

To get ready, you will need a group that you can manage. If you do not have one, please go back to the *Creating groups* section and set one up.

Now, we will take a look at how to manage groups. Follow these steps:

1. When you click on your group, you will gain access to all its settings and configuration details:

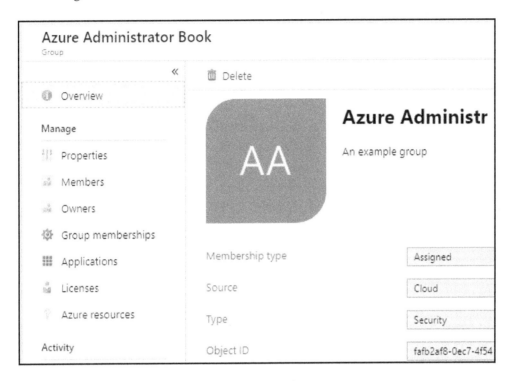

Figure 4.23 - Group overview

From this screen, you will be able to perform the following activities:

- Change the group name, its description, or its membership type by using the **Properties** button
- Manage members
- Manage owners (if you create an Office 365 group and assign it an expiration time, an owner will be notified before a group is expired)
- Assign a group to other groups
- Check which applications, licenses, and Azure resources a group is assigned to

2. Since this is a newly created group, we do not have any assignments. To assign a group to a resource, you will have to go to it and access its **Access control (IAM)** blade.

 I am assuming that you already have a resource that you want to change. If you do not have one, please create one before continuing. If you do not know how to create a resource, go back to `Chapter 2`, *Managing Azure Resources*, and `Chapter 3`, *Configuring and Managing Virtual Networks*, where we created various services such as Azure Storage and Azure Virtual Network.

All Azure resources have the aforementioned blade displayed right after the overview section. In the following screenshot, you can see it in the Azure Storage resource:

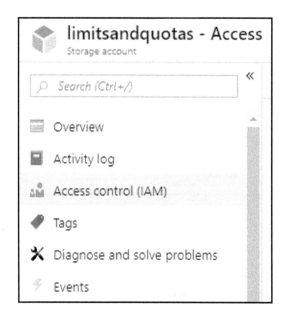

Figure 4.24 - Access control (IAM) blade

3. To assign a group to it, you will have to click on the **+ Add** button and select the **Add role assignment** option:

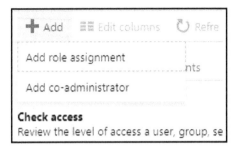

Figure 4.25 - Add role assignment option

4. In the displayed form, you can select a role and the assignment target. Since we want to assign a role to a group, the value of the **Assign access to** field should be set to **Azure AD user, group, or service principal**:

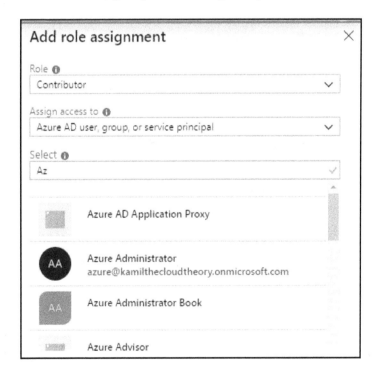

Figure 4.26 - Searching for a group and role selection

5. You will have to find a group you are searching for and click on it to see it as a *Selected member*:

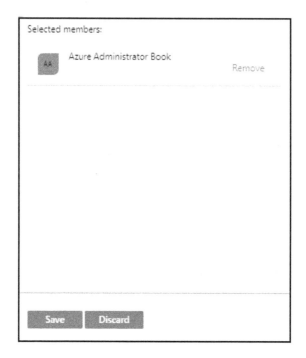

Figure 4.27 - Members selected for role assignment

6. Once you are ready, you can click on the **Save** button and wait a moment until the assignment is created.

Congratulations – your group is now assigned to a resource and can perform the activities allowed by its role permissions!

Groups are quite simple to manage as they have limited possibilities when it comes to giving them identity. However, since they act as containers, they simplify access management. By assigning a group to a resource with a specific role, all the members of a group are given immediate access to it based on the role's permissions. This means that you can control access to a specific service in Azure with a certain level of granularity using groups.

Remember that, in many ways, groups behave like a simple identity. This means that you can assign them the very same set of roles as you would do for a user and you do not need any special functionality to do so.

In this section, you learned how to manage a group in an Azure AD tenant. The important thing here is to remember the value that groups bring to your directory – you can be more productive and manage access with ease (as you do not have to track all the users assigned to resources).

In fact, using groups is the only way to ensure that you have things under control – when you have hundreds or thousands of users inside your directory, managing all of them individually would be really tiresome.

In the next section, we will cover roles in Azure Active Directory. This will help you understand how to configure access properly.

Managing directory roles

There are two different sets of roles in Azure – one reflects permissions defined by different services, while the other is designed to operate on Azure AD directory and give you the possibility to decide who can perform a specific management task (such as access audit logs or register an application).

In this section, you will learn how to use that functionality and assign different users to different directory roles.

To get started, you will have to access your Azure AD tenant in the Azure portal. To do so, search for `Azure Active Directory` in the search box located at the top of the portal:

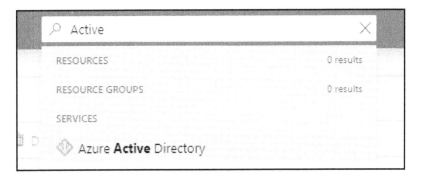

Figure 4.28 - Searching for the Azure Active Directory blade

Now, you will have to find the **Roles and administrators** blade:

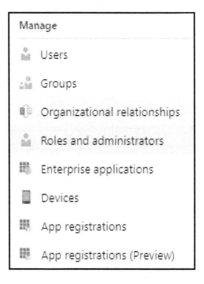

Figure 4.29 - Roles and administrators blade

On the next screen, you should be able to see all the available roles and your current role. From here, you will be able to check who has a particular role assigned and its description.

When browsing the available roles, you will see that there's plenty of them available to you (including some that, initially, may not be self-explanatory). In fact, they cover Azure and other services (such as Office 365 or Power BI) as well:

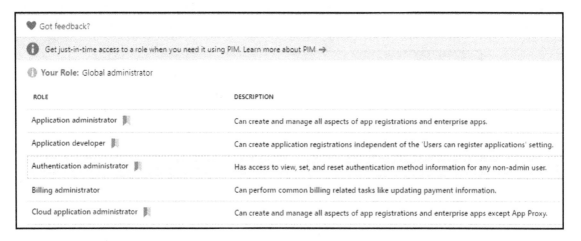

Figure 4.30 - Available directory roles

A role, which has a little ribbon next to its name, is a recently introduced or updated role that you may want to check out in order to understand it better.

Note that these particular roles reflect your Azure AD directory – you cannot use them for better control over your provisioned resources, but you can use them for easy assignment of permissions when it comes to performing tasks such as application registrations, auditing, or user management. To check what permissions are assigned to the role, click on it and go to the **Description** blade:

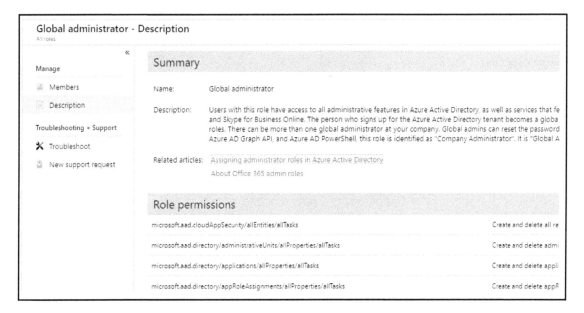

Figure 4.31 - The description of the Global administrator role

When we know what a specific role grants to a user, we can learn how to assign it to a directory entity.

Remember that assigning a directory role to a specific user often means that it has granted extended permissions. Always take into consideration the possible damage that can be done via this particular set of functionalities and ensure that the user's credentials cannot be stolen.

Let's assume that we want to assign a user to a role named `Application developer` so that we can register applications even if a global administrator will turn off that possibility globally. To do so, we need to go to the specific role and click on the **+ Add member** button:

Figure 4.32 - The + Add member button

Now, I only need to search for a specific user and click on the **Select** button to finish the setup process:

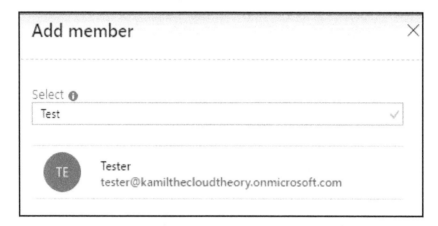

Figure 4.33 - Selecting a member

Once a user has been added, you should be able to see them on the list of members of this particular role. Once this role is assigned to the user, you will be able to see it when you access the user's **Directory role** blade.

Directory roles are one of the most useful features when you want to quickly set up proper roles within your Azure tenant. Thanks to them, you can easily assign different users to different sets of permissions and allow them to perform proper management tasks.

The important thing here is to always make sure that you have implemented proper security policies when it comes to passwords and user credentials. By assigning an important role (such as the global administrator role) to a person, which then loses its account, you may lose access to the whole directory.

Depending on the characteristics of your company, you may or may not need custom roles in your directory. For many scenarios, the extensive list of available roles in Azure is everything an administrator needs, but you still may face a situation where it is not enough. Apart from your case, remember that directory roles cover a separate set of permissions than resource roles and do not affect effective permissions a user has when accessing a resource. The next section will help you understand the actual behavior of users by helping you learn how to monitor their actions.

Monitoring and auditing users

Being an administrator means that you often need to check some data related to a user. This can be for different things – their saved information, assigned permissions, or access to Azure resources. Another important thing will be also auditing them and checking what was changed. In Azure AD, there are a few different methods for monitoring your users such as sign-ins logs and activity logs. We will cover these in this section so that you are familiar with how to audit people accessing your tenant.

To get started, you will need to go to your Azure AD tenant in the Azure portal and access the **Users** blade. To do so, search for `Azure Active Directory` using the search box at the top of the portal:

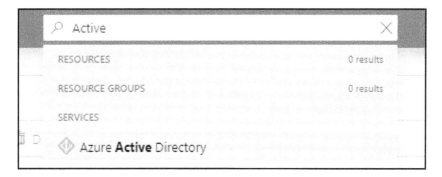

Figure 4.34 - Searching for the Azure Active Directory blade

Then, find the mentioned blade and click on it:

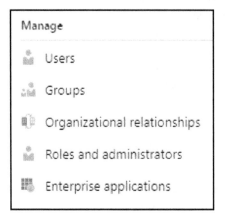

Figure 4.35 - Users blade

 If you have followed the previous sections, you should be familiar with the displayed view. If you haven't, then I strongly recommend that you go back and go through them so that you have a better understanding of how users in Azure AD work.

The following steps will walk you through the process of monitoring and auditing users:

1. From the **Users** blade, you will able to access the **Activity** section, where you can find two features to audit your users, **Sign-ins** and **Audit logs**:

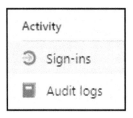

Figure 4.36 - Sign-ins and audit logs blades

To access the **Sign-ins** feature, you will need to upgrade your Azure AD plan to at least P1. If your organization does not have it, you can request a free trial.

2. Those two functionalities can be used for the following purposes:

   - Validating how and when a user has signed in, in case of any suspicious activity
   - Checking whether this particular user was really signed in
   - Auditing all the operations made against your Azure AD tenant

3. You can check, for example, all the activities under the **User Management** category:

DATE	SERVICE	CATEGORY	ACTIVITY	STATUS	TARGET(S)
3/27/2019, 4:21:27 PM	Core Directory	UserManagement	Add user	Success	user8@kamiltheclo
3/27/2019, 4:21:17 PM	Core Directory	UserManagement	Add user	Success	user7@kamiltheclo
3/27/2019, 4:21:07 PM	Core Directory	UserManagement	Add user	Success	user6@kamiltheclo
3/27/2019, 4:20:56 PM	Core Directory	UserManagement	Add user	Success	user5@kamiltheclo
3/27/2019, 4:20:47 PM	Core Directory	UserManagement	Add user	Success	user4@kamiltheclo
3/27/2019, 4:20:37 PM	Core Directory	UserManagement	Add user	Success	user3@kamiltheclo
3/27/2019, 4:20:15 PM	Core Directory	UserManagement	Add user	Success	user2@kamiltheclo
3/27/2019, 4:20:05 PM	Core Directory	UserManagement	Add user	Success	user1@kamiltheclo
3/27/2019, 4:19:48 PM	Core Directory	UserManagement	Add user	Failure	user1@kamiltheclo

Figure 4.37 - User activity logs

4. When you check the **Activity** dropdown, you will see that there are lots of possible activities available to you:

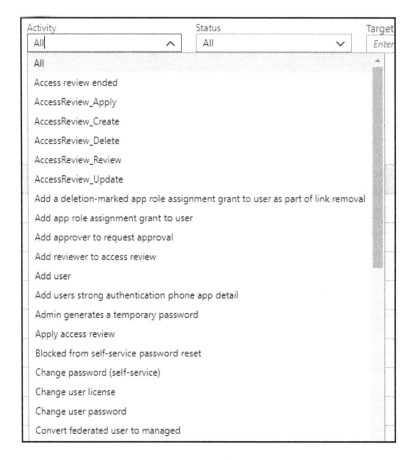

Figure 4.38 - Filtering different activities

As you can see, this particular set of functionalities gives you total control over your tenant in Azure. The important thing here is the fact that you can download the audit logs. This will be especially helpful when you need to provide evidence of your user's activities (or for the sake of the reports you are generating). To download the log, click on the **Download** button:

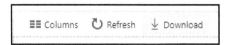

Figure 4.39 - Download button

This functionality becomes especially important if you have external tools that you can use to analyze logs and search for particular actions. As you can see, with only a few clicks, you have direct access to your tenant audit logs – you do not have to log into a machine or extract them from an external database.

Each time a user signs in or performs an operation against a tenant, it is recorded and saved to an internal database in your Azure AD directory. That information is then available to all the directory administrators (or people who have permission to access it), so it does not have to be you who is responsible for analyzing and downloading them.

Use that information to check your user's behavior (or even check for suspicious behavior) anytime you need to audit the tenant or monitor them.

One more option for auditing what is happening inside your directory is the IAM functionality, which is available for all the resources in Azure:

Figure 4.40 - Access control ((IAM) blade

This will give you access to the data of a particular resource so that you can do any of the following:

- Check who can access it
- Validate the assigned roles
- Ensure who is disallowed from accessing it

This feature provides the options that are available to you when validating operations inside the tenant.

With proper monitoring and auditing users inside your tenant, you will be able to deeply understand their actions and have proof that a specific action was undertaken. However, this feature will not extend the security features of your directory – to get the most from Azure Active Directory, proceed to the next section, where you will learn how to enable MFA authentication.

Enabling MFA authentication

Nowadays, using only a username and a password is not enough when securing access to our accounts. When you have an Azure subscription under your control that holds many different production environments, you cannot rely only on the fact that an attacker does not know your password.

This is where MFA comes into play – the abbreviation stands for **Multi-Factor Authentication** and describes an additional method of authentication that leverages extra components during the sign-in process (such as a mobile phone or a token device). Fortunately, MFA is one of the features of Azure AD and can be enabled to enhance the security of your tenant.

To get started, you will need to go to your Azure AD tenant in the Azure portal and access the **Security** blade. To do so, search for `Azure Active Directory` using the search box at the top of the portal:

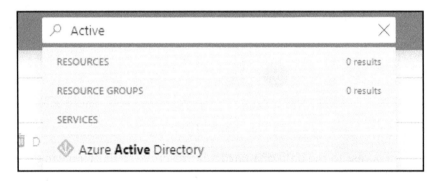

Figure 4.41 - Searching for the Azure Active Directory blade

In the **Manage** section, find the **Security** blade:

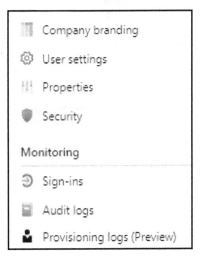

Figure 4.42 - Security blade

Now, you need to access the **MFA** blade in the **Manage** section:

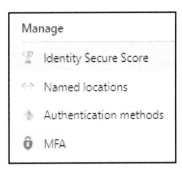

Figure 4.43 - MFA blade

 Note that you will need at least a P1 version of Azure Active Directory to access this feature.

You will see a new screen where all the MFA settings can be accessed. From here, we will able to configure it and check all the available features such as account blocking, fraud alert, or even allow for rules to be bypassed temporarily.

There are two ways to enable MFA for your organization:

- Deploy an Azure MFA service (which is the recommended way to do things for new deployments)
- Use your own infrastructure to manage the MFA components

We will focus on the first solution. To get started, follow these steps:

1. Click on the **Additional cloud-based MFA settings** link on the **Overview** section of the MFA feature:

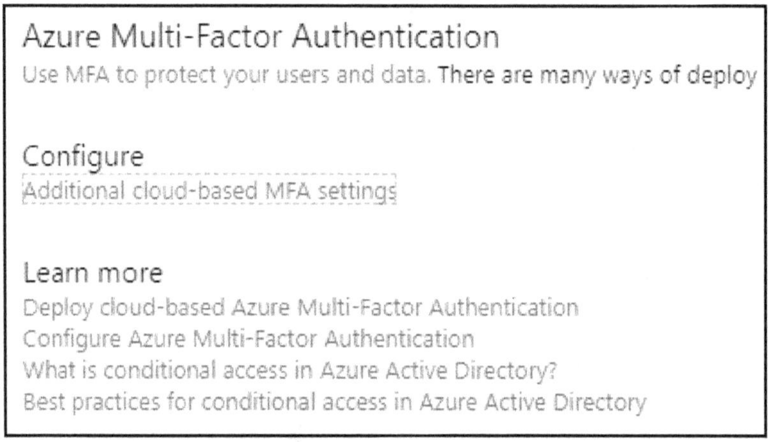

Figure 4.44 - Additional cloud-based MFA settings

2. You will see a new screen where you will be able to configure different options available for the MFA, such as trusted IPs or the verification options:

Figure 4.45 - MFA authentication settings

3. When you are done with the configuration, you can click on the **Save** button. Now, we will have to enable the MFA feature on the user. To do so, go to the **Users** blade and search for the **Multi-Factor Authentication** button:

Figure 4.46 - Multi-Factor authentication button

4. From the new screen, select all the users you want to have MFA enabled for and click on the **Enable** button:

Figure 4.47 - Enabling MFA for a user

Now, each time a user is authenticated, they will be asked to provide an additional way to validate their credentials. The available options will depend on the configuration of the MFA feature you have set.

During the first user authentication process, you will be asked to provide the details of the extra authentication method that a user would like to use (in my case, this is a mobile phone number):

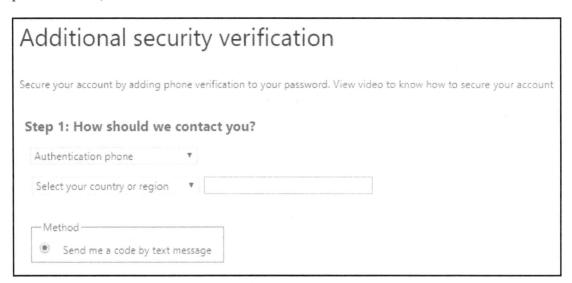

Figure 4.48 - Configuring an additional factor for authentication

From this point, each time a user signs in, they will see a screen that asks them to enter an additional security code (depending on the authentication method, this can be an SMS, a code from a mobile app or hardware token, and so on). The following screenshot shows that the selected authentication method is a mobile application:

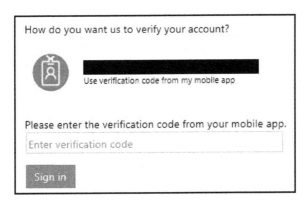

Figure 4.49 - Verification screen

If the authentication method is SMS, each time a user signs in, they will see a message similar to the following:

Figure 4.50 - Authentication code sent to a mobile device

From this point, the user's account will be much more secure. This method of authentication is especially important for accounts that have been assigned a wider set of roles (such as for administrators and all the systems operators). By enabling this, you lower the chance of someone taking control of them and attacking your company.

At `https://docs.microsoft.com/en-us/azure/active-directory/authentication/ howto-mfa-mfasettings`, you will find more information about the MFA feature in Azure Active Directory. I strongly recommend that you read this so that you are familiar with all the features available. In this section, we covered only the basic configuration and authentication flow of MFA in Azure. This should inspire you to check the other functionalities that come with it (such as blocking the account after `N` failed authentication attempts or fraud alerts) so that you can make your system even more secure.

Remember to enable the MFA security feature on your admin accounts so that you can be sure that breaking your account will require access to a physical device you own or an additional account. The last section in this chapter will cover Azure Service Fabric security features, which is a topic of its own due to the complexity of Service Fabric services.

Securing an Azure Service Fabric cluster

Azure Service Fabric is a microservice platform that allows you to host your services in a reliable and durable manner, without the need to replicate them. One of the most important features of Service Fabric is its security capabilities – regardless of whether you're using certificates or Azure AD.

In this section, you will learn how to secure access to your cluster and ensure that only a limited number of people can access it.

 For this section, I am assuming that you have already created a Service Fabric cluster in a resource group.

Before we continue, I would like to remind you of the process of creating a cluster:

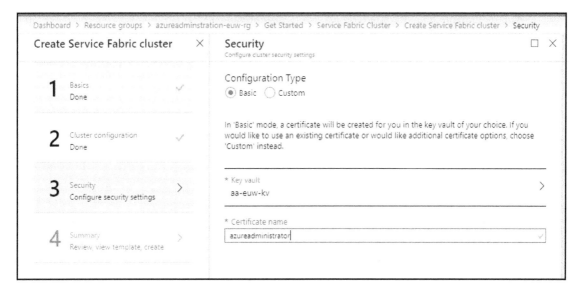

Figure 4.51 - Security tab for creating a Service Fabric cluster

One of the required steps is to configure the available security features. For node-to-node communication, Azure Service Fabric uses certificates, which you can either generate or provide custom ones. Whichever option you choose, Azure Key Vault is used to securely store them. By default, the provided certificate will be your key to access the cluster explorer via a browser (to log into VMSS, you will only need to know the administrator password).

The following steps demonstrate the process of securing the Azure Fabric cluster:

1. Access the security features of your cluster via the **Security** blade in the **Settings** section, as shown in the following screenshot:

Figure 4.52 - Security blade

2. When you click on it, you will see all the available security configuration options, including linked certificates and Azure AD parameters:

Figure 4.53 - Security configuration of a cluster

3. To configure a new way of securing access to the cluster, click on the +
   Add button. You will see a new screen where you can select an authentication
   type and authorization method. Depending on the option selected, different
   options will need to be entered:

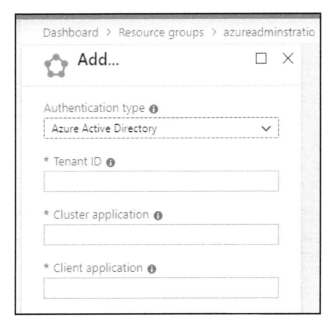

Figure 4.54 - Configuring authentication for a cluster

You have four different options here:

- **Secondary certificate thumbprint**: Not available via the Azure portal. If you
  want to ensure that you have a secondary certificate (which can be used if the
  primary has been revoked), use this option to preserve a healthy and working
  cluster.
- **Admin client**: If you want to allow another certificate holder to perform admin
  tasks on the cluster, add its thumbprint using this option.
- **Read-only client**: The same as the previous option but with limited access rights.
- **Azure Active Directory**: If you do not want to manage certificates for cluster
  access, you can use Azure AD as the authentication method.

In this section, we will focus on the fourth one as it is one of the most popular ways of
securing SF clusters.

When a new certificate is added, it is safely stored in the Azure Key Vault, which is connected to the SF cluster. However, for Azure AD to work, you will have to configure three parameters:

- **Tenant ID**
- **Cluster application**
- **Client application**

Basically, you have to provide the identifier of your tenant (which is a GUID value) and the IDs of two applications that have been created inside it. While you can perform such an operation manually, there is a simpler way: using a ready script (which can be found here: `https://docs.microsoft.com/en-us/azure/service-fabric/service-fabric-cluster-creation-setup-aad`). The concept here is simple – you have to run the following PowerShell scripts. You will have to pass your tenant identifier, cluster name, and application reply URL to correctly configure the cluster. You can obtain the tenant ID using the Azure CLI and the `az account show` command, as follows:

```
$Configobj = .\SetupApplications.ps1 -TenantId ';tenant-id;' -ClusterName
';cluster-name;' -WebApplicationReplyUrl
'https://;cluster-name;.eastus.cloudapp.azure.com:19080/Explorer/index.html
' -AddResourceAccess
.\SetupUser.ps1 -ConfigObj $Configobj -UserName 'TestUser' -Password
'P@ssword!123'
.\SetupUser.ps1 -ConfigObj $Configobj -UserName 'TestAdmin' -Password
'P@ssword!123' -IsAdmin
```

Once you've run the preceding code, you will get the following JSON object in response:

```
"azureActiveDirectory": {
  "tenantId":";guid;",
  "clusterApplication":";guid;",
 "clientApplication":";guid;"
},
```

These values will have to be provided in the security configuration in order to enable Azure AD authentication. This will allow you to skip the browser window warning you that the connection is not secure (because of an invalid certificate). For example, in the Chrome browser, it will look like this:

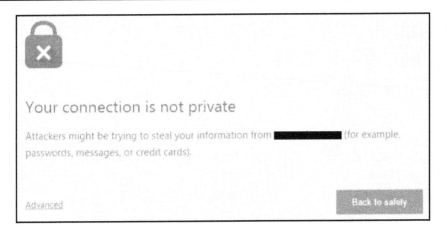

Figure 4.55 - Certificate validation error in Chrome

The preceding message is displayed each time you try to browse a resource that your browser cannot trust. In order to access it, you have to select a certificate that's available inside your certificate's store. To access a Service Fabric cluster, you have to download a certificate that was generated (or attached) during cluster creation and install it.

Then, you will be able to select it while you're connecting to a cluster. To avoid this, Azure AD can be enabled so that you can use your credentials to authenticate while connecting. This approach makes much more sense than simple certificate authorization as you can easily use groups to set access to multiple entities at once.

To get more insight into Azure Service Fabric's security features, go to `https://docs.microsoft.com/en-us/azure/service-fabric/service-fabric-cluster-security`. The important thing to remember here is the proper configuration of Azure AD – can prepare it on your own, but it is easy to make a mistake. To avoid confusion or outages, leverage the script provided in the previous paragraphs, which automates the process and can also be used in your CD pipelines.

Azure Service Fabric, being a really complex service, is a real challenge for Azure administrators as it requires managing certificates, virtual machine access, and different user identities. If in doubt, make sure to take a look at the extensive documentation that this Azure service provides – it may help you understand the most common errors and best practices when it comes to cluster configuration.

Summary

In this chapter, we started by creating users in Azure AD. We also learned how to assign a user to a role and registered an application in Azure AD. We then learned how to create and manage groups. We also learned how to manage directory roles, along with monitoring and auditing users, and also learned how to enable MFA authentication.

This chapter should have given you a basic understanding of how to manage users in Azure AD tenant and how they are reflected in Azure resources. Robust management of users is quite important as without the proper procedures in place, you may introduce security holes or grant wide access to a specific group of people.

In the next chapter, we will cover more topics regarding access management, which is one of the main roles of many Azure and system administrators.

5
Access Management

Whether you are an Azure administrator, a developer, an IT pro, or an architect, you always want to make your provisioned resources secure. This is a common problem for multiple environments – how to manage access from a single place using common policies and defined roles. In this chapter, we will focus on solving access management problems, including custom roles, RBAC, SAS tokens, and MSI. You will also learn how to secure and define access for popular Azure services such as Azure App Services.

In this chapter, we will begin by creating a custom role and then configure access to Azure resources and configure MSI. The next step will be learning how to use and revoke Shared Access Policies, along with generating SAS tokens for different services.

In this chapter, we will cover the following topics:

- Creating a custom role
- Configuring access to Azure resources
- Configuring MSI
- Using and revoking Shared Access Policies
- Generating SAS tokens for different services

Let's get started!

Technical requirements

To complete the exercises in this chapter, you will need the following:

- Access to an Azure subscription (created in Chapter 1, *Getting Started with Azure Subscriptions*)
- Azure PowerShell installed on your computer: https://docs.microsoft.com/en-us/powershell/azure/azurerm/other-install?view=azurermps-6.13.0

- The Azure CLI: `https://docs.microsoft.com/en-us/cli/azure/install-azure-cli?view=azure-cli-latest`
- Microsoft Azure Storage Explorer: `https://azure.microsoft.com/is-is/features/storage-explorer/`

Creating a custom role

In each computer system, you want to make managing permissions as easy as possible. Assigning individual permissions to an individual person or an entity is cumbersome and error-prone. This is why, in most cases, you should aim to create a role that describes a scoped list of permissions and then assign it to a group.

In this section, you will learn how to create a custom role that you will be able to use in your Azure subscription. However, before we proceed, let's take a look at the most basic in-built roles that you can find in Azure (`https://docs.microsoft.com/en-us/azure/role-based-access-control/built-in-roles`). The in-built roles are useful in many standard scenarios, but unfortunately, they are often too general and require adjustment – this is why we need custom roles.

The easiest way to create roles in Azure is by using either the Azure CLI or PowerShell. For the CLI, you can use the following command:

```
$ az role definition create
usage: az role definition create [-h] [--verbose] [--debug]
                                 [--output
{json,jsonc,table,tsv,yaml,none}]
                                 [--query JMESPATH] --role-definition
                                 ROLE_DEFINITION
                                 [--subscription _SUBSCRIPTION]
```

The preceding command will create a new role definition, which can be used later for identity and access management. For Azure PowerShell, you will be interested in this command (you can find details about its usage and remarks on it here: `https://docs.microsoft.com/en-us/powershell/module/azurerm.resources/new-azurermroledefinition?view=azurermps-6.13.0`) as it is the direct equivalent of the Azure CLI command mentioned previously:

```
New-AzRoleDefinition
```

Both methods will lead to the same result. The choice is yours here – in most cases, I am using the Azure CLI as it works on any environment that supports running Python scripts.

To create a role, you will need to describe it in JSON. Optionally, you can provide a path to a file that contains such a definition. An example definition looks like this:

```
{
  "Name": "Custom Reader",
  "IsCustom": true,
  "Description": "Custom reader role",
  "Actions": [
    "*/read"
  ],
  "NotActions": [],
  "DataActions": [],
  "NotDataActions": [],
  "AssignableScopes": [
    "/subscriptions/<subscription-id>"
  ]
}
```

There are a few things that need to be explained here:

- Each custom role has defined actions that describe the scope of permissions assigned to it. To get actions assigned to a particular service, you can use the `Get-AzProviderOperation` cmdlet or use the Azure CLI and input `az provider operation list`.
- You must provide your subscription ID to the `AssignableScopes` property to be able to assign a role along with your subscription. To obtain the ID, use the `Get-AzSubscription` cmdlet or use the Azure CLI and input `az account list --output table`.

When you have the JSON ready, either copy it or save it to a file. To create it inside your subscription, pass it to the mentioned commands. For the Azure CLI, the full command will look like this:

```
$ az role definition create --role-definition "<path-to-a-file-containing-role-definition>"
```

As you can see, we are using the `--role-definition` parameter to point to a JSON definition of a role.

 Note that the `--role-definition` parameter value has to be a resource that can be accessed from your computer – whether it is a local file or a remote one.

Once the command has finished running, you will see confirmation of this, along with some JSON output:

```json
{
  "assignableScopes": [
    "/subscriptions/..."
  ],
  "description": "...",
  "id":
"/subscriptions/.../providers/Microsoft.Authorization/roleDefinitions/e0267
2f3-97d4-4c82-a830-8d3d49d7109a",
  "name": "e02672f3-97d4-4c82-a830-8d3d49d7109a",
  "permissions": [
    {
      "actions": [
        "*/read"
      ],
      "dataActions": [],
      "notActions": [],
      "notDataActions": []
    }
  ],
  "roleName": "Custom Reader",
  "roleType": "CustomRole",
  "type": "Microsoft.Authorization/roleDefinitions"
}
```

Note that I provided a role description as a file and, as a result, got the full resource description. Running a PowerShell script will look like this:

```
PS C:\> New-AzureRmRoleDefinition -InputFile C:/customrole.json
```

The output of running the preceding command will look like this:

```
Name : Custom Reader 2
Id : 1768f02c-01cf-4760-a0d4-f8b58ee36062
IsCustom : True
Description : Second custom role
Actions : {*/read}
NotActions : {}
DataActions : {}
NotDataActions : {}
AssignableScopes : {/subscriptions/...}
```

Congratulations! You have just created your very own role, which can be used when defining access to Azure resources.

By creating a custom role, you are adding it to the defined scope (which will be a single or multiple subscriptions). Once it has been configured, it will be visible when browsing all the roles that have been defined at the assigned scope level. For example, if you set the `AssignableScopes` field as your subscription, this role will be available for assignment only at the subscription level. In the following screenshot, you can see my custom role available among the list of in-built Azure roles:

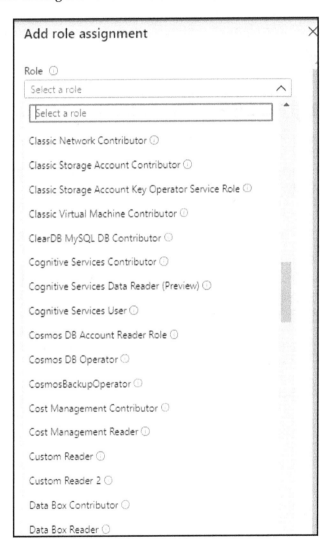

Figure 5.1: List of roles available at a subscription level

By using custom roles, you are greatly improving the management capabilities of subscriptions as you can quickly and easily define multiple sets of permissions.

In more complicated cases, custom roles will be a must-have as the in-built ones probably won't satisfy your requirements.

In this short section, you have learned how to create a custom role. The more you are proficient with the Azure cloud, the more custom roles you will be able to start using. In the next section, you will learn how to configure access to Azure resources – how to leverage RBAC and IAM to set access accordingly to your company policies.

Configuring access to Azure resources

In the previous section, you learned how to create a custom role. The next step is to actually use it in Azure resources. Configuring access in Azure is really simple as it is mostly covered by the **Identity and Access Management (IAM)** feature, which is available both in the portal and through the command line.

In this section, we will show you how quickly we can configure access for your services and validate who has permissions to read or modify them. You are going to learn what **role-based access control (RBAC)** is and how to use it.

RBAC, as its name implies, relates to controlling access to resources via roles. Each role consists of one or more permissions that describe individual operations a user or an application may perform. You may think of a role as a container for available (or not permitted) operations or actions. While you could assign each permission to each individual identity, it would be a real burden to manage them on larger sets of identities. This is why the preferred way of access management is through roles.

To get ready, go to any Azure resource you want and search for the **Access control (IAM)** blade:

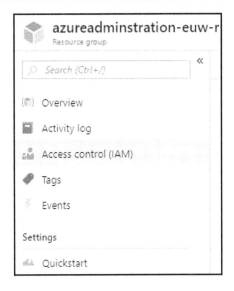

Figure 5.2: Access control (IAM) blade

For the purpose of this section, we have decided to show the functionality of using a resource group. Very often, RGs are the best place to define access as they are logically grouped, dependent resources that act as a container for them. However, you are free to proceed with any service or element of your choice. Follow these steps to add a role:

1. To add a role in Azure portal, simply click on the **+ Add** button and select **Add role assignment**:

Figure 5.3 - Add role assignment button

2. On the new screen, you will be asked to select a role, the type of identity, and the actual identity that will be assigned to the resource:

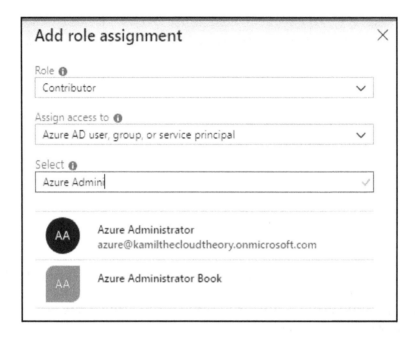

Figure 5.4 - Selecting who is going to have a role assigned to them

3. Once you click the **Save** button, an assignment will be created and the selected identity will gain limited access to the resource.

The same can be achieved using the Azure CLI. To do so, use the following command:

```
$ az role assignment create --role "Contributor" --scope
"/subscriptions/.../resourceGroups/azureadministration-euw-rg"
```

With the preceding command, you will create an assignment – a link between an identity and a role in a specific scope (which can be a subscription, a resource group, or an individual resource). Once a role has been assigned, you will see the following result:

```
"/subscriptions/.../resourceGroups/azureadminstration-euw-rg" --assignee
"<object-id|sp-name|sign-in-name>"
{
  "canDelegate": null,
  "id": "/subscriptions/.../resourceGroups/azureadminstration-euw-
rg/providers/Microsoft.Authorization/roleAssignments/1fb672c8-2116-482b-
ac69-dc5bbbbe23af",
  "name": "1fb672c8-2116-482b-ac69-dc5bbbbe23af",
```

```
"principalId": "fafb2af8-0ec7-4f54-a88e-c696a15d7c0d",
"resourceGroup": "azureadminstration-euw-rg",
"roleDefinitionId":
"/subscriptions/.../providers/Microsoft.Authorization/roleDefinitions/b2498
8ac-6180-42a0-ab88-20f7382dd24c",
   "scope": "/subscriptions/.../resourceGroups/azureadminstration-euw-rg",
   "type": "Microsoft.Authorization/roleAssignments"
}
```

 Remember that if you do not provide a subscription ID in commands that accept that optional parameter, they will be executed in the scope of the default subscription.

Just like in most Azure CLI commands, once a role assignment has been created, you will get the full description of it as an Azure resource. Then, you can validate the parameters that were evaluated, such as scope, resource group, or principal ID.

Once an assignment has been created, you will be able to see it when using the **Check access** functionality:

Figure 5.5 - Checking access

Depending on the selected role, a different set of permissions will be assigned to an identity. Three of the most popular roles are as follows:

- **Owner**: Gives you full control of a resource
- **Contributor**: Can access all the available features but cannot manage access to a resource
- **Reader**: Can only read the settings and configuration options

Of course, you are not limited to these roles – there are plenty of different in-built ones (see `https://docs.microsoft.com/en-us/azure/role-based-access-control/built-in-roles`) that can satisfy your requirements if you need more granular access.

 Remember that you can also assign your custom roles here, which basically gives you unlimited control over access management.

The feature we've described in this section is called RBAC and is something you have to understand to be able to administer Azure resources and identities. Fortunately, it is very easy to understand since most of the features are really intuitive. To give you even more insight into it, take a look at `https://docs.microsoft.com/en-us/azure/role-based-access-control/overview`, which describes various details of the functionality in the Azure documentation.

Configuring MSI

In Azure, you can often get access to a resource by getting its service key or connection string, which contains a token. While such an approach is super simple and saves time, it is really problematic when it comes to security management and granular access to the different features of a service.

 At the time of writing this, a few months ago, **Managed Identity** (**MI**) was named **Managed Service Identity** (**MSI**). In some older publications, you can still see the old name but do not be confused – it is still the same feature.

Before we get started, I want to ensure that you understand all the pros and cons of MSI:

- Addresses the problem of revoking access to services, which has limited capabilities when it comes to security (such as Azure Storage or Azure Cosmos DB)
- Allows you to introduce identities to resources that did not have them previously
- Gives you the capability to declare access to different services using RBAC and custom roles
- Uses service principals to configure the feature, which is a well-understood feature of Azure
- Complicates the process of delivering software as you have to configure all the identities first and define proper access
- Introduces complexity when configuring local and cloud environments

Nonetheless, in most cases, the advantages outweigh the disadvantages. There is one more important feature here that you should become familiar with. MSI gives you two different types of identities:

- **System assigned identity**: This particular identity is assigned to an Azure resource and tied to its whole life cycle.
- **User assigned identity**: This is a kind of identity that can be attached and detached from a resource.

In this section, you will learn what MSI is and how you can use it. It's one of the newer features available that introduces identities to Azure services and your applications, all of which can be managed via RBAC. Depending on your use case, different kinds of identities will suit your needs.

 MSI is a feature that is still under development for many Azure services. Before you decide to implement your own method of authentication, consult the MSI documentation to make sure that it is not available for the services you are using.

To get started, you will need an actual resource that works with the MSI feature. One example of such a resource is Azure Virtual Machine. It is also available for other services such as Azure Cosmos DB and Azure App Services. For the purpose of this section, we will cover how to work with MSI using the latter service.

The main feature of MSI is giving an identity to a resource so that it can access other services without implementing the whole authentication logic. This can be done via provided endpoints, which allow a service to obtain an authentication token. That token allows services to access other resources (assuming you have granted access to them). Now, let's learn how to use MSI to secure Azure App Services.

Securing Azure App Services

To get started with MSI, you will need a principal that can be used (or let Azure create an identity for us by using the system-assigned identity). To access this feature in Azure App Service, you will have to find the **Identity** blade in the portal:

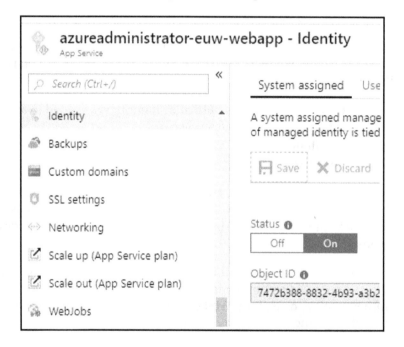

Figure 5.6 - Identity blade

As you can see, by enabling a system-assigned identity on Azure App Service, it gets an **Object ID**, which is the identifier or the resource in Azure AD. If you go to the **Enterprise applications** feature in your Azure AD tenant, you will be able to find the application here:

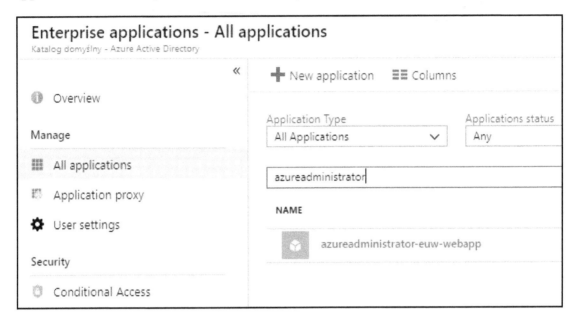

Figure 5.7 - Enterprise applications blade

Of course, you do not have to assign a system identity to a resource – in all cases, you can leverage an identity you created previously by using a user-assigned identity.

 Remember that services with identities can access all the Azure AD secured resources. If you assign it a wide set of permissions, you may face security issues.

When MSI is enabled, a service obtains a token from a special endpoint by using the object ID it has been assigned. By using the token, the service no longer has to store all the passwords and important configuration inside it – it can connect to Azure Key Vault and introduce itself as a service with a particular set of permissions. To read more about Azure Key Vault, go to `https://azure.microsoft.com/en-us/services/key-vault/`.

If you access, for example, **Kudu** (which is an additional layer for Web Apps hosted on Azure App Services) for Azure App Service, you will see that it now contains environment variables that can be leveraged to use the MI feature inside your application:

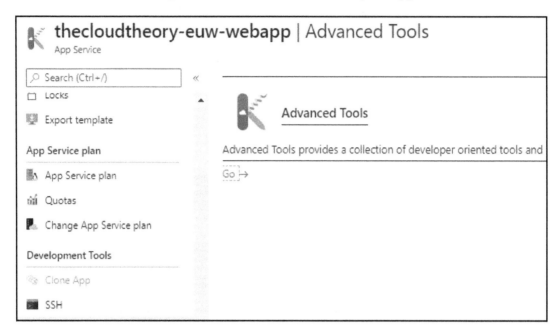

Figure 5.8 - Accessing Kudu from Azure portal

Unfortunately, to obtain a token from the endpoint, you will still have to implement a short snippet inside the application code (written in C#):

```
public static async Task <HttpResponseMessage> GetToken(string resource,
string apiversion) {
   var request = new
HttpRequestMessage(HttpMethod.Get,String.Format("{0}/?resource={1}&api-
version=2019-      08-01",
Environment.GetEnvironmentVariable("IDENTITY_ENDPOINT"), resource));
   request.Headers.Add("X-IDENTITY-HEADER",
Environment.GetEnvironmentVariable("IDENTITY_HEADER"));

   return await _client.SendAsync(request);
}
```

The preceding snippet is written in C#, but the feature will work with basically any language. It will be able to do one thing – send a REST request to the provided endpoint.

 To find more examples, consult the following page in the documentation: `https://docs.microsoft.com/en-us/azure/app-service/overview-managed-identity?tabs=dotnet`.

The response will look like this:

```
HTTP/1.1 200 OK
Content-Type: application/json

{
    "access_token": "eyJ0eXAi...",
    "expires_on": "1586984735",
    "resource": "https://vault.azure.net",
    "token_type": "Bearer",
    "client_id": "5E29463D-71DA-4FE0-8E69-999B57DB23B0"
}
```

Let's explain this in more detail:

- We are constructing the endpoint URL from the environment variable.
- We are adding the `X-IDENTITY-HEADER` header to help the server secure itself against **Server-Side Request Forgery** (**SSRF**) attacks.
- Once the access token is returned, we are returning it as the result of the method. The value of the `resource` parameter is the URL of the Azure service you want to get the token for (for example, `https://vault.azure.net`).
- The actual token is passed via the `access_token` parameter.
- When the response is returned, you can use it to authenticate your request to other resources by passing it in the `Authorization` header and prepending `Bearer` as the schema.

Using the access token only will not give you immediate access – you will have to give principal access to a service. To do so, consult the previous section about assigning roles to different identities. The scenario is a little bit different when using Azure Key Vault as you will have to explicitly assign a principal to the service by giving it a defined set of permissions. To do this, follow these steps:

1. Go to your Azure Key Vault instance and find the **Access policies** blade:

Figure 5.9 - Access policies blade

2. When you click on it, you will see a new screen that shows all the policies that have been assigned to this particular instance of Key Vault. From here, you can click on the **+ Add new** button, which will display the following form:

Figure 5.10 - Configuring an access policy

Once an application has been assigned to a Key Vault instance, it will be allowed to, for example, get and list keys or secrets. On the screen shown in the preceding screenshot, you will have to configure the following:

- **Select principal**: The service principal who will have that policy assigned to them.
- **Key/Secret/Certificate permissions**: Configuration of permissions for different areas inside Key Vault.

This pattern is really helpful when you have many applications that store passwords in databases or other systems and want to improve security. I strongly recommend that you use it so that you can be sure that they are stored in a secure fashion and that only a limited number of entities can access them.

In this section, you had a chance to use the MSI feature to configure access to your services without implementing your own logic. The next section will cover how to secure access in Azure using Shared Access Policies, which are available for Azure Storage.

Using and revoking Shared Access Policies

When you need granular access to Azure Storage services, you can use **Shared Access Signature (SAS)** tokens, which can be explicitly shaped and designed for a particular client. However, there is always a need to find a way to revoke them so that you can get rid of compromised tokens. You can achieve this by using Shared Access Policies, which are one of the security features of Azure Storage.

When generating a SAS token, you can decide whether it is an **ad hoc SAS** (which stores all its information about its start, expiration time, and permissions inside it) or a **SAS with stored access policy** (which is attached to a container and inherits its configuration). The choice directly implies which features are available to you:

- When using ad hoc signatures, you will have to have a way to revoke them when compromised.
- Ad hoc SAS tokens can be created at any time and do not rely on the configuration of a container.
- Signatures with policies need initial configuration.
- When a policy is attached to a container and the generated signature is based on it, you can control all the parameters of the SAS and adjust them if needed.
- Policies let you control many signatures at once, while ad hoc signatures have to be managed individually.

You may wonder why we cannot just use Storage Account keys for authorizing access. Well, there are some caveats for leveraging them for production scenarios:

- You are unable to segment access to your accounts.
- If one key becomes compromised, you need to revoke both keys and rotate the old ones out of usage.
- You need to keep an eye on their lifetime and refresh them from time to time.
- They grant full access to the resource.

On the other hand, SAS tokens require much more attention and experience if we wish to use them effectively:

- They still require you to implement some way to refresh compromised tokens and fix the leak.
- You need to offload refreshing a token to your clients or allow them to automatically grant new tokens.
- You need to design access in the most efficient way. Relying on SAS tokens as a magic bullet is rarely a good idea.

Nonetheless, when it comes to compliance rules, SAS tokens are much more important than plain keys as they provide much more functionality and granularity in terms of their usage.

Creating and managing Shared Access Policies

To create and manage Shared Access Policies, we will use the Azure CLI and the following command:

```
az storage container policy
```

Note that policies management and generating tokens based on them is also possible when using SDKs for different programming languages. However, this book is trying to provide you with a generic way of controlling them, so we are not tied to a specific language.

To create a policy connected to a container, we will use the following command:

```
$ az storage container policy create -c "<container-name>" -n "<policy-name>" --account-name "<account-name>" --permissions "rl"
```

Creating a policy using the Azure CLI will result in JSON output similar to the following:

```
{
  "etag": "\"0x8D6BAB88E733C7D\"",
  "lastModified": "2019-04-06T17:51:54+00:00"
}
```

For the `--permissions` parameter, you can use any combination of the following values:

- `r` : Read
- `d` : Delete
- `l` : List
- `w` : Write

The same functionality can be achieved when using Microsoft Azure Storage Explorer. When you navigate to a container you want to define a policy for, right-click on it and select **Manage Access Policies...**:

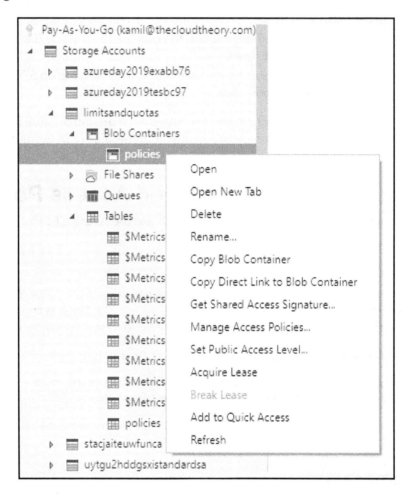

Figure 5.11 - Managing access policies with Azure Storage Explorer

In the displayed window, you will be able to define a new access policy. This is a much easier way to manage them as you do not have to remember the command:

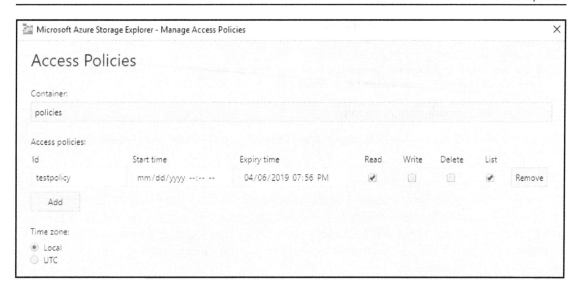

Figure 5.12 - Access Policies screen

Currently, we have a policy that's been created and is attached to a container. There are two more things we need to do – we need to create a SAS token based on this policy and revoke it so that no one can access a Storage Account anymore.

To generate a SAS token, you will have to use the `az storage container generate-sas` command, as follows:

```
$ az storage container generate-sas -n "<sas-name>" --account-name
"<account-name>" --policy-name "<policy-name>"
```

Generating a SAS will result in a string representing a token:

```
"sv=2018-03-28&si=<policy-
name>&sr=c&sig=k3dUIz81JJOHjOPW92LwGL1bYQB1SPkbCnI%2BEAojCXQ%3D"
```

To run the preceding command, you will have to define the name of the signature (which can be any string), the account name you wish to assign the SAS to, and a custom policy name. The result of running it is a short string that contains some parameters:

- `sv`: The version of the service API
- `si`: SAP identifier
- `sr`: The scope of the generated token
- `sig`: The signature of the token

Let's compare this with a token that's been generated without using a stored policy (ad hoc signature):

```
$ az storage container generate-sas -n "<sas-name>" --account-name
"<account-name>" --permissions "rl"
```

You should see a result similar to mine:

```
"sv=2018-03-28&sr=c&sp=rl&sig=HcL5Mo8ri8WMZtfpjTjINsh6nirYswBw06Bw4qj1fgY%3
D"
```

As you can see, it no longer contains an identifier for the policy. Instead, it has defined the permissions that have been assigned to it by the `sp` parameter. The obvious downside of this solution is the lack of the ability to revoke it. However, if your SAS token has a policy assigned to it, you can remove it (or shorten the expiry time) so that no-one is able to use it to connect to a service. To perform that operation, use the `az storage container policy delete` command.

It is important to decide whether you need ad hoc SAS tokens or the ones with a policy assigned to them. To understand tokens fully, consult the following documentation page: `https://docs.microsoft.com/en-us/azure/storage/common/storage-sas-overview`. It deeply describes the functionality of SAS tokens and is an important lecture for anyone interested in using the proper security features for Azure Storage.

In the next section, you will learn how to generate SAS tokens with granular access to different services so that you can control access to Azure Storage services even better.

Generating SAS tokens for different services

Proper usage of SAS tokens is an important task, especially when leveraging multiple services of Azure Storage such as blobs, tables, and queues. The better you manage them, the easier it is to properly secure resources and the data stored in them. In this section, you will learn how to generate tokens for different parts of your storage and ensure granular access to them.

To generate a SAS token, you can use one of the following tools:

- Use the commands available in the Azure CLI and create a SAS for different services
- Use the SDK for the programming language of your choice and execute a program that generates a token
- Use Microsoft Azure Storage Explorer to easily generate the token with just a few clicks

For the purpose of this book, I have made no assumptions when it comes to a programming language you are familiar with, so we will focus on the first and the last solutions (using the Azure CLI or Azure Storage Explorer).

In the previous section, we presented an `az storage container generate-sas` command, which lets us create a SAS token for a container. However, there are different options available to you:

```
az storage table generate-sas
az storage blob generate-sas
az storage queue generage-sas
```

Now, let's focus on Table Storage. To create the *most basic* SAS token, run the following command:

```
$ az storage table generate-sas --account-name "<account-name>" --name "<table-name>"
```

A SAS token that's been generated for Table Storage will look like this:

```
"sv=2017-04-17&tn=<table-name>&sig=enBO5zlJwzE%2BdXSrYe2VFb7tSEhIQrPYQ5emT6TMHfo%3D"
```

As you can see, I configured none of the optional parameters such as the range of Partition Keys or Row Keys, which these particular SAS tokens grant access to, or the expiry time. Here is a more advanced example:

```
$ az storage table generate-sas --permissions "r" --expiry "2020-04-10" --account-name "<account-name>" --name "<table-name>"
```

Note how more advanced example differs from the previous one:

```
"se=2020-04-10&sp=r&sv=2017-04-17&tn=<table-name>&sig=R6ozQlaqFhoFv/OUmjc9by/8jXs81UmfbN%2BSK7ZAYgo%3D"
```

Using the preceding command, we configured some extra parameters:

- The permission is set to `r`, which means that only read/query operations are possible.
- The expiry time is set to `2020-04-10`.

Now, let's try to generate even more granular access. I will add the **Partition Key** (**PK**) and **Row Key** (**RK**) ranges so that a service (or a person) that uses this SAS token will not have access to the full content of a table:

```
$ az storage table generate-sas --permissions "r" --expiry "2020-04-10" --
account-name "<account-name>" --name "<table-name>" --start-pk "colors" --
end-pk "colors" --start-rk "1" --end-rk "100"
```

Since we added additional parameters for our SAS token, it will look different to the one generated without them:

```
"se=2020-04-10&sp=r&sv=2017-04-17&tn=<table-
name>&spk=colors&srk=1&epk=colors&erk=100&sig=MkUHFArwgDb2IbzjsfEsXrdFoEy5N
U37HOYssfZpdjI%3D"
```

As you can see, besides a limited set of permissions and defined expiration time, we have also limited access to the available ranges of PKs and RKs. The preceding SAS token will only let you access records from the `colors` partition and rows between `1` and `100`.

 SAS tokens allow you to define a range of PKs or RKs, which makes it impossible to exclude specific rows from access.

The very same functionality can be achieved using Storage Explorer. Go to **Storage Accounts** and then a table you are interested in. Right-click on it and select the **Get Shared Access Signature...** menu item:

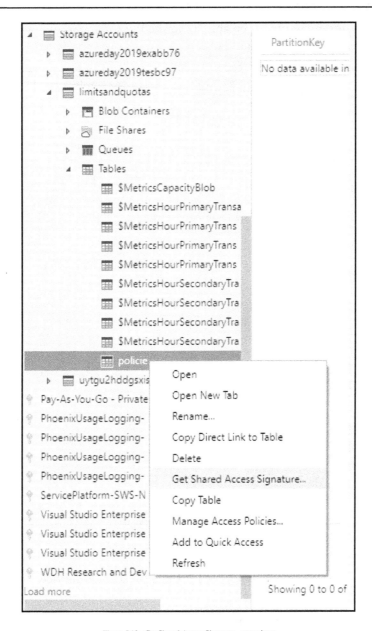

Figure 5.13 - Get Shared Access Signature... menu item

On the displayed window, you will be able to define the same parameters you were defining using the Azure CLI commands:

Figure 5.14 - Generating a Shared Access Signature

Similar functionality is, of course, available for the blob storage service. The following is a simple example:

```
$ az storage blob generate-sas --account-name "<account-name>" --container-
name "<container-name>" --name "<blob-name>"
```

The output of the preceding command should look like this:

```
"sv=2018-03-28&sr=b&sig=pU95OJrxFGS/khiyjBs%2BgOIG/6BcgUzZvBh9oCUkonY%3D"
```

With the preceding SAS token, I have limited access to a specific blob stored inside a specific container. We can extend this access restriction to additional permissions or even protocol requirements:

```
$ az storage blob generate-sas --account-name "<account-name>" --container-
name "<container-name>" --name "<blob-name>" --https-only --permissions "r"
```

A SAS token that's been generated with additional restrictions for blob storage will look similar to the following:

```
"sp=r&spr=https&sv=2018-03-28&sr=b&sig=5XQBP6tXZXfgnVDF0o9Hdd4YJ8AsrcSFqsi2
CsmmcSQ%3D"
```

Using the preceding SAS token, I will be limited to the following traits:

- Forced to use HTTPS instead of HTTP when accessing the blob
- Must attach read (r) permissions so that only this particular operation can be performed against it

With Azure Storage Explorer, we can generate the token in an even easier way. Go to the blob you are interested in and click on the **Get Shared Access Signature...** menu item:

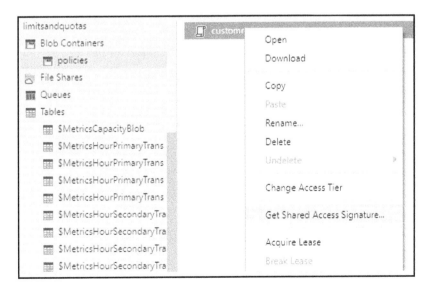

Figure 5.15 - Get Shared Access Signature... menu item at the file level

On the displayed window, you will able to generate a SAS token for a file. The obvious downside of this method is the lack of additional parameters (such as enforcing access via HTTPS):

Figure 5.16 - Generating a Shared Access Signature for a file

The last service – Azure Storage Queue – enables you to generate SAS tokens in the same manner. Consider the following examples:

```
$ az storage queue generate-sas --account-name "<account-name>" --name
"<queue-name>"
```

The preceding command will result in an output similar to the following:

```
"sv=2018-03-28&sig=z88nEawuUzOb9No8HRG8MEq8cPLadaFJ6iHJeqfvzqk%3D"
```

Let's see what happens to the output when we use the `--permissions` parameter in this command:

```
$ az storage queue generate-sas --account-name "<account-name>" --name
"<queue-name>" --permissions "r"
```

Using the `--permission` parameter will result in a little bit of a different output:

```
"sp=r&sv=2018-03-28&sig=aiHTvLJAjESFBZs/LlTvx8tOC%2BGBVeYuvXz8xcpYnTQ%3D"
```

Now, we will limit access to `HTTPS` and a specific IP address:

```
$ az storage queue generate-sas --account-name "<account-name>" --name
"<queue-name>" --permissions "r" --https-only --ip "127.0.0.1"
```

Note how the generator signature differs when limiting access to `HTTPS` and a specific IP address:

```
"sp=r&sip=127.0.0.1&spr=https&sv=2018-03-28&sig=jFouDlGHQsI9F7sYsSF19AUnnSp
ujYqabHuvrrjJcys%3D"
```

Each of the generated SAS tokens gives access to a queue in some specific way:

- The first one gives generic access to the service.
- The second one extends the security and limits access to reading messages only.
- The third one adds another layer of security by enforcing `HTTPS` and a particular IP address.

Using Storage Explorer here will be similar to the previous services – once you've found a queue you want to generate a token for, click on the **Get Shared Access Signature...** menu item and generate a new token:

Figure 5.17 - Generating a Shared Access Signature for a queue

Note that on all the screens for generating a SAS token using Microsoft Azure Storage Explorer, you can select an access policy. In the previous section, I described the process of creating policies – you can attach them to SAS tokens using either the command line or the application in order to easily manage them once they've been passed to the clients.

Once you have generated a SAS token, you can use it as follows:

```
https://account.table.core.windows.net/container?se=2020-04-10&sp=r&sv=2017
-04-17&tn=<table-name>&sig=R6ozQlaqFhoFv/OUmjc9by/8jXs81UmfbN%2BSK7ZAYgo%3D
```

The preceding example is used for Table Storage and consists of two sections:

- The `HTTP` endpoint of a container
- A SAS token

Those two fragments create a SAS URI, which is used to connect to a resource. In the same manner, you can use the token when connecting from applications. The service will ensure that the connection respects the attached set of permissions or protocol and will forbid unauthorized access to your resources.

Summary

In this chapter, we started by creating a custom role. We then learned how to configure access to Azure resources and how to configure MSI. We also learned how to use and revoke Shared Access Policies, along with how to generate SAS tokens for different services. With the skills you have gained in this chapter, you are now able to secure your resources with ease. You can define roles and various policies for all your users, depending on their needs, which will help you conveniently handle security.

In the next chapter, we will start learning how to manage virtual machines in Azure, as well as data disks, network interfaces, and desired configuration. We will also cover things such as deployments, security, and connectivity.

Managing Virtual Machines

6

Virtual machines (**VMs**) are both very popular on-premises and in the cloud. This chapter is designed to give you all the information you need to manage VMs so that you can start deploying and configuring them without hesitation. We will provide answers to problems such as vertical/horizontal scaling, monitoring, configuring networking, and connecting to different machines.

In this chapter, we will start by adding additional disks to a VM and configuring its network and configuration. You will also learn how to manage monitoring, availability, and the number of instances of working machines. The last part of this chapter will cover the security features of VMs, along with different ways to connect to them.

In this chapter, we will cover the following topics:

- Adding data disks
- Adding network interfaces
- Using Desired State Configuration
- Scaling VMs up/out
- Configuring monitoring
- Configuring high availability
- Deploying VMs
- Securing access to VMs
- Connecting to a VM

Let's get started!

Technical requirements

To complete the exercises in this chapter, you will need the following:

- Access to an Azure subscription (created in Chapter 1, *Getting Started with Azure Subscriptions*)
- Azure PowerShell installed on your computer: https://docs.microsoft.com/en-us/powershell/azure/azurerm/other-install?view=azurermps-6.13.0
- The Azure CLI: https://docs.microsoft.com/en-us/cli/azure/install-azure-cli?view=azure-cli-latest

Adding data disks

Each Azure VM has to have a disk configured for it that it uses to store the various operating systems and your files. However, you may want to configure an additional disk that you can utilize for additional files or application data. These disks are called **data disks** and can be attached to VMs, depending on their size. In this section, you will learn how to add such a disk and configure it so that it works with your VM.

In fact, in Azure, each VM can have two types of disks attached to it:

- An OS disk (required), which contains the operating system of the machine
- A data disk (optional), which is an additional disk that offers extended disk space

You can create a VM without a data disk if it is not required and add it later when you run out of space on your OS disk. Technically, when you work with your VM, all the data from the OS disk is saved in the Azure storage account that contains the disk. Thanks to that, the whole state of the machine is persisted and once it is rebooted, your data is still there. There is, however, a second type of OS disk called **ephemeral**, which does not persist data to Azure Storage. If you use this option and your machine gets rebooted, all the data will be erased and you will need to start with a *fresh* OS installation.

 Take a look at the following article for more information on ephemeral disks. There are some differences between them and *normal* OS disks that are not covered in this chapter: https://docs.microsoft.com/en-us/azure/virtual-machines/windows/ephemeral-os-disks.

Now, let's learn how to create a data disk in Azure.

Creating a data disk

To get started, you will need a working VM. If you do not have one, you can quickly deploy one. To do so, use the following Azure CLI command:

```
# You can find all the available options for this command by running `az vm
create -h`
az vm create --size VmSku -n MyVm --resource-group MyResourceGroup --image
VmImage
```

The same functionality is available via a PowerShell cmdlet:

```
#
https://docs.microsoft.com/en-us/powershell/module/azurerm.compute/new-azur
ermvm
New-AzureRmVM
```

Remember to pass all the required parameters and enter the expected VM size (see the preceding Azure CLI command) and wait a few minutes for the process to complete. If you want, you can also use the Azure portal and create a machine using a step-by-step wizard:

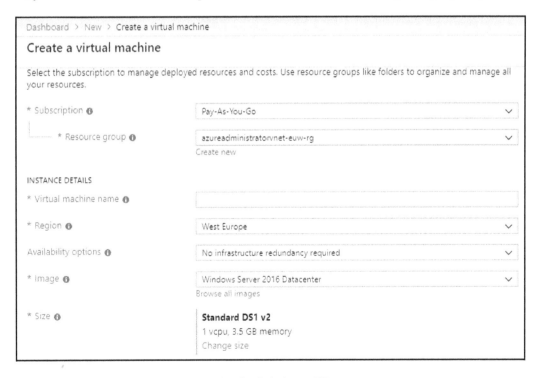

Figure 6.1 – Configuring a new VM

To attach a data disk to a VM, you will have to create one. To do so, use the following command:

```
az disk create --resource-group "<resource-group-name>" --name "<disk-name>" --size-gb "<size>"
```

Since we are creating an empty disk, we have to pass its size using the `--size-gb` parameter. Of course, by using the preceding command, you can configure the disk so that it uses a specific type (Standard/Premium, SSD/HDD) or even set its IOPS:

- `--sku`: For determining disk performance (Premium_LRS, StandardSSD_LRS, Standard_LRS, UltraSSD_LRS)
- `--disk-iops-read-write`: Only allowed for UltraSSD disks

To create a disk with PowerShell, use the following command:

```
New-AzureRmDisk
```

Once the disk has been created, we have to attach it. To do so, run the following command in the Azure CLI:

```
az vm disk attach
```

For example, to attach a disk to a VM named ch06-euw-vm, I used the following parameters:

```
$ az vm disk attach --vm-name "ch06-euw-vm" --name "<disk-name>" --resource-group "<resource-group-name>"
```

You can create and attach a disk in the same moment by using the az vm disk attach command with the --new switch, as follows: az vm disk attach --vm-name "ch06-euw-vm" --name "<disk-name>" --resource-group "<resource-group-name>" --new

Once the disk is attached, you will be able to see it in the Azure portal:

Figure 6.2 – View of both the OS and data disks attached to a machine

Data disks, similar to OS disks, can be encrypted, and their performance depends on the disk type (if you chose the Premium_SSD type, you will benefit from much better performance than using Standard_HDD disks).

Once the data disk is attached to a VM, it is registered as an SCSI drive and can be used by your VM. All the attached disks are, in fact, **Virtual Hard Disks** (**VHDs**) stored as Page Blobs on storage accounts (this is why a storage account is always created along with a VM). Data disks are one of the available types of Managed Disks, which is a special offering for VMs. It enables you to be responsible only for the provisioning part of the storage – Azure takes care of the rest.

In the next section, you will learn how to configure an additional feature related to VMs: networking interfaces.

Adding network interfaces

In the previous section, you had a chance to add data disks, which can be used as external storage for your data. However, VMs are not only about storage – they are also a part of a network that you have to configure properly to ensure proper access. In this section, you will learn what network interfaces are and how they work to deliver a proper VM security model.

This section requires you to have a VM already deployed. For detailed instructions, go back to the *Adding data disks* section, where I described the process step by step.

Network interfaces are a feature of Azure that aggregates the following configurations:

- IP configuration
- DNS servers
- **Network Security Groups** (**NSGs**)

They act as an interface to your VM and ensure the proper communication between it and other components. To create a **network interface** (**NIC**), use the following Azure CLI command:

```
az network nic create --resource-group "<resource-group-name>" --name
"<interface-name>" --subnet "<subnet-name>" --vnet-name "<vnet-name>"
```

As you can see, to create a NIC, you have to have a **virtual network** (**VNet**) already created with a subnet configured.

If you need instructions on how to create a VNet and a subnet, refer to Chapter 3, *Configuring and Managing Virtual Networks*, where we covered managing and configuring them.

A NIC is always created with each VM you provision in Azure and is available in the **Networking** blade in the Azure portal:

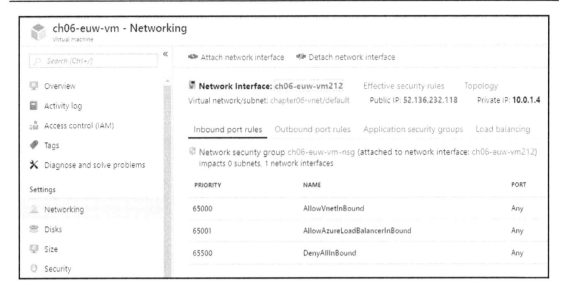

Figure 6.3 – A view of a NIC attached to a machine

As you can see, you can have more than a single interface attached to the machine. To attach an additional one, you will have to run the following command:

```
$ az vm nic add --resource-group "<resource-group-name>" --vm-name "<vm-name>" --nics "<names-or-ids-of-nics>"
```

Using multiple NICs allows you to configure additional public IP addresses or network rules. A NIC is a logical Azure resource that, by itself, does not imply any cost. It can be defined as follows:

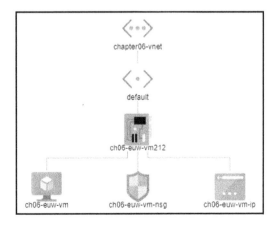

Figure 6.4 – Network infrastructure of a machine

As you can see, it clearly describes the functionalities of NICs – they aggregate the configuration and rules from multiple components so that they act as a single entity. This greatly simplifies management and allows you to control things from a single point of view.

The next section is about a feature or practice that can be described as **Infrastructure as Code (IaC)**. We will discuss a component called Desired State Configuration, which will help you automate deploying your machines by providing reusable configuration.

Using Desired State Configuration

Desired State Configuration (DSC) is a feature of Azure that allows you to ensure that a given VM has a desired state configured. What is the desired state? All the machines you deploy in Azure should have a specific set of features and tools already installed and enabled. By using DSC, you can automatically turn on different capabilities and make sure that you can deploy your application to them without any additional steps being required.

 To get started, you will need a VM deployed in your subscription. To create a new one, please reference the *Adding data disks* section of this chapter. The feature described in this section requires a machine that supports the Windows Management Framework. A list of such machines can be found here: https://docs.microsoft.com/en-us/powershell/scripting/dsc/getting-started/wingettingstarted?view=powershell-7.

To be able to run DSC scripts, you will have to install the **PowerShell Desired State Configuration** extensions on the desired VM. You can do this in a variety of ways, as follows:

- You can install it via the Azure portal (using the **Extensions** blade):

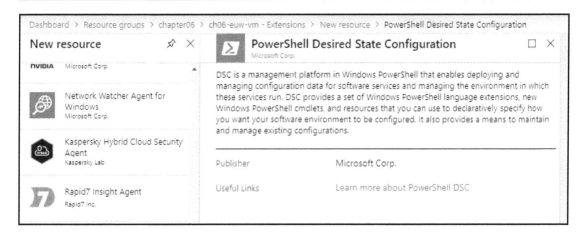

Figure 6.5 – DSC extension in the Extensions list

- Another option is using the Azure CLI (or PowerShell cmdlets). By using the `az vm extension set` command, you can easily add a particular extension to a VM of your choice:

```
$ az vm extension set --publisher "Microsoft.Powershell" --vm-name
"<vm-name>" --name "DSC" --resource-group "<resourve-group-name>"
```

You can get all the required information regarding an extension (its publisher and a name) by running the `az vm extension image list` command.

However, there is one gotcha with the preceding command – it will just install the extension without a proper configuration. To leverage all the features of DSC, use the following command variation:

```
$ az vm extension set --publisher "Microsoft.Powershell" --vm-
name>" --name "DSC" --resource-group "<resourve-group-name>" --settings
'{"ModulesURL":"<zip-archive-location>", "configurationFunction":
"<configuration>", "Properties": {"prop1": "value1"} }'
```

This is the very same command we described a few lines prior. The only difference is the `--settings` parameter, where you can provide the extensions configuration. As you can see, before the extension is installed, we have to write a DSC script. A configuration that is passed via DSC is a specific PowerShell structure and looks like this:

```
configuration IISInstall
{
    node "localhost"
    {
        WindowsFeature IIS
        {
            Ensure = "Present"
            Name = "Web-Server"
        }
    }
}
```

The preceding script makes sure that we have **Internet Information Services** (**IIS**) on our machine. This is a Microsoft web server that's installed and running. To run it, we will use a PowerShell script, as follows:

```
$resourceGroup = 'chapter06'
$location = 'westeurope'
$vmName = 'ch06-euw-vm'
$storageName = 'chapter06diag'

Publish-AzureRmVMDscConfiguration -ConfigurationPath C:\installiis.ps1 -
ResourceGroupName $resourceGroup -StorageAccountName $storageName -force
Set-AzureRmVMDscExtension -Version '2.76' -ResourceGroupName $resourceGroup
-VMName $vmName -ArchiveStorageAccountName $storageName -ArchiveBlobName
'installiis.ps1.zip' -AutoUpdate -ConfigurationName 'IISInstall'
```

At the time of writing this book, the `Publish-AzureRmVmDscConfiguration` cmdlet had an issue of caching a current subscription, so it could not find a resource group when executed after signing into a different one. Make sure you are starting with a fresh environment when running this command.

In the preceding code block, first, we defined some variables. Then, we published the configuration script to a VM and scheduled its execution. Once the extension is installed, we can verify whether it actually changed something on the machine:

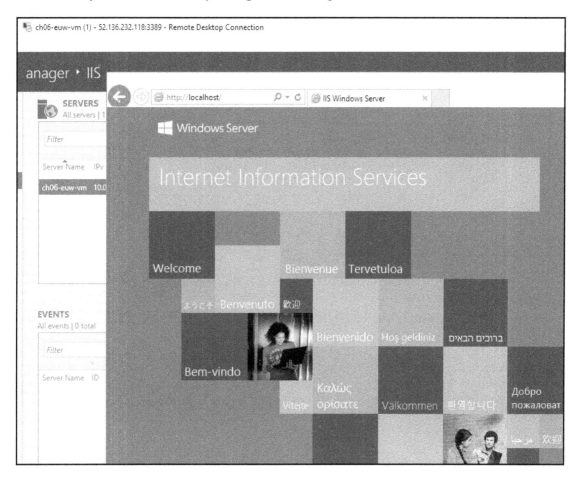

Figure 6.6 – Working IIS on a VM after running a script

As you can see, after running the script, IIS is working (by default, I am unable to access a welcome screen by going to the `localhost` page). Of course, such a page is not accessible from the internet – I have to add an inbound rule that accepts traffic from port 80 to be actually able to see it.

A DSC script is an actual PowerShell module and works in a similar fashion. Let's check out another example script (you can find the full example at `https://gist.github.com/kamil-mrzyglod/2aa0f0ce2188684b4f70a01fdd9ffa1e`):

```
Configuration ParametersExample
{
    param(
        [Parameter(Mandatory=$true)]
        [string] $FeatureName,
        ...
    )

    Node 'sample'
    {
        WindowsFeature ($FeatureName + 'Feature')
        {
        }
    }
}
```

As you can see, it contains a few areas:

- **Parameters**: You can pass a parameter to a DSC script as if it was a typical PowerShell script.
- **Logic**: You can write logic as if it was a typical PowerShell script.
- **Node description**: Contains all the features to be enabled on a machine.

DSC is a part of Azure Automation accounts. This is another Azure service that lets you configure automation for things such as onboarding machines, update management, and configuration provisioning. Currently, all these features are part of VMs in Azure:

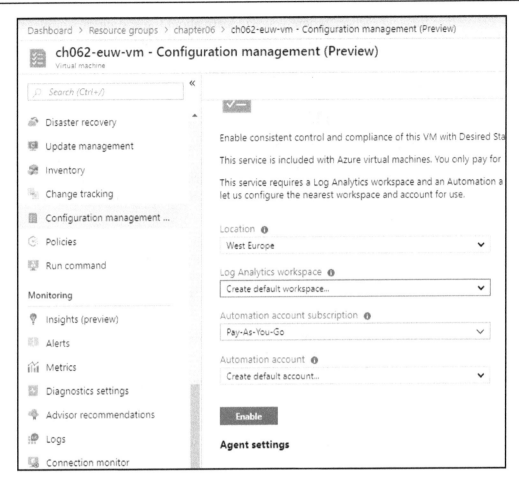

Figure 6.7 – Enabling configuration management

As you can see, you can enable DSC directly from a machine. This will, however, force you to create a Log Analytics workspace and Automation account (but will improve the overall capabilities of the feature). Remember that there are two features related to DSC:

- DC scripts for VMs.
- Azure Automation State Configuration, which extends the DSC capabilities and lets you manage the modules, import them, and configure them using Azure's capabilities.

The important thing with DSC is the fact that you can deploy the scripts using **Azure Resource Manager** (**ARM**). By doing this, we can ensure that we have a fully automated pipeline for deploying VMs and ensure that they are configured properly.

Please proceed to the next section, where you will learn about the scaling capabilities of VMs. Even if you are not proficient with them yet, it will help you understand the capabilities of horizontally and vertically scaling VMs in Azure.

Scaling VMs up/out

The biggest power of cloud computing is the seamless possibility to scale your workloads in seconds, without the need to provision new hardware. Any time you need more power for your applications, you can either add a VM to the workload or scale it up so that it gets better hardware. In this section, you will learn how easy it is to perform such actions and manage your machines.

 To get started, you will need a VM deployed in your subscription. To create a new one, please reference the *Adding data disks* section of this chapter. The feature described in this section works for both Windows and Linux machines, so do not worry and select whichever you prefer to work with.

Scaling up an instance is as easy as running a single command. Here, you can find an example of scaling a VM with the Azure CLI:

```
$ az vm resize --size Standard_DS2_V2 --resource-group "<resource-group-
name>" --name "<vm-name>"
```

The preceding command takes a --size parameter to define a new VM SKU value. Once run, the process of scaling up (upgrading the hardware) will start immediately.

 Note that not all VM sizes are available in each region. To know which are available for you, go to `https://aka.ms/azure-regions`.

The process of scaling up may take a while, so be patient. This operation, however, allows you only to scale up – how about scaling out? Well, to perform such an operation, we will need a **Virtual Machine Scale Set** (**VMSS**). To create a VMSS, use the following command:

```
az vmss create -n "<vmss-name>" -g "<resource-group-name>" --instance-count
<instance-count> --image Win2016Datacenter
```

The preceding command will create a VMSS containing a specific number (according to the `--instance-count` parameter) of the same VMs created from the Windows Server 2016 Datacenter image. Now, to add some more instances (or remove them), use the following command. The difference between this and the previous command is that, here, we are scaling the whole scale set (we're scaling more than a single VM at once):

```
az vmss scale --name "<vmss-name> --new-capacity <new-capacity> --resource-
group "<resource-group-name>"
```

When performing a scale-up/down operation, Azure will provision brand new machines that will have your data attached to them. This doesn't happen with scaling out since, during that operation, you are only adding/removing machines from a workload. In most cases, you do not want to use scaling up (vertical scaling) as it may cause data loss and, in general, it is a much more complicated operation.

Vertical scaling (as opposed to horizontal scaling) has far more limitations as both possible hardware and CPU and memory utilization, in most cases, have upper bounds. It is easier to write code for parallel processing than putting all the power into a single machine.

Scaling caveats

Please note that when you scale up/down a VM, it is restarted prior to allocating new resources to it. As it is difficult to alter provisioned CPU and memory for a working machine, it is highly possible that such an operation will restart your workloads or pause them. This is why you should do that with caution – wait for a window of opportunity or low-peak hours to limit users affected by the scaling operation.

Remember that a scaling operation may fail due to various reasons:

- Temporary data center capacity quota
- Service outage
- Reaching limits on your subscription

Take these into account when you plan to make any changes to the production subscription to avoid disruptions to your services.

Soon, you will see that scaling is one of the most common operations you can perform when working with cloud services. In the next section, I will show you how to configure another important feature of cloud services, which is monitoring for VMs.

Configuring monitoring

Monitoring VMs is one of the most important features available as there are many different parameters to analyze and watch for. In Azure, when designing IaaS architectures, you can use different services and features – this is why the initial choice may be difficult to make. In this section, you will learn how you can monitor different VM aspects and create dashboards to display them.

 To get started, you will need a VM deployed in your subscription. To create a new one, please reference the *Adding data disks* section of this chapter.

In Azure, the way you monitor different aspects is based mostly on two things:

- Performance counters collected by the running OS
- Installed extensions

As performance counters are OS-specific, you may get different results for Linux and Windows machines. When it comes to extensions, their interface is more or less OS-agnostic. Remember that Azure Monitoring collects data for all your machines, regardless of whether there is additional software installed or not. The downside of this solution is the fact that the data that's collected is available only for the machine – you cannot easily send it to other monitoring solutions or dashboards.

Configuring guest-level monitoring

With guest-level monitoring enabled, you can collect additional data and send it to destinations other than Azure. To enable this feature, go to the **Diagnostics settings** blade and click **Enable guest-level monitoring**:

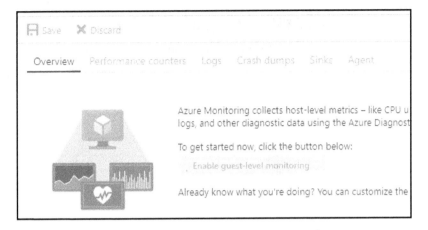

Figure 6.8 – Diagnostic settings blade before enabling it

Now, if you go to your deployed VM in the Azure portal, you will see that the very first monitoring feature of a VM is available immediately when you go to its **Overview** section:

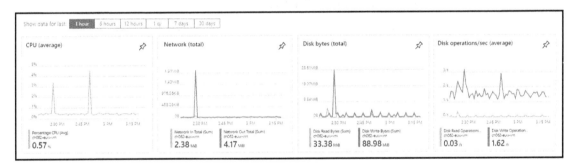

Figure 6.9 – View of a machine's workload

As you can see, this gives you an immediate insight into parameters such as CPU, network, and disk utilization. By using the pin icon next to each chart, you can attach it to your main dashboard inside the Azure portal.

Extending monitoring capabilities

More interesting capabilities can be found in the **Monitoring** section:

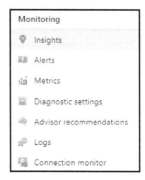

Figure 6.10 – Insights blade

Most of the features are made available by another Azure service named Azure Monitor. By going to the **Insights** section, you will be able to enable this feature:

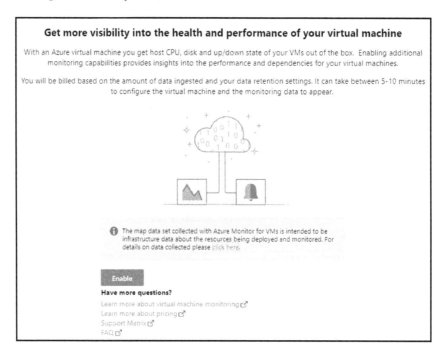

Figure 6.11 – Getting started with Insights

When you click the **Enable** button, this functionality will be onboarded onto the VM (this can take a few minutes, so be patient). With Insights and a workspace installed, you will be able to see additional things regarding your machine, such as the topology of the system:

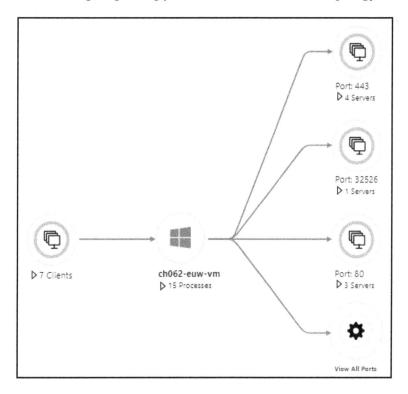

Figure 6.12 – Topology of your network traffic

As you can see, you are able to analyze all the open ports and active processes running on the machine. Installing the extension also allows you to query collected data using the **Logs** blade:

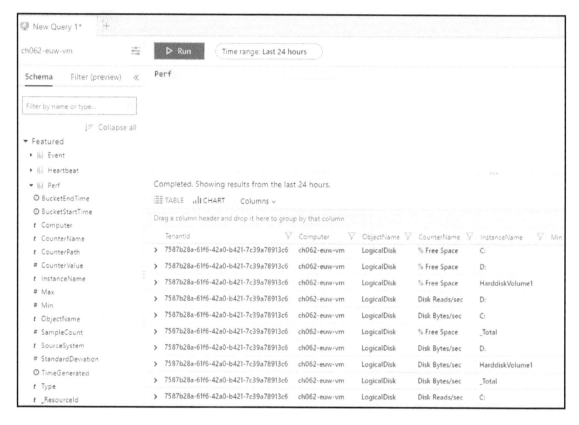

Figure 6.13 – Data gathered by monitoring extensions on a machine

Azure VMs can be also configured to monitor network latency and topology changes so that you are notified when such a situation occurs.

Enabling connection monitor

Connection monitor enables you to monitor communication between two separate VMs so that you're notified when there are any issues in the network connection between them. To use this feature, go to the **Connection monitor** blade and click on the **+ Add** button to install the monitor:

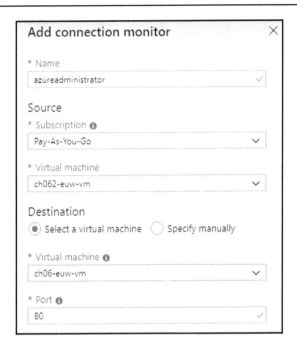

Figure 6.14 – Adding a connection monitor

Besides the aforementioned fields, you can use advanced settings such as a source port and probing interval. This will allow you to leverage custom configuration (if you have very specific requirements when it comes to open ports). Check out the following link for a more detailed approach: https://docs.microsoft.com/en-us/azure/network-watcher/connection-monitor-preview.

Note that this service works not only for Azure VMs but also for applications (by using Application Insights). Proper monitoring configuration is crucial for all the systems as it allows you to quickly react to issues and investigate them properly. Take into consideration that you are not limited to Azure services only – you can install your own monitoring solutions on VMs that can collect and send data to any data sink you like.

Here, you could try some additional capabilities when it comes to monitoring VMs. You may find them interesting when you're heavily working on IaaS architectures and seeking built-in tools for gathering insights.

To learn about how to achieve high availability for VMs, please proceed to the next section, where we'll discuss Availability Zones and Availability Sets.

Configuring high availability

In many scenarios, you can live with only a single instance of your VM available. This may include low-priority systems, asynchronous processing, or non-production resources. Things are much more difficult when we consider failover and business continuity scenarios. In such cases, you have to ensure that your VMs are properly configured and that even if one of them fails, the rest are still operating. In this section, I will show you how to achieve **high availability** (**HA**) for Azure VMs and configure it for resiliency scenarios.

Depending on the settings, you will end up with a machine in either an Availability Set (which you will have to configure on your own by adding additional VMs to it) or a VM provisioned in each available zone in the region.

 Note that **Availability Zones** (**AZ**) are not available in all the Azure regions. You can find all the available regions at `https://azure.microsoft.com/en-us/global-infrastructure/regions/`.

In Azure, the availability of a VM can only be configured while you're creating it:

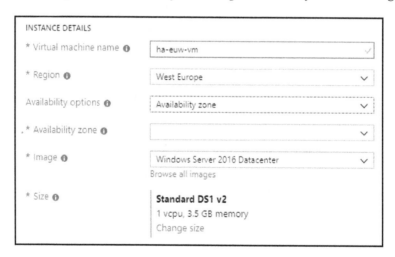

Figure 6.15 – Configuring availability options

Currently, you have two options:

- **Availability set**
- **Availability zone**

The difference between them is based on the technical details found behind each of the solutions. Depending on your choice, you will achieve different levels of availability and resiliency for your machines:

- Availability Sets ensure that, during planned or unplanned maintenance events in Azure, at least one VM will be running to meet the described SLA. This is done via upgrade and fault domains, which you will have to select. This can protect you from local outages, but will not secure your workloads in the case of region-wide issues.
- AZs make your VM resilient to zone failures but cannot protect you from a region-wide disaster. They are based on a single region that is designed in a way that even a local accident should not affect all your data centers.

To achieve HA across regions, you would have to implement at least two sets of VMs hosted in different regions and leverage AZs. This is beyond the scope of this section, but you can consult the following article for more: https://docs.microsoft.com/en-us/azure/virtual-machines/windows/manage-availability.

Now, let's learn how to create a VM with an Availability Set and see what it looks like:

1. During the creation of a VM, select the availability option of your choice. For the purpose of this example, I went for **Availability set** (when you select this option, you will be asked to create a new set or select an existing one):

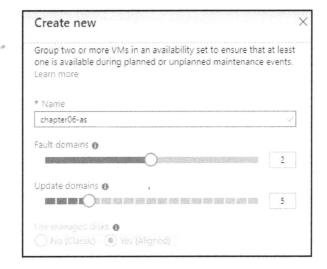

Figure 6.16 – Configuring an Availability Set

2. Select the number of fault/update domains you are interested in. The difference between them is as follows:
   - **Fault domains** separate your VMs physically so that they are not affected by the same network or power issues.
   - **Update domains** allow you to update VMs one by one.
3. When you are done, click the **OK** button. The rest of the process is the standard VM creation process – you will have to provide network settings and choose disks for the machines.

Note that using AS/AZ does not mean you are paying less for a machine – you will still pay for each VM individually (what you are not paying for is the availability feature itself). When it comes to ensuring HA globally, you will have to introduce an entry point that will be able to point to a proper set of machines in the working region (such as Azure Traffic Manager or Azure Front Door). In general, there are some major differences between local and geographical replication:

- Services leveraging AZs are replicated synchronously, so you do not have to worry about data integrity.
- Services replicated globally, in most cases, give you only asynchronous replication (unless stated otherwise), which does not ensure proper data replication. They also introduce greater latency and system fragmentation.

Depending on your requirements, you will have to choose the proper solution. Many applications can flawlessly work using only AZs as the whole region failing is something rather uncommon. Remember that you should always consider the most likely scenario when considering the replication model. If your system does not require 100% uptime, you do not have to replicate it globally (when only the availability parameter is considered).

So far, we have focused mostly on deploying VMs either using the Azure portal or the Azure CLI. In the next section, you will learn about additional tools that can be used to create a VM in Azure.

Deploying VMs

In this chapter, we have covered two ways of deploying VMs to Azure. Of course, these aren't the only options we have because, in CI/CD pipelines (which are basically **continuous integration/continuous deployment** automation scripts implemented with various tools), you will need more sophisticated solutions to ensure the desired level of automation. In this section, we will discuss other possibilities available, including Azure Resource Manager, the Azure Fluent API, and Terraform.

Browsing the solutions

Depending on the selected solution, different steps will be required to perform proper VM deployment. When it comes to using ARM, take a look at the ARM reference page at `https://docs.microsoft.com/en-us/azure/templates/microsoft.compute/2019-03-01/virtualmachines`, where you can find the complete schema of a VM deployment:

```
{
    "name": "string",
    "type": "Microsoft.Compute/virtualMachines",
    "apiVersion": "2019-03-01",
    "location": "string",
    "tags": {},
    "plan": {
        "name": "string",
        "publisher": "string",
        "product": "string",
        "promotionCode": "string"
    },
    "properties": {
        "hardwareProfile": {
            "vmSize": "string"
        },
        ...
    }
}
```

The preceding schema will be similar to any other Azure resource that's deployed via ARM. The common properties are as follows:

- name
- type
- apiVersion
- location
- tags
- properties

The `plan` property comes directly from the VM schema.

The reason for using ARM templates here is the fact that it is a native way of deploying resources to Azure. Unfortunately, ARM templates (especially for resources such as VMs) tend to be quite complicated and unclear. This is where the other two solutions come into play as they allow you to use your favorite programming language to create a deployment pipeline. Take a look at the following links, where I've put SDKs for three different platforms – .NET, Java, and Python (though there are also packages for Go and PHP available):

- .NET: https://docs.microsoft.com/en-us/dotnet/azure/sdk/
- Java: https://docs.microsoft.com/en-us/azure/developer/java/sdk/
- Python: https://docs.microsoft.com/en-us/azure/developer/python/

An example Fluent API description for a VM deployment written in C# looks like this:

```
IAzure azure = Azure.Authenticate(credFile).WithDefaultSubscription();
var windowsVM = azure.VirtualMachines.Define("myWindowsVM")
    .WithRegion(Region.USEast)
    .WithNewResourceGroup(rgName)
    .WithNewPrimaryNetwork("10.0.0.0/28")
    .WithPrimaryPrivateIPAddressDynamic()
    .WithNewPrimaryPublicIPAddress("mywindowsvmdns")
    .WithPopularWindowsImage(
        KnownWindowsVirtualMachineImage.WindowsServer2012R2Datacenter
    )
    .WithAdminUsername("tirekicker")
    .WithAdminPassword(password)
    .WithSize(VirtualMachineSizeTypes.StandardD3V2)
    .Create();
```

The preceding code presents a fluent way of creating a VM by describing the deployment with easy-to-read functions. We can define all the properties (region, resource group name, VM image, and authentication) using one of the supported programming languages.

As you can see, the syntax is much simpler than writing a JSON document. By using a simple console application, you can greatly improve the overall maintenance capabilities of your deployment pipeline. The third option will require you to understand how the basics of Terraform work (please refer to https://www.terraform.io/docs/index.html to get a better picture of the technology). An example Terraform script for deploying a VM in Azure looks like this:

```
resource "azurerm_virtual_machine" "main" {
  name = "${var.prefix}-vm"
  location = "${azurerm_resource_group.main.location}"
  resource_group_name = "${azurerm_resource_group.main.name}"
  ...
```

```
    storage_image_reference {
      publisher = "Canonical"
      ...
    }
    storage_os_disk {
      name = "myosdisk1"
      ...
    }
    os_profile {
      computer_name = "hostname"
      ...
    }
  }
```

In Terraform, you can define a `resource` that will contain all the supported properties, all of which are used later during deployment. The preceding fields, such as `name`, `location`, and `resource_group_name`, can be found when using SDKs or ARM templates.

All the solutions have their pros and cons, so the choice is yours. Let's quickly summarize them:

- Using ARM templates is the native for Azure and is a widely supported approach that gets the most updates and support from Microsoft. The downside of these templates is their limited readability.
- Terraform is a third-party tool that requires an additional language to be mastered. It manages the configuration state on its own and offers much better readability. Until recently, it had one advantage over standard ARM templates – it could perform a what-if analysis.
- The Management SDK is a great tool for staying within a specific language stack. It is preferred by developers over other tools and it allows us to use standard programmatic language constructs to deploy infrastructure.
- The imperative approach using Powershell/Azure CLI is another alternative that helps in rapid development. However, it can be tricky when implementing more complicated logic.

When selecting a proper tool, you always have to take factors such as your current technology stack, the audience of the scripts, and their use into account. Depending on the answers, one tool may suffice more than another.

Deploying resources using various tools

To deploy a VM using ARM, you will need to use either the Azure CLI or Azure PowerShell. Depending on the technology, you will have to use a different command. For the CLI, use the following command:

```
az group deployment create --resource-group <resource-group-name> --template-file <path-to-template>
```

For PowerShell, the following command should do the job:

```
New-AzResourceGroupDeployment -ResourceGroupName <resource-group-name> -TemplateFile <path-to-template>
```

Both of these commands take the provided parameters and deploy a template file in a specified resource group. Remember to enter all the required fields to perform a correct deployment (they are all described in the ARM reference). Another thing to note is the fact that a VM requires other resources to also be provisioned (such as VNet, a public IP address, or a load balancer). You will have to include all of them inside your template to finish the deployment. The very same requirement works for the Fluent API and Terraform – for example, to deploy a VNet, which you will be able to use later in a VM deployment, run the following syntax:

```
var network = networks.Define("mynetwork")
  .WithRegion(Region.USEast)
  .WithNewResourceGroup()
  .WithAddressSpace("10.0.0.0/28")
  .WithSubnet("subnet1", "10.0.0.0/29")
  .WithSubnet("subnet2", "10.0.0.8/29")
  .Create();
```

Here, we defined a new network called `mynetwork` and provided a bunch of parameters (such as its region/address space). Note that we also declared a need to deploy it inside a new resource group. A nice thing when it comes to using the Fluent API is the variety of available methods – all the VM required resources can be either passed as a reference or you can instruct the syntax to create a resource for you. Here is an example method for creating a VNet. By using a VM name as a reference, we can quickly instruct the SDK to create a new primary network for it:

```
var windowsVM = azure.VirtualMachines.Define("myWindowsVM")
  .WithNewPrimaryNetwork("10.0.0.0/28")
```

When using Terraform, things look really similar – you can create a resource similar to a VNet before creating a VM. To do so, you need to define your resource in the same manner as you would in an ARM template (in Terraform, you need to use the `resource` block and provide the parameters you want):

```
resource "azurerm_virtual_network" "main" {
  name = "${var.prefix}-network"
  address_space = ["10.0.0.0/16"]
  location = "${azurerm_resource_group.main.location}"
  resource_group_name = "${azurerm_resource_group.main.name}"
}

resource "azurerm_network_interface" "main" {
  name = "${var.prefix}-nic"
  location = "${azurerm_resource_group.main.location}"
  resource_group_name = "${azurerm_resource_group.main.name}"

  ip_configuration {
    name = "testconfiguration1"
    subnet_id = "${azurerm_subnet.internal.id}"
    private_ip_address_allocation = "Dynamic"
  }
}
```

Then, you can reference it (see the `network_interface_ids` parameter). We are basically creating a new VM with a name, location, and VM size. We are also using other resources to link them to that specific one:

```
resource "azurerm_virtual_machine" "main" {
  name = "${var.prefix}-vm"
  location = "${azurerm_resource_group.main.location}"
  resource_group_name = "${azurerm_resource_group.main.name}"
  network_interface_ids = ["${azurerm_network_interface.main.id}"]
  vm_size = "Standard_DS1_v2"
}
```

All the possibilities end up with us deploying a VM of the desired size, with the configuration included. No matter which solution meets your requirements, all of them use ARM under the hood. Currently, there is no other way to deploy resources to Azure (besides the classic model of deployment, which is currently being deprecated). Using ARM templates is a native way of creating deployments, but being so close to the API means that you have to deal with cumbersome syntax and complicated schema. The Fluent API and Terraform are mostly on the same level in terms of maturity and development – they require additional work to be compatible with new resources and often lack support for services that have not reached **General Availability (GA)** status.

Since we're nearing the end of this chapter, in the next section, we will cover more advanced topics and provide more details regarding common actions. We will cover securing access to VMs so that you can ensure no one without the required authority will be able to access your machines.

Securing access to VMs

A VM that is accessible to everyone is worse than having no VM at all. In this section, you will learn how VMs in Azure can be secured and how to enhance and use their security features. We will also discuss the proper security approach when it comes to designing network topologies.

To get started, you will need a VM deployed in your subscription. To create a new one, please reference the *Adding data disks* section of this chapter. The feature described in this section works for both Windows and Linux machines, so do not worry and select whichever you prefer to work with.

By default, when a VM is created in Azure, there is no way to access it – all the ports are closed for both inbound and outbound connections. You can find confirmation of this when creating a machine directly from the Azure portal:

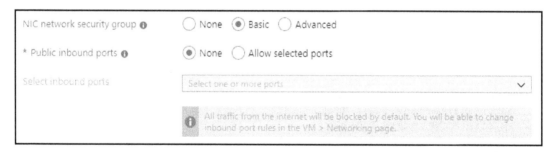

Figure 6.17 – Information about ports blocked by default

This means that you will not be able to access both a Windows machine (using RDP) or a Linux machine (using SSH). To change this, you can go to the **Networking** blade of the selected machine and add a proper port rule using the **Add inbound port rule** button:

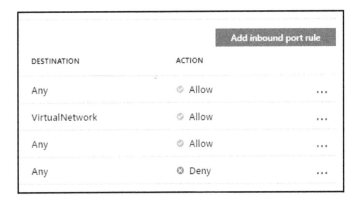

Figure 6.18 – Inbound rules configuration

 We covered working with NSGs and VNets in `Chapter 3`, *Configuring and Managing Virtual Networks*. Take a look at it if you are not familiar with the networking concepts available in Azure.

This applies to all the inbound or outbound ports that you may consider when deploying your application to a VM. If you have a web server running on a VM, you will have to open port `80` (and `443` if you are planning to use secured connections). The same applies to web servers or databases – with the default configuration, you will not be able to communicate with the machine. The effective security rules are described by a NIC attached to a machine. Take a look at the following screenshot:

Inbound security rules

Priority	Name	Port	Protocol	Source	Destination	Action	
1000	⚠ default-allow-3389	3389	TCP	Any	Any	⊘ Allow	•••
65000	AllowVnetInBound	Any	Any	VirtualNetwork	VirtualNetwork	⊘ Allow	•••
65001	AllowAzureLoadBalancerInBo...	Any	Any	AzureLoadBalancer	Any	⊘ Allow	•••
65500	DenyAllInBound	Any	Any	Any	Any	⊗ Deny	•••

Outbound security rules

Priority	Name	Port	Protocol	Source	Destination	Action	
65000	AllowVnetOutBound	Any	Any	VirtualNetwork	VirtualNetwork	⊘ Allow	•••
65001	AllowInternetOutBound	Any	Any	Any	Internet	⊘ Allow	•••
65500	DenyAllOutBound	Any	Any	Any	Any	⊗ Deny	•••

Figure 6.19 – Inbound/outbound rules

As you can see, all the rules are divided into a few columns:

- **NAME**: The custom name of a rule
- **PRIORITY**: The lower the rule is, the more important it is
- **SOURCE**: The origin of a request
- **SOURCE PORTS**: The origin ports
- **DESTINATION**: The endpoint type for a request
- **DESTINATION PORTS**: Endpoint ports
- **PROTOCOL**: The type of protocol (TCP/UDP/ICMP) allowed by that rule
- **ACCESS**: Either allowed or denied

In production environments, you should consider closing all the unused ports (for example, you do not want to have port 80 open if you are not using a web server).

When configuring a production environment, you can consider a thing called a **jumpbox**. It is a VM and is the only machine that allows you to log into it to diagnose other system components. From a jumpbox VM, you can then RDP/SSH to other machines inside the same VNet to understand the issue or access internal logs.

 There is also a new service available to achieve a secure connection when connecting with VMs, which is called Azure Sentinel. You can read more about it here: https://docs.microsoft.com/en-us/azure/sentinel/overview.

The last section of this chapter will help you understand the ways to connect to a VM. We will cover connecting both via RDP and SSH so that you can select a protocol that suits your needs.

Connecting to a VM

When you provision a VM in Azure, it has some settings already configured and ready to be used. In many cases, you won't want to log into it as there are often easier ways to diagnose a problem or install the software. However, there are still moments when you just need to use RDP or SSH and get your hands on the internal console of a machine. This may include a lack of proper monitoring and the unavailability of certain tools that may automate running a command or debugging. In this section, you will learn how to connect to a VM from a Windows or Linux machine.

To get started, you will need a VM deployed in your subscription. To create a new one, please refer to the *Adding data disks* section of this chapter. The feature described in this section works for both Windows and Linux machines, so do not worry and select what you prefer to work with.

With your VM deployed, we can make an attempt to connect to it.

Connecting to a VM

Connecting to Azure VMs is pretty simple as the Azure portal comes with a wizard that helps you with this. Whether you have a Windows or a Linux machine, you will need to use the **Connect** button, which can be found on the **Overview** page of your machine:

Figure 6.20 – Connect button

Note that you will use different ports for RDP (3389) and SSH (22) connections as per the default settings of those services.

 For using SSH, you will need an SSH client that can handle the connection. For most use cases, I recommend using PuTTy, which is free and popular.

After clicking on the **Connect** button, you will be able to select the desired option:

Figure 6.21 – Connecting to a machine

Depending on your choice, the process of signing into a VM will be slightly different:

- For RDP, you will either use an RDP file or will have to provide the IP address and the port number to your RDP client.
- For SSH, you will have to provide the IP address, port number, and login details to your SSH client.

Note that for Windows machines, you have two options available because connecting with both RDP and SSH is possible.

Using RDP and SSH to connect

When it comes to Linux machines, by default, only SSH is enabled – to use remote desktop, you will have to install and configure a proper package. Click on **Download RDP file** to quickly log into your VM. After accepting the connection, you will be asked to provide the admin credentials that were passed during the VM's creation:

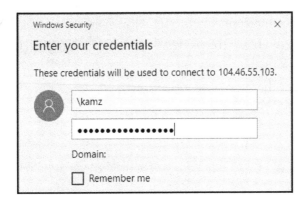

Figure 6.22 – Windows RDP login prompt

Here, you can see how the process of connecting looks for SSH with PuTTy:

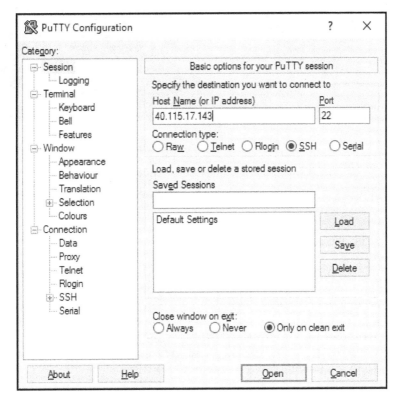

Figure 6.23 – Connecting to a machine via SSH with PuTTy

Here, we are using port 22 to connect via SSH. However, remember that it is just a default port number and that, under specific circumstances (such as security issues), it can be altered.

 Remember that you need either port 3389 or 22 open to be allowed to access the VM.

After correctly logging into a VM via SSH, you will see a console that you can use to browse the system:

```
The programs included with the Ubuntu system are free software;
the exact distribution terms for each program are described in the
individual files in /usr/share/doc/*/copyright.

Ubuntu comes with ABSOLUTELY NO WARRANTY, to the extent permitted by
applicable law.

To run a command as administrator (user "root"), use "sudo <command>".
See "man sudo_root" for details.

kamz@ubuntu-euw-vm:~$
```

Figure 6.24 – Login prompts when using SSH and a Linux machine

For RDP, you will see a desktop for the operating system of your choice. Take into consideration that the performance of using a remote desktop may be affected by the size of your VM and its utilization.

 Avoid using RDP for small machines running production workloads. Azure services such as Azure Service Fabric may be affected by your attempts using a machine with Remote Desktop, even resulting in the failure of your service. Also, note that you can always change the configuration of the remote desktop so that it is not available behind the default 3389 port.

When it comes to remote access, always consider remapping the default port (for example, by using NSGs) so that a potential attacker won't know that a specific OS service is a possible vector of attack.

Connecting to VMs is one of the easiest steps when it comes to managing and monitoring them. However, always consider the security factor – ports 3389 or 22 are well-known ports and should not be opened on production machines unless really necessary.

In this section, you learned how to connect to your VMs. In production systems, the whole setup may be quite different (as your VMs may be connected to your domain controllers or require a jumpbox to actually connect with them). Personally, I still heavily leverage the simplest ways to connect, especially when prototyping things.

Summary

In this chapter, we covered how to connect to managing VMs hosted in Azure. You learned about ways to secure machines, how to enhance storage capabilities with additional disks, and how to extend networking using network interfaces. We also talked about configuring software on VMs using DSC and achieving HA. All these basics are really important from an administrator's point of view as you will often face a ticket mentioning one of those capabilities.

In the next chapter, we will cover advanced networking concepts such as load balancing, VNets for managed services, and DDoS protection.

Section 3: Advanced Topics

3

With the basics in place thanks to the previous sections, we are able to move on to more advanced topics. In this section, you will learn how to work with data migration, high availability, and even automation for your daily tasks.

This section consists of the following chapters:

- Chapter 7, *Advanced Networking*
- Chapter 8, *Implementing Storage and Backup*
- Chapter 9, *High Availability and Disaster Recovery Scenarios*
- Chapter 10, *Automating Administration in Azure*

Advanced Networking

7

Networking in Azure is a big topic that requires a solution to diverse problems. This chapter is designed to solve advanced problems that an Azure administrator may face, such as proper DDoS protection, load balancing, or networking for containers. After this chapter, you should be familiar with configuring VNets even for more complicated infrastructures.

This chapter will help you understand more advanced networking topics relating to various Azure services, such as **Azure Kubernetes Service** (**AKS**) or **Azure Container Instances** (**ACI**). We will also describe features such as DDoS protection and monitoring.

The following topics appear in this chapter:

- Implementing load balancing
- Monitoring networks
- Configuring DDoS protection
- Enabling VNets for AKS
- Enabling VNets for ACI
- Enabling VNets for Redis Cache

Technical requirements

To perform the exercises in this chapter, you will need the following:

- Access to an Azure subscription (created in `Chapter 1`, *Getting Started with Azure Subscriptions*)
- Azure PowerShell installed on your computer: `https://docs.microsoft.com/en-us/powershell/azure/azurerm/other-install?view=azurermps-6.13.0`
- The Azure CLI: `https://docs.microsoft.com/en-us/cli/azure/install-azure-cli?view=azure-cli-latest`

Implementing load balancing

None of the more complex systems can work without proper load balancing. The process and implementation of handling bigger loads may differ depending on the components you use, the characteristics of your system, and the overall requirements of the whole solution. In this section, we will cover different ways to load balance your workloads, including different OSI layers and Azure resources. Just to refresh your knowledge, there are seven layers in the OSI model:

- Layer 1 – The physical layer
- Layer 2 – The data link layer
- Layer 3 – The network layer
- Layer 4 – The transport layer
- Layer 5 – The session layer
- Layer 6 – The presentation layer
- Layer 7 – The application layer

To get started, we have to understand what our capabilities are when it comes to load balancing in Azure:

- **Azure Load Balancer**: Works on layer 4 and is designed to work directly with **Virtual Machines** (**VMs**) in Azure by handling TCP/UDP packets.
- **Azure Application Gateway**: Works on layer 7, allowing you to perform URL routing, SSL offloading, and other application-level features.

- **Azure Traffic Manager**: For DNS-level load balancing, you use Traffic Manager. It works on a DNS level, which basically means that it resolves a proper URL address for your clients depending on the selected settings.
- **Azure Front Door**: Working on layer 7, this is a global load balancer. It is similar to Azure Traffic Manager in terms of resiliency as even a region-wide failure will not put it down.

To select a proper load-balancing method, you should consider the following cases:

- Do you want to load-balance traffic on an application level? If so, use Application Gateway.
- Do you have multiple VMs inside a **Virtual Network** (**VNet**) and want to ensure that they are evenly utilized? For that scenario, use Load Balancer.
- Do you need to load-balance requests geographically? This scenario is covered by Traffic Manager.
- Is SSL termination something you care about? If so, use Application Gateway.
- Do you seek global traffic distribution using HTTPS? Front Door looks like the best choice for you.

To perform the exercises in this section, you will need the aforementioned resources. To create them, I will use the Azure CLI with the following commands:

```
$ az network lb create -n "<lb-name>" -g "<rg-name>"
$ az network application-gateway create -n "<ag-name>" -g "<rg-name>"
$ az network traffic-manager profile create -n "<tm-name>" -g "<rg-name>" -
-routing-method Priority --unique-dns-name "<unique-dns-name>"
```

The preceding code snippet covers three different things:

- Creating a load balancer with `az network lb create`
- Creating an Application Gateway instance with `az network application-gateway create`
- Creating a Traffic Manager profile with `az network traffic-manager profile create` and a priority routing method, which will be described in detail later in this chapter

Note that besides the provisioned resources, you will also need VMs or applications to perform the load balancing. What is more, do not be surprised by extra resources created when provisioning Load Balancer or Application Gateway—they need public IPs and VNets to work properly.

 The process of creating an instance of Application Gateway may take a while. Be patient!

Depending on the service, there will be different ways to configure it to achieve a proper load-balancing solution. We will start with Azure Load Balancer—to add any load-balancing rules, you will need to create a health probe:

```
$ az network lb probe create -g "<rg-name>" --lb-name "<lb-name>" -n
"myprobe" --protocol TCP --port 80
```

The preceding command will create a probe named `myprobe`, which will use TCP protocol to probe a destination VM on port `80`. One more thing needed here is the actual pool of machines that we want to load-balance. By default, a single backend pool is created for your needs, so the only thing needed here is the rule creation:

```
$ az network lb rule create -g "<rg-name>" --lb-name "<lb-name>" -n
"myrule" --protocol TCP --frontend-port 80 --backend-port 80
```

 Before creating a rule, make sure at least one backend pool and probe exists as they are required to create it.

The preceding rule will forward traffic coming on port `80` to port `80` on all the machines in the attached backend pool.

 A backend pool can be attached to either a single machine, Availability Set, or **Virtual Machine Scale Set** (**VMSS**). This gives you a quick configuration option without the need to manually attach a dozen of your machines.

In the portal, the configured rule looks like this:

Figure 7.1 – Configuring a load-balancing rule

As you can see, you can configure additional properties such as **Session persistence** or **Floating IP**. They will be helpful for more advanced scenarios (such as a need for sticky sessions). For Application Gateway, the concept is very simple—once it is provisioned, you will have default options already configured. Once more, you will need a backend pool, which describes attached VMs, VMSS, or app services by declaring its targets (for example, by using the IP addresses of your VMs or their FQDN):

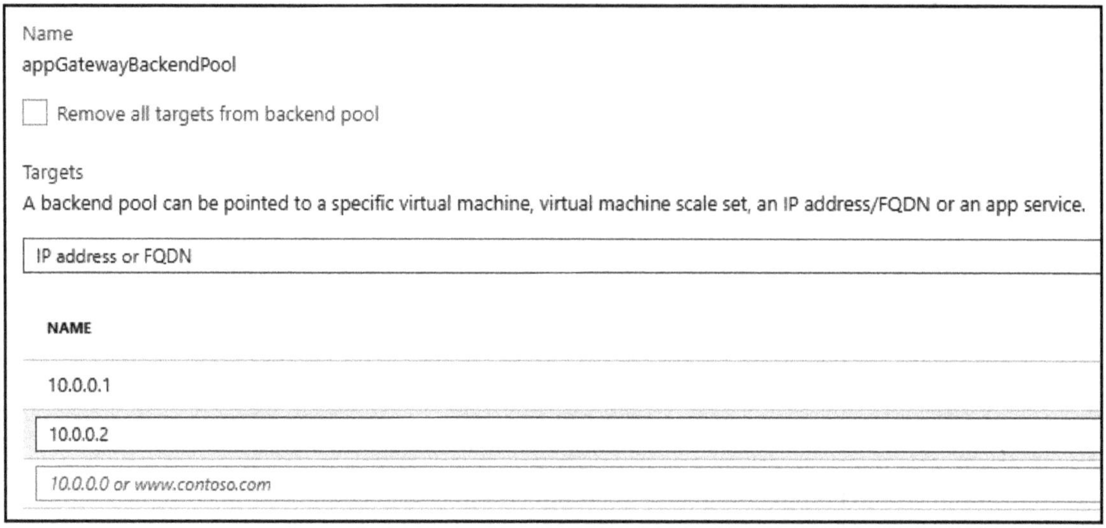

Name
appGatewayBackendPool

☐ Remove all targets from backend pool

Targets
A backend pool can be pointed to a specific virtual machine, virtual machine scale set, an IP address/FQDN or an app service.

IP address or FQDN

NAME

10.0.0.1

10.0.0.2

10.0.0.0 or www.contoso.com

Figure 7.2 – Configuring a backend pool for Application Gateway

In Application Gateway, load-balancing rules are named HTTP settings:

Figure 7.3 – Application Gateway load-balancing rule

As you can see in *Figure 7.3*, all the parameters available are related to the HTTP protocol—this is why you can see settings such as **Cookie based affinity**, **Request timeout**, and **Override backend path**. Conceptually, they are the very same thing as load-balancing rules in Azure Load Balancer—the difference here is the OSI model layer. In Load Balancer, we operate on TCP/UDP packets, whereas for Application Gateway, we work with HTTP. The extra thing needed here is a listener:

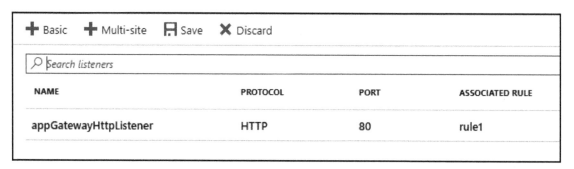

Figure 7.4 – Application Gateway listener

Listeners combine load-balancing rules with the port and selected protocol, ultimately making the feature work. Things are slightly different in Azure Traffic Manager—each instance consists of a profile and attached endpoints. To attach an endpoint, use the following command:

```
$ az network traffic-manager endpoint create -g "<rg-name>" --profile-name
"<tm-name>" -t externalEndpoints -n "myendpoint" --priority 1 --target
<target-ip>
```

The preceding command may differ depending on the profile of Traffic Manager and your selected endpoint type. As done previously, I selected **Priority** as the profile type and I had to provide the `priority` parameter, which defines the order in which an endpoint will be selected. What's more, because the endpoint type I selected was `externalEndpoints`, I had to provide a correct IP address to which traffic will be forwarded.

Depending on the selected resource and routing method, things will work differently for your scenarios:

- Azure Load Balancer leverages the public IP address, which is attached to it to act as a front door to your system. It probes the attached machines to make sure that they are responsive and they can receive the traffic. It can be used as a part of a highly available solution (thanks to using the Standard tier) by integrating with availability zones in Azure.

- Azure Application Gateway is similar to Load Balancer but operates on a higher layer of the OSI model. Once more, it acts as a front door to your system, and each client will connect to it instead of communicating with other system components. It allows you to also use Azure **Web Application Firewall** (**WAF**), which can protect you from many common threats.
- Azure Traffic Manager has a different concept. To use it, you have to configure your DNS server by adding a `CNAME` record, which will point from your domain to the Traffic Manager domain. Your client's request will be redirected to an instance of Traffic Manager for the final DNS resolution. Depending on the rules defined and the current status of your system, your client will be pointed to one of the available locations.

It is important to select the proper solution for your needs, as there is a variety of different services (and each of them offers different capabilities), so a deeper understanding of how things should be done is crucial for decent management operations. Keep in mind that each of the load-balancing solutions mentioned here has its pros and cons (refer to `https://docs.microsoft.com/en-us/azure/architecture/guide/technology-choices/load-balancing-overview`) and you will not always be able to apply them in all of the scenarios. Note that these are not the only available options in Azure—you can deploy your VMs and install any kind of load balancers you want (for example, Traefik). The advantage of native Azure load balancers is easy integration with existing services and much easier configuration.

This section should help you understand different ways to achieve load balancing in Azure and what the implications of using various services are. Proceed to the next section for insights regarding tools and features to monitor and diagnose networks.

Monitoring and diagnosing networks

Being able to monitor what happens inside your network is always a crucial thing. It helps you investigate outages, security issues, and the flow of your applications. The more applications and elements your system has, the more difficult is to monitor things in a manual manner. This is why being able to leverage external components and automation is always an important feature of any ecosystem of your choice. In this section, we will focus on one Azure service, Network Watcher, which is an extra Azure service that can be enabled for remote network monitoring, packet capturing, and network logs. To understand this section fully, you will have to have deployed an architecture that consists of multiple VMs and that is connected to a VNet. To get to that point, you can refer to `Chapter 3`, *Configuring and Managing Virtual Networks* and `Chapter 6`, *Managing Virtual Machines*, where we discussed both the VM and networking topics.

In my scenario, I had two VMs load-balanced using Application Gateway. They were deployed to the same subnet in the same VNet and both had ports 3389 and 80 opened for management and communication. The actual architecture can be seen in the following diagram:

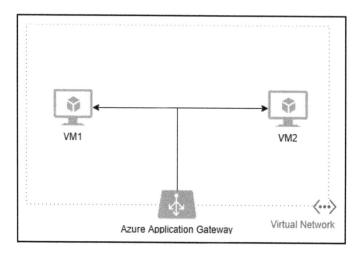

Figure 7.5 – The architecture of two VMs load-balanced by Application Gateway

The reason to have a little more advanced architecture is to be able to really implement a solution that can be monitored in terms of network traffic. If you deploy only a single machine, there will be nothing to watch.

We will start with Network Watcher. Before you use it, make sure it is enabled in your subscription and your region. It is a regional service, which means that once enabled, it will be available for all the networks inside a single region. To check which regions are enabled, search for Network Watcher and verify the regions:

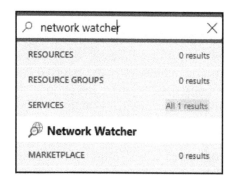

Figure 7.6 – The Network Watcher service in the search box

By default, Network Watcher is enabled automatically in each region to which you have deployed a network. However, there is a possibility to disable this feature—although this has important implications, as you will be forced to contact support to opt back in.

When you check the menu on the left, you will see the available features of Network Watcher:

Figure 7.7 – Network Watcher features

We can briefly explain them before diving deeper:

- **IP flow verify**: Allows you to create a configuration determining whether a packet should be approved or blocked
- **Next hop**: Determines the next place where a packet will go
- **Effective security rules**: Allows you to quickly validate your security setup
- **VPN troubleshoot**: A tool for validating your VPN connection
- **Packet capture**: Allows you to analyze packet flowing by your network
- **Connection troubleshoot**: A tool for checking the correctness of the network setup

Let's now describe all the features in detail.

IP flow verify

By using **IP flow verify**, you can check whether a packet is accepted or blocked based on the provided configuration and attached security rules:

Figure 7.8 – The IP flow verify settings

This feature consists of the following fields:

- **Subscription**: Determining the availability of particular resources
- **Resource group**
- **Virtual machine**

- **Network interface**: The actual network card that we are interested in
- **Protocol** and **Direction**: The actual communication flow
- Local and remote address and port: Communication origin and destination

The advantage of this feature is the fact that it displays the result and the name of the rule that provided it.

Next hop

The next feature, **Next hop**, makes it easier to understand what the next checkpoint is when reaching the provided destination IP address:

Figure 7.9 – The Next hop functionality

By using **Source IP address** and **Destination IP address**, we can decide the actual route of packets. It is a great feature when you want to quickly check whether you are communicating with a VNet, the internet, or any other kind of network resource.

Effective security rules

The **Effective security rules** feature grants you the possibility to gather all the rules defined for a VNet and inbound/outbound connections. If you want to check whether a machine accepts a connection on port 80, this is the place to start.

VPN troubleshoot, Packet capture, and Connection troubleshoot

VPN troubleshoot and **Packet capture** are more advanced tools for analyzing connections handled by VPN gateways or transferred packets, respectively.

 VPN troubleshooting is a long-running operation that gives results only when it is finished. When using it, be patient and wait for the analysis to be completed.

The last feature, **Connection Troubleshoot**, allows you to understand what exactly is happening when connecting from one place to another. It works by sending packets from the source VM to the destination VM and checking the result. It will also display the topology and all the hops to give you a better picture of the current situation:

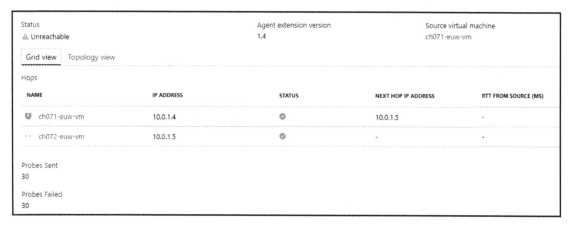

NAME	IP ADDRESS	STATUS	NEXT HOP IP ADDRESS	RTT FROM SOURCE (MS)
ch071-euw-vm	10.0.1.4	⊘	10.0.1.5	-
ch072-euw-vm	10.0.1.5	⊘	-	-

Status
⚠ Unreachable

Agent extension version
1.4

Source virtual machine
ch071-euw-vm

Grid view   Topology view

Hops

Probes Sent
30

Probes Failed
30

Figure 7.10 – Connection troubleshooting

The Network Watcher connection monitor can be added from a VNet instance itself. You can follow these steps to add it:

1. Go to your VNet and search for the **Connection monitor** blade:

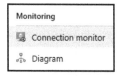

Figure 7.11 – The Connection monitor blade

2. From this screen, you will be able to add a new monitor to diagnose your connection:

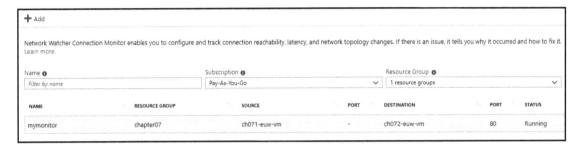

Figure 7.12 – Configured monitors

Connection monitors diagnose traffic on particular ports and display insights about network behavior. These features are not always enough to define a problem (as there might be issues such as a local network configuration problem or errors on the ISP side, which cannot be told just by using Azure's capabilities), but should suffice for most of the troubles you may face. Network diagnosis and monitor features in Azure work by being installed on machines' extensions, which gather the data:

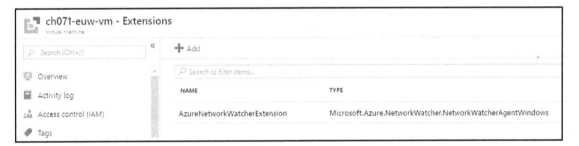

Figure 7.13 – VM installed extensions

Some of them use in-built or native storage, but still, there are extra features (such as VPN troubleshooting) that require you to provide external storage such as Azure Storage. Thanks to those extensions working on your VMs (and internal features of other Azure services such as Azure Load Balancer), you can gather enough data to diagnose a problem. What's more, they generate the full topology of your network:

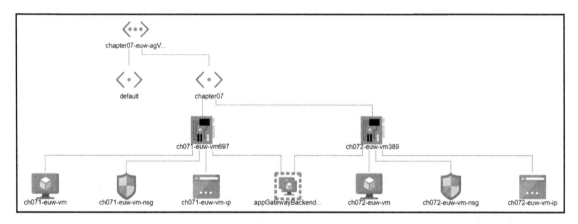

Figure 7.14 – Network infrastructure

You can access this by going to the **Topology** blade in your VNet. For bigger networks, this feature will be especially helpful as it gives you a full picture of all the connections.

Diagnosing and monitoring networks in Azure is a really big topic and there is no way to describe it in only one section. Here, you will find some more information about Network Watcher, which we only briefly described in this chapter: `https://docs.microsoft.com/en-us/azure/network-watcher/`. Besides packets and connection monitoring, you will be able to also find information on how to monitor the performance of your network, or even ExpressRoute.

Monitoring and diagnosing networks when using in-built features in Azure makes the management task much easier. You do not have to implement your own tools to analyze traffic and maintain them—everything is provided as additional components available in the cloud. The next section will describe in detail one of the most common features when it comes to securing a network, which is DDoS protection.

Configuring DDoS protection

Security should always be something that you're concerned about, especially if you are responsible for the proper administration and management of Azure resources. As in this chapter, we are covering networking topics, so now is a good moment to describe DDoS protection of Azure VNets. DoS attacks can be really dangerous as they are not aimed (at least not always) at breaking into your system—they are focused on interrupting your business, which can be even more painful than dealing with a security breach. In this section, we will talk a little about different levels of DDoS protection of VNets and how to use them.

 To get started, you will need a VNet that you can configure. If you do not know how to do this, refer to `Chapter 3`, *Configuring and Managing Virtual Networks*, where I described the process of creating VNets at the very beginning of the chapter.

Let's now check how to configure the feature:

1. Once you have a VNet, go to the Azure portal and search for the **DDoS protection** blade:

Figure 7.15 – The DDoS protection blade

You will see two radio buttons:

- **Basic**
- **Standard**

There are some major differences between these two versions of DDoS protection. While the basic option may be just about okay for most standard workloads that do not need an external level of security, the standard option gives you some really nice benefits:

- Application availability guarantee
- Attack metrics
- Post-attack reports
- Access to DDoS experts

In general, the case where you would choose **Standard** over **Basic** is for when you have to deal with more sophisticated DDoS attacks such as SYN floods, UDP floods, or HTTP protocol violations. As mentioned earlier, this all depends on the actual level of security and reliability that your application requires. Choosing the Standard tier does not guarantee that your application will stay alive during an attack—it just gives you better analysis and monitoring and the opportunity to be more adjusted to your application.

2. To change the level of DDoS protection, switch the **DDoS protection** option to **Standard**:

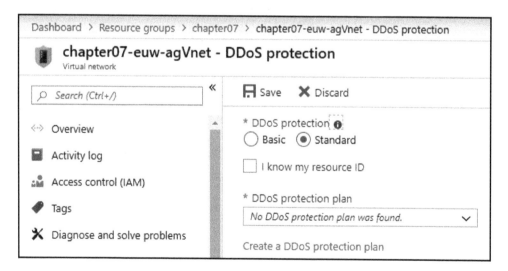

Figure 7.16 – Switching to the standard level of DDoS protection

You will be asked to provide a DDoS protection plan. This is an additional service, which will be deployed to your resource group and paid for separately. This service will be responsible for protecting resources inside your VNet.

 Before creating a DDoS protection plan, take into consideration its pricing. The basic price for a month is exactly $2,944 plus data processing costs.

3. To create a new protection plan, click on the **Create a DDoS protection plan** link. It will redirect you to a new window, where you can provide information related to it:

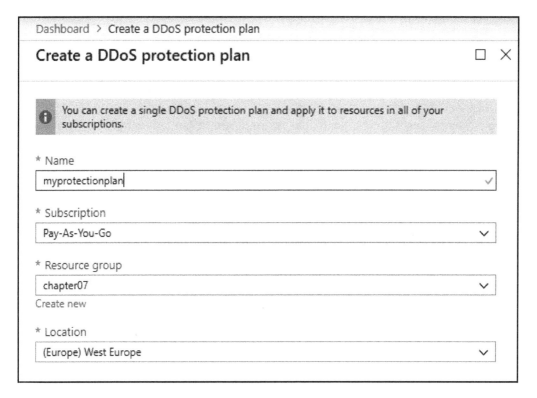

Figure 7.17 – Creating a new DDoS protection plan

4. By clicking on the **Create** button, you will start the provisioning process of your new protection plan.

Consider reusing your protection plan for multiple VNets. Using multiple protection plans may be required when you have to clearly calculate the cost of the architecture or when you exceed the 1 PB limit for the data processed.

When a **Standard** protection level is enabled, it will be its responsibility to analyze and verify traffic coming into your applications inside a VNet. That means that if an attack is detected, the following checks are performed:

- Verifying packets to ensure they are not malformed.
- Communication with a client is initialized to check whether it is an attacker.
- Ultimately, some limits are applied to accept only part of the incoming traffic.

When using the **Standard** tier, a few minutes after the attack starts, you will be notified via Azure Monitor.

There are many different mitigation policies implemented in the DDoS protection service—they all depend on the actual attack vector and its intensity. The advantage of securing your services with this particular Azure resource is the fact that it comes as a single product—you do not need to implement the policies on your own, manage the monitoring of your network, and mitigate the attack if it happens. The important fact here is the actual knowledge about DDoS attacks. If you are not familiar with different DoS attacks such as DRDoS, fork bombs, or SYN floods, make sure to update your knowledge, starting with the following article: `https://www.us-cert.gov/ncas/tips/ST04-015`. Knowing how they work will be crucial for you to properly implement DDoS protection policies.

DDoS protection is one of the most common features when it comes to securing a network as many attackers want to exploit the lack of security in this particular area and cripple a website or an application. This is why it is important to understand how you can secure your services with Azure. The next section will cover VNet integration in a managed version of Kubernetes called AKS.

Enabling VNets in AKS

AKS is a PaaS offering from Microsoft that enables you to use and manage a Kubernetes cluster without actually provisioning your VMs and the configuration on your own. It greatly enhances the productivity of a team and application flexibility, as you do not have to be concerned by the burden of updates, infrastructure, and networking. In this section, I will show you how you can configure a VNet in AKS by leveraging a feature called Azure **Container Networking Interface** (**CNI**).

To get ready, you will have to start with an actual Kubernetes cluster. There are a few ways for doing that—either by using the Azure portal or CLI commands. We will focus on using the portal, but I will also add the appropriate commands that you will be able to use. To create a cluster, you can follow these steps:

1. Search for `Kubernetes Service` in the marketplace and click on the **Create** button:

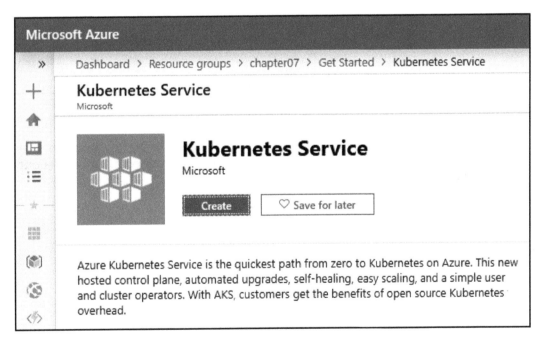

Figure 7.18 – Creating a new Kubernetes Service instance

2. You will have to provide multiple options, such as the size of the nodes, the Kubernetes version, or the authentication options. In fact, when it comes to the required fields, only the **Basics** tab has to be configured. You can find an example here:

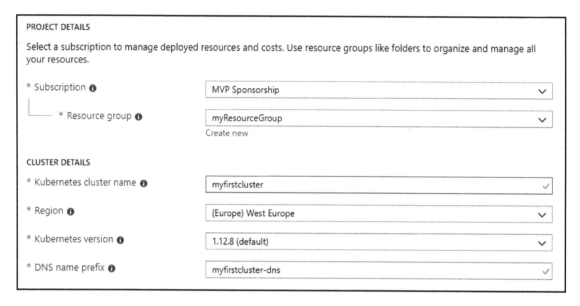

Figure 7.19 – Configuring a Kubernetes cluster

3. However, what we are interested in in this section is the **Networking** tab, which allows us to change the advanced settings of the network configuration of our Kubernetes cluster:

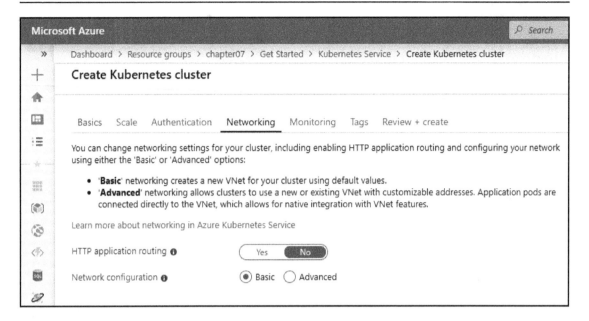

Figure 7.20 – Configuring networking for the Kubernetes cluster

The important thing to consider here is the ability to use either a **Basic** or an **Advanced** network configuration. The difference between them is simple—you can either use the default configuration with kubenet or leverage Azure CNI with a customizable VNet. We will go for the second option here.

4. **Azure CNI** allows each pod to get an IP address from a subnet and be addressed directly. This is quite the opposite to using kubenet, where the IP is attached from a subnet to a node, and then each pod has its IP translated by **Network Address Translation** (**NAT**).

 While using Azure CNI requires much more advanced configuration and an understanding of networking features, it actually allows much more flexible infrastructures. By giving each pod its own IP address, you can natively integrate them with Azure VNet features.

When we change the radio button value from **Basic** to **Advanced**, we will see new options available to be set:

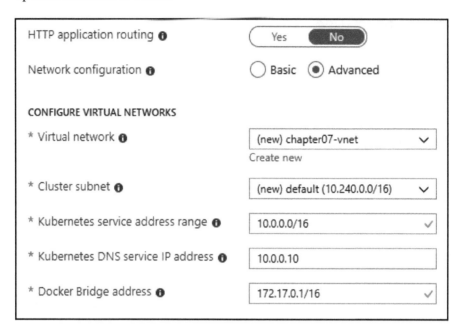

Figure 7.21 – Configuring a VNet

These parameters are required to get started with Azure CNI. Besides quite obvious things, such as a VNet instance or a subnet, there are three additional things to be configured:

- The IP range for the cluster service so that you know how many services you can host
- The IP address for a Kubernetes DNS service in case you have to explicitly pass its address to your services
- The address of the Docker bridge to interconnect between services

Once the cluster is created, IP addresses will be automatically assigned to your pods based on the IP range of the assigned subnet.

 By default, Azure CNI configures 30 IP addresses, which are available for your pods per node. When the cluster is scaled, new addresses are configured dynamically.

The advanced networking feature can be also configured and enabled from the Azure CLI. The following command will create an AKS cluster with `--network-plugin` set to `azure`. That means that the created cluster will have advanced networking enabled (as it will be using Azure CNI for networking):

```
az aks create --resource-group <rg-name> --name <cluster-name> --network-plugin azure --vnet-subnet-id <subnet-id> --docker-bridge-address 172.17.0.1/16 --dns-service-ip 10.2.0.10 --service-cidr 10.2.0.0/24
```

Whether you run the preceding command or enable advanced networking in the portal, the output will be the same—the network in your cluster will be configured with the values provided by yourself. Thanks to that, you will be able to properly set the cluster IP range (so you know it will not overlay reserved IP addresses in a particular subnet) or its DNS service (for custom discovery scenarios).

When using Azure CNI, you have to pay attention to the IP address uniqueness and plan the network ahead. In the case of growing demands, you may face a situation where you need to rebuild a cluster to continue using the feature. However, this has its own advantages, as follows:

- Direct communication between pods—you do not have to communicate through a NAT service to reach the destination.
- You can configure service endpoints for different pods for secure communication with native Azure services.
- You can leverage all the native features of VNets, such as traffic routing and IP range configuration.

With Azure CNI, the communication happens via the Docker bridge, which acts as a door to pods hosted on each node. It communicates with CNI to consult the IP address of a pod. The following diagram should help you understand the infrastructure:

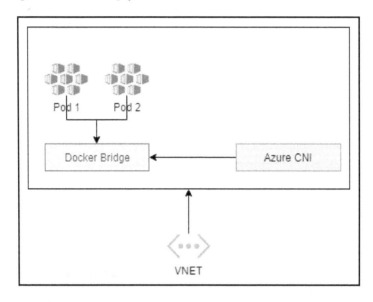

Figure 7.22 – Networking in Kubernetes with Azure CNI enabled

As you can see, there is no translation feature of NAT, which exists with the basic networking in AKS. However, as IP addresses of pods are assigned from the pool of available IP addresses of a subnet, you have to consider additional factors:

- If you deploy an internal Azure load balancer, its front-door addresses will also be assigned from the subnet that Azure CNI uses.
- If you are planning to upgrade or scale your cluster, you should set a valid range of a subnet to avoid a need to rebuild a cluster.

Because of the preceding considerations, when selecting a range of a subnet, do not aim at the minimal range to avoid problems. When making a choice about whether you should use basic or advanced networking in AKS, always ask yourself whether you need to natively integrate your pods with Azure VNet. Advanced networking for Kubernetes in Azure is meant for more sophisticated scenarios with a need for direct communication between pods and Azure services and will require a detailed approach for network design.

The next section will help you understand how ACI integrates with VNets so that you can make them private services.

Enabling VNets for ACI

If you have your applications packed as a container and do not want to maintain the infrastructure, you can use ACI. This Azure service allows you to host your containers without the need to handle things such as proper VM configuration, installing hosts, and ensuring proper resources. By default, those deployed containers are hosted inside a public network and there is no native possibility to secure them without implementing logic directly in the application. In this section, you will learn how to deploy ACI to a VNet, which will give you additional features.

To get ready, you will need an instance of the ACI service. There are multiple ways to get it—using either the portal or the Azure CLI:

```
$ az container create
```

If you have not had a chance to deploy this service previously, I strongly recommend trying it from the portal first and reading the following article: `https://docs.microsoft.com/en-us/azure/container-registry/container-registry-intro`. The command for creating ACI is quite complicated as it allows you to provide several different parameters. They will be much easier to understand after deploying the service from the Azure portal. To deploy this particular resource from the portal, go to the marketplace and search for `Container Instances`. The last thing required here (besides configuration) is clicking on the **Create** button:

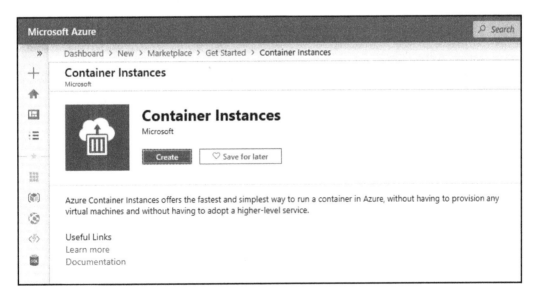

Figure 7.23 – Creating ACI

Once you are familiar with the service, you can proceed with this section where we discuss the process of assigning a VNet using the proper commands.

 Deploying ACI to a VNet was still in preview when I was writing this chapter. At the moment you are reading, the UI or naming of the parameters might have changed.

To deploy ACI to a VNet, you can use the following command:

```
az container create --name <aci-name> --resource-group <rg-name> --image
<name-of-image> --vnet <vnet-name> --vnet-address-prefix 10.0.0.0/16 --
subnet <subnet-name> --subnet-address-prefix 10.0.0.0/24
```

Take into consideration the following things:

- The preceding command deploys ACI to a new VNet and configures it accordingly. This is why we passed the address prefixes for both a VNet and a subnet.
- The deployment can take a while as it has to deploy additional Azure resources.

Once the preceding command is finished, you can query it for the private IP address, which can be used for further deployments:

```
az container show --resource-group <rg-name> --name <aci-name> --query
ipAddress.ip --output tsv
```

In my case, the output was `10.0.0.4`. Your output may be different depending on the address prefixes you used in the previous command. Once the first deployment is complete, you can add new Azure container instances to the same VNet just like this:

```
az container create --resource-group <rg-name> --name <aci-name> --image
<image-name> --vnet <vnet-name> --subnet <subnet-name>
```

When you deploy other ACI resources to the same VNet, they will be able to communicate with each other, even though they are not using the public IP address to do so. Deploying container instances to the same VNet works in the same manner as other Azure services. Once your containers are inside a VNet, they can leverage the private addressing space and be secured against unauthorized access. You can also confirm that your container instances are inside a private network in the portal by confirming its private IP address:

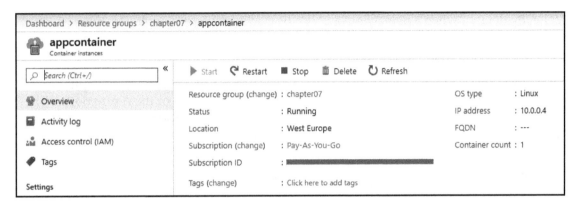

Figure 7.24 – Running container instances

As you can see, the same IP address that was displayed by querying the resource is available here as the **IP address** parameter on the right. Once a VNet is assigned to your Azure container instances, you can extend their functionality to the following:

- Connecting containers with Azure resources via service endpoints
- Enabling your container to connect to on-premises networks via VPN gateways
- Direct communication between containers inside the same VNet

By using this feature, you can enforce more advanced scenarios when it comes to connecting to your containers. If you are planning to use ACI and find its networking features lacking, the ability to deploy a service to a VNet should do the trick.

The last section about VNet integration will explore Redis Cache as one of the managed services of this popular database.

Enabling VNets in Redis Cache

Redis Cache is one of the PaaS/SaaS offerings in Azure, which gives you a well-known product that can be easily configured and provisioned. Thanks to that option, you can quickly deploy a Redis Cache instance and focus on using it in your application. As it very often acts as the first-level storage (or in other words, the first-level cache) of an application, you may want to secure it and improve its performance by colocating it inside a single VNet. By default, when a managed Azure Redis Cache instance is deployed, there is no way to isolate it from the public internet. In this section, I will show you how a network integration can be achieved with just a few clicks.

To perform this exercise, we will need a Redis Cache instance. There are a few options to do so, but we will consider two of them—either using the Azure CLI or the Azure portal. The important thing here is the fact that VNet integration can only be added when deploying the cache. To create Redis via the command line, run the following snippet:

```
$ az redis create --resource-group "<rg-name>" --name "<redis-name>" --
location "<location>" --sku <Basic|Standard|Premium> --vm-size
<c0|c1|c2|c3|c4|c5|c6|p1|p2|p3|p4|p5>
```

The preceding command will create a Redis Cache instance with the following settings:

- `--resource-group`: The name of your resource group
- `--name`: The name of your Redis Cache instance
- `--location`: The region where an instance will be deployed
- `--sku`: The version of Redis Cache
- `--vm-size`: The size of the VM hosting your instance of Redis Cache

For the Azure portal, you will have to search for `Azure Cache for Redis` in the marketplace. Once you find the resource, click on the **Create** button and fill in the form:

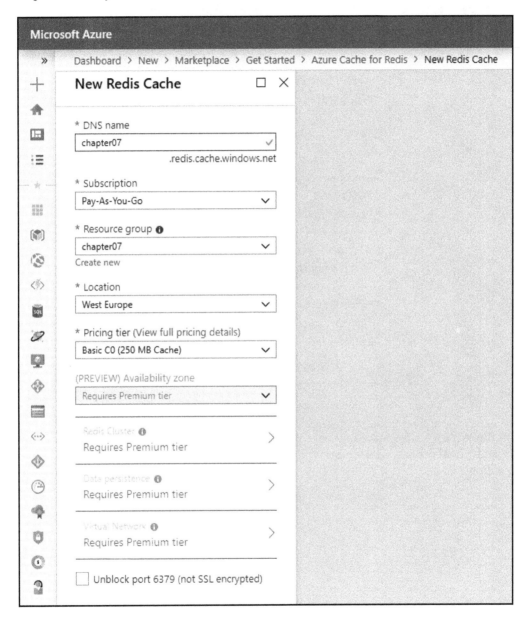

Figure 7.25 – Creating a new Redis Cache instance

As you can see, the `--vm-size` parameter is linked to the **Pricing tier** parameter in the portal. It defines the actual memory amount and available features (such as replication, **Service Level Agreement (SLA)**, or overall performance). However, if you want to go for VNet integration, you will need to choose the **Premium** tier to enable advanced features. In the portal, if you have chosen the **Premium** tier, you will see some additional options:

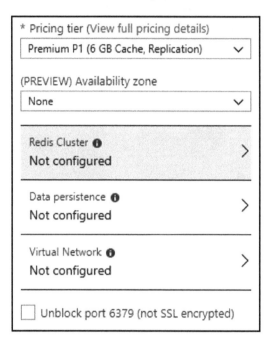

Figure 7.26 – Additional options for Premium SKU Redis Cache

One of the extra features available here is VNet integration. When you click on it, you will see an additional screen, where you will have to put in some extra configuration information:

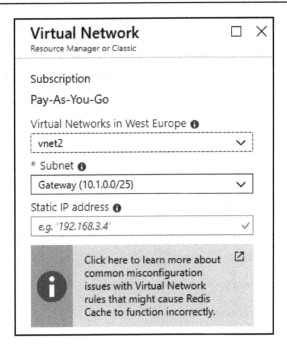

Virtual Network □ ✕
Resource Manager or Classic

Subscription

Pay-As-You-Go

Virtual Networks in West Europe ❶

vnet2 ⌄

* Subnet ❶

Gateway (10.1.0.0/25) ⌄

Static IP address ❶

e.g. '192.168.3.4' ✓

ⓘ Click here to learn more about ☒
common misconfiguration
issues with Virtual Network
rules that might cause Redis
Cache to function incorrectly.

Figure 7.27 – Configuring the VNet

 Remember that the selected VNet has to be in the same location as your cache.

There are some things to be considered:

- The selected subnet has to be dedicated to your instance of Redis Cache.
- There are some port requirements, which will be discussed further in this section.
- When VNet integration is enabled for Redis Cache, your client will have to be deployed to the same VNet, or VNet peering has to be configured.

The same functionality can be achieved using the Azure CLI and two additional parameters: `--subnet-id` and `--static-ip`. The actual command will look just like this:

```
$ az redis create --resource-group "<rg-name>" --name "<redis-name>" --
location "<location>" --sku <Basic|Standard|Premium> --vm-size
<c0|c1|c2|c3|c4|c5|c6|p1|p2|p3|p4|p5> --subnet-id "<subnet-id>" --static-ip
"<ip-address-of-instance>"
```

After running the preceding command, wait a while until your Redis Cache instance is deployed. Depending on the current region status and its availability, this may take from several seconds to a few minutes. Once your instance of Redis Cache is deployed with VNet integration, you will see it in the **Virtual Network** blade in the portal:

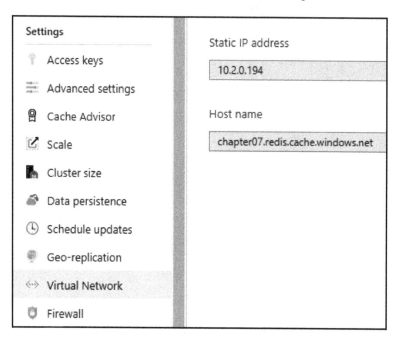

Figure 7.27 – VNet configuration for Redis Cache

Remember that if you did not provide the static IP address, it will be assigned automatically once the integration is complete. You can also use the Azure CLI to obtain that information:

```
$ az redis show --resource-group <rg-name> --name <redis-name>
{
  ...
  "staticIp": "10.2.0.194",
  "subnetId":
"/subscriptions/.../resourceGroups/.../providers/Microsoft.Network/virtualN
etworks/<vnet-name>/subnets/<subnet-name>",
  ...
}
```

As you can see, some of the fields returned are `staticIp` and `subnetId`—both tell us that VNet integration has been completed.

When using this feature, consider the following limitation and issues:

- Ports such as `8443`, `10221–10231`, `20226`, and some more are used internally by Redis for outbound connections. They should not be blocked by any means to ensure proper Redis communication.
- The same applies to inbound ports (`6379`, `6380`, `8443`, `10221–10231`, and some more).
- Your VNet should support connecting to the `ocsp.msocsp.com`, `mscrl.microsoft.com`, and `crl.microsoft.com` hosts to support SSL functionality.
- The same applies for resolving DNS domains for Azure Storage: `table.core.windows.net`, `blob.core.windows.net`, `queue.core.windows.net`, and `file.core.windows.net`.

As Azure Cache for Redis is a PaaS offering from Microsoft, enabling VNets for it works seamlessly and is only a matter of selecting a proper tier and configuring the network. However, there are many to-do points that have to be checked before enabling the feature. Once everything is set, you may want to test the connection. To do so, there are some options available:

- Using `tcping` for testing whether a port is open with the following command: `tcping.exe contosocache.redis.cache.windows.net 6380`
- Using a simple console application that connects to the host

Redis is very popular in caching scenarios, yet it is important to ensure that it is secure so that no one will exploit its interface or degrade its performance. By using the steps in this section, you were able to do so with only a few steps. This is the power of PaaS/SaaS components, where you are focusing on business values, rather than fighting the infrastructure.

Summary

This chapter was intended to help you build strong foundations for networking in Azure. Topics such as advanced networking, monitoring, and load balancing should help you understand how to manage more complex setups in Azure. You are now able to configure VNets for more complicated infrastructures, as well as use services such as AKS and ACI. Now, you can proceed on to the next chapter, where you will learn more about storage and backup functionalities in the cloud.

8
Implementing Storage and Backup

Azure administrators can use the Azure Storage service for multiple actions, such as setting up a file server, managing and storing backups, or synchronizing their organization's files. While these concepts are simple, everyone has to understand the implications of their choices. In this chapter, you will find a lot of information for migrating files between local servers and the cloud, monitoring the service, and configuring the network for limiting access and improving security. More and more companies are starting their journey with cloud providers—some of them have terabytes of data that has to be migrated to the cloud at some point. As you will see, there are many ways to achieve the same result—the only difference may be time or the amount of money consumed.

The following topics will be discussed in this chapter:

- Configuring network access for Azure Storage accounts
- Enabling monitoring and finding logs for Azure Storage accounts
- Managing the replication of Azure Storage accounts
- Setting up Azure file shares
- Transferring large datasets with no or low network bandwidth
- Transferring large datasets with medium or high network bandwidth
- Periodic data transfer
- Enabling security for Azure Storage

Technical requirements

To perform the exercises in this chapter, you will need the following:

- Access to an Azure subscription (created in `Chapter 1`, *Getting Started with Azure Subscriptions*)
- Azure PowerShell installed on your computer: `https://docs.microsoft.com/en-us/powershell/azure/azurerm/other-install?view=azurermps-6.13.0`
- The Azure CLI: `https://docs.microsoft.com/en-us/cli/azure/install-azure-cli?view=azure-cli-latest`
- Azure Storage Explorer: `https://azure.microsoft.com/en-us/features/storage-explorer/`

Configuring network access for Azure Storage accounts

Azure Storage is one of the most basic and most important services available in Azure. Combined with Azure virtual machines, it is the backbone of most cloud applications hosted in Azure. By default, each storage account is available publicly—however, in many cases, you will want to limit access possibilities by encapsulating it inside a virtual network. That may be enforced by policies in your company, an InfoSec audit, or the industry you are working in. In this section, we will discuss the actual solution of enabling **Virtual Network (VNet)** integration and its features.

To get ready, you will need a Storage account that we will use for this exercise—to create one, we will use the Azure CLI with the following commands:

1. Creating a new Azure Storage instance is pretty simple—all you will need is this basic command:

```
$ az storage account create --resource-group "<rg-name>" --name
"<account-name>"
```

2. Once the account is created, you can test that you are able to connect to it by sending a request to its public endpoints:

```
$ az storage account show --resource-group "<rg-name>"--name
"<account-name>" --query secondaryEndpoints
```

Running the preceding command will result in the following output. Note that it contains some HTTPS endpoints that are provided, while others are set to null. This is related to the default settings of Storage accounts where initially, you have only the `blob`, `queue`, and `table` services configured:

```
{
  "blob":
"https://<account-name>-secondary.blob.core.windows.net/",
  "dfs": null,
  "file": null,
  "queue":
"https://<account-name>-secondary.queue.core.windows.net/",
  "table":
"https://<account-name>-secondary.table.core.windows.net/",
  "web": null
}
```

Note that I used the `--query` parameter in the preceding command. This allowed me to get only a specific subset of the JSON result, which I would normally get by running the preceding command.

3. As all the endpoints are standard HTTP endpoints, we can just paste the URL or use tools such as `curl` to get the result. Let's now add a table to the account—to do so, we will use the `az storage table create` command to create a table and continue with `az storage entity insert` to insert data using key-value parameters passed via the `--entity` parameter:

```
$ az storage table create --name "chapter08" --account-name
"<account-name>"
{
  "created": true
}

$ az storage entity insert --table-name "chapter08" --entity
PartitionKey=user RowKey=1 Name=John Surname=Doe --account-name
"<account-name>"
"W/\"datetime'2019-05-11T16%3A36%3A09.2502542Z'\""
```

4. Finally, once the entity is added, we can check that we can query it without any additional features:

```
$ az storage entity query --table-name "chapter08" --account-name
"<account-name>"
```

Querying an entity should give you the following result:

```
{
  "items": [
    {
      "Name": "John",
      "PartitionKey": "user",
      "RowKey": "1",
      "Surname": "Doe",
      "Timestamp": "2019-06-10T09:46:43.049078+00:00",
      "etag": "W/\"datetime'2019-06-10T09%3A46%3A43.0490789Z'\""
    }
  ],
  "nextMarker": {}
}
```

As you can see, it contains the fields that we provided (`PartitionKey`, `RowKey`, `Name`, and `Surname`) plus some technical fields (`Timestamp` and `etag`), which are populated automatically. Now, we are ready to implement the feature, which will allow us to block access to an account from external networks. Let's start by configuring the network access for Azure Storage accounts. We will take the following steps to do so:

1. In the Azure portal, you can find the **Firewalls and virtual networks** blade, which, by default, is configured to allow access from all networks, including the internet:

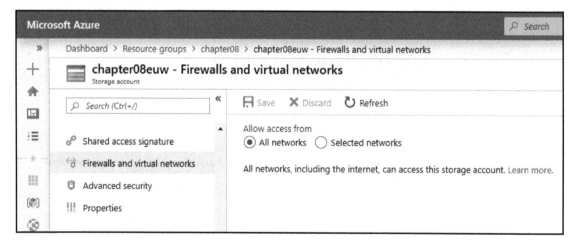

Figure 8.1 – The Firewalls and virtual networks blade

2. To limit access, we will have to change the **Allow access from** value to **Selected networks**. You have two options here:
   - Either configure the feature via the portal by providing an existing VNet or by creating a new one (see Chapter 3, *Configuring and Managing Virtual Networks*, for managing and configuring VNets).
   - Use the command from the next step to configure access using the CLI.

3. To add a new network rule with a proper VNet, run the following Azure CLI command:

```
$ az storage account network-rule add --account-name "<storage-account>" --vnet-name "<vnet-name>" --subnet "<subnet-name>"
```

> To perform the preceding operation, you will need a VNet created with a subnet and a service endpoint configured for the Microsoft Storage service. You can find the information on how to configure your network in Chapter 3, *Configuring and Managing Virtual Networks*.

4. However, the preceding command is not all you need to finish configuring the feature. By default, if no rule matches a request, the default action allows access to an account. To change that, you will have to update your account with the following command:

```
$ az storage account update --default-action Deny --name "<account-name>"--resource-group "<rg-name>"
```

Now, when you query a table storage instance, you will see that it no longer accepts requests from external networks. Once you update your Storage account with a new default action and a network rule, you are blocking access to it by encapsulating it inside a VNet. This implies that the IP address of the service is no longer public—instead, it is switched to the private one, which can be discovered by other services that are also inside the same network. The whole functionality is based on the two following commands:

```
az storage account network-rule add
az storage account update
```

While the first just adds a new network rule (so basically, it attaches a subnet inside a network to a Storage account), the second one reconfigures an account, so it correctly handles scenarios when somebody from outside a network tries to access its records.

The described feature is based on the service endpoints feature of Azure VNet. Basically, it integrates a network with your Storage account by switching its IP address from the public one to the private one. With that switch, you are losing public access to Storage services such as tables, blobs, or queues, but only after you deny all the traffic by updating the account with a new default rule.

The additional feature of Storage and VNet integration is limiting access using configured IP addresses. If you want to access the account from your corporate network (which is not peered with the network integrated with the account), you can allow access by adding a specific set of IP addresses (or CIDR blocks).

In the next section, you will learn about another Azure Storage feature, which is monitoring and logging everything related to operations performed against that service.

Enabling monitoring and finding logs for Azure Storage accounts

Azure Storage accounts often process millions of entities, messages, or blobs. As they are often the backbone of your systems, proper diagnosis and monitoring will be crucial for understanding the issues you are facing. In this section, we will focus on enabling logging features and finding logs, which should be helpful when diagnosing problems in your applications.

To perform this exercise, you will need a Storage account. You can use Azure PowerShell, the Azure portal, or the Azure CLI for that, depending on your expertise and what you are used to. To create an account with the Azure CLI, go to the first section of this chapter, where there are detailed instructions on how to do so. However, remember that the same can be done with Azure PowerShell by using the `New-AzureRmStorageAccount` cmdlet with the required parameters, listed as follows:

```
New-AzureRmStorageAccount -Location <location> -Name <name> -
ResourceGroupName <rg-name> -SkuName <selected-sku> -AccessTier <selected-
tier>
```

We will walk through the following steps to enable monitoring and finding logs for Azure Storage accounts:

1. To enable logging, run the following command:

```
$ az storage logging update --log rwd --services bqt --retention 7 --account-name "<account-name>"
```

   There are two parameters that require additional description:

   - `--log`: Select operations to be logged with the possible `r` (read), `w` (write), or `d` (delete) values.
   - `--services`: Select services to monitor with the `t` (table), `b` (blob), or `q` (queue) values.

2. The same functionality can be achieved by using the portal. If you go to your Storage account, select the **Diagnostic settings (classic)** blade:

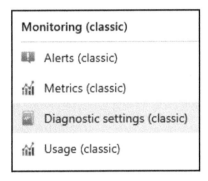

Figure 8.2 – The Diagnostics settings blade

3. You will see the following screen containing various logging and monitoring options. From that point, we can select what metrics should be included, what the retention period is, and what operations should be included:

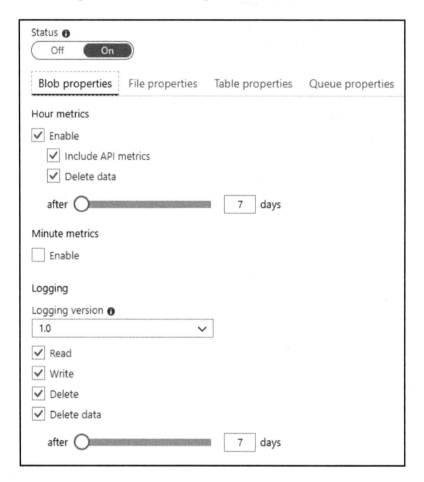

Figure 8.3 – Various logging and monitoring options

4. Now, we are ready to find and read the gathered logs. Of course, log for operations performed before enabling the feature will not be available—this is why you should consider enabling it right after deployment.

Gathered metrics are stored in special system tables, which are not visible from the Azure portal. In fact, they are also not available by using the Azure CLI or Azure PowerShell. All of the mentioned tables start with the dollar sign ($):

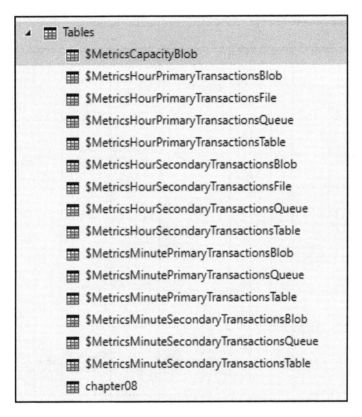

Figure 8.4 – The systems tables visible in Azure Storage Explorer

 There are two types of metrics—primary and secondary. Secondary metrics are related to additional instances of Azure Storage when geo-replication is enabled (so, GRS/RA-GRS options).

Tables contain all the information about operations performed against your services as availability, latency, or error counts. Once the metrics are enabled, each action on the Storage account is logged and stored in the following format—you can reference the following article for the table schema: `https://docs.microsoft.com/en-us/rest/api/storageservices/Storage-Analytics-Metrics-Table-Schema`:

1.0	2019-05-12T12:01:29.0241580Z	QueryEntities	Success	200	302	123	authenticated	chapter08 euw	chapter08 euw	table	https://chapter08euw.table.core.windows.net:443/$MetricsHourPrimaryTransactionsTable?%24top=1000
1.0	2019-05-12T12:01:29.5061543Z	QueryEntities	Success	200	175	16	authenticated	chapter08 euw	chapter08 euw	table	https://chapter08euw.table.core.windows.net:443/$MetricsHourPrimaryTransactionsTable?%24top=1000
1.0	2019-05-12T12:01:51.2239975Z	QueryEntities	Success	200	34	34	authenticated	chapter08 euw	chapter08 euw	table	https://chapter08euw.table.core.windows.net:443/$MetricsMinuteSecondaryTransactionsTable?%24top=1000
1.0	2019-05-12T12:01:53.8909824Z	QueryEntities	Success	200	8	8	authenticated	chapter08 euw	chapter08 euw	table	https://chapter08euw.table.core.windows.net:443/$MetricsMinutePrimaryTransactionsTable?%24top=1000
1.0	2019-05-12T12:01:58.8309427Z	QueryEntities	Success	200	140	23	authenticated	chapter08 euw	chapter08 euw	table	https://chapter08euw.table.core.windows.net:443/$MetricsHourSecondaryTransactionsFile?%24top=1000
1.0	2019-05-12T12:01:59.1019429Z	QueryEntities	Success	200	125	11	authenticated	chapter08 euw	chapter08 euw	table	https://chapter08euw.table.core.windows.net:443/$MetricsHourSecondaryTransactionsFile?%24top=1000

Figure 8.5 – Metric Table

As Azure storage tables are NoSQL databases, different records may be saved using different schemas while still in the same table. This is important in the case of processing the data—you want to ensure that you are not expecting the rows to follow the same strict schema rules.

Based on the gathered data, you can build your own charts for monitoring, or you can correlate a particular value with some issues you were facing. Additionally, besides metrics data, there are some additional logs stored inside your account with more granular information. If you go to the containers of your Storage account, you will see that there is an additional container named `$logs`. Inside it, you will find files for each of the services holding the gathered data.

Using the following link, you will find more information about logs stored inside Azure Storage accounts and how to read them: `https://docs.microsoft.com/en-us/azure/storage/common/storage-monitor-storage-account`.

The most important thing is the schema described in the previous link—based on it, you will be able to read all the columns and incorporate log files into your diagnosis pipelines. There is one more problem to be solved—how to download all the files in the correct way so that we are not affected by their size or network limitations. We will address those issues in other sections in this chapter. They will describe the proper ways of downloading files from Storage accounts depending on their size and the overall network bandwidth.

This section should have helped you to get a better understanding of how things are monitored for Storage accounts. The next section is about one of the most crucial features of this service—data replication.

Managing the replication of Azure Storage accounts

Azure Storage offers six different levels of replication, which should be considered when both architecting and maintaining a solution. You can often start with local replication called **Locally Redundant Storage (LRS)** and switch for the geo-paired region with **Geographically Redundant Storage** (**GRS**) or RA-GRS (read-only) models. If you seek the highest level of consistency and durability, you should consider the GZRS/RA-GZRS models, which are **Zone Redundant Storage** (**ZRS**) models in geo-paired regions. In this section, we will discuss how to switch the replication model and what the possible issues when performing such an operation are.

Basically, we can divide the replication models into two main categories:

- **Local replication**: LRS and ZRS
- **Global replication**: GRS, RA-GRS, GZRS, and RA-GZRS

The number of replicas can be presented as follows:

- **Three local replicas**: LRS and ZRS
- **Three local replicas and three replicas in paired regions**: GRS, RA-GRS, GZRS, and RA-GZRS

When using the global replication model, your Storage account will be paired with its geographic twin. You can find all the regions' twins in the following article: `https://docs.microsoft.com/en-us/azure/best-practices-availability-paired-regions`.

To choose the right replication model, you also have to understand one more thing—which model represents a synchronous replication approach and which represents an asynchronous replication approach. The difference between the former and the latter is crucial from a data integrity point of view—for asynchronous replication, you have a lower guarantee when it comes to being sure that all the data was copied before an incident happened. We can divide the replication models up as follows:

- **Synchronous**: LRS and ZRS
- **Asynchronous**: GRS, RA-GRS, GZRS, and RA-GZRS

If you use, for example, GZRS, you will have three replicas of your record copied synchronously across the local data center. Then, an asynchronous operation comes in and copies the remaining three replicas to the paired region. If an outage in the primary region happens before the asynchronous operation completes, you may miss some data in the secondary one.

If you require strong data consistency and still want to leverage Azure Storage, it is a much better option to use Azure Cosmos DB with a strong consistency setting and the Table API. You can read about it here: `https://docs.microsoft.com/en-us/azure/cosmos-db/table-introduction`.

Let's now see how you can select or change the replication mode in Azure Storage.

Selecting the replication mode

To perform this exercise, you will need a Storage account. You can use Azure PowerShell, the Azure portal, or the Azure CLI for that, depending on your expertise and what you are used to. If you want to learn what commands you should use, refer to the previous sections of this chapter.

Remember that, by default, if you do not provide the replication model value, you will end up with a `Standard_RAGRS` account:

```
$ az storage account show --name "<account-name>" --query sku.name
"Standard_RAGRS"
```

To change that, you will have to provide the `--sku` parameter, which supports the `Standard_LRS`, `Standard_GRS`, `Standard_RAGRS`, `Standard_ZRS`, `Standard_RAGZRS`, `Standard_GZRS`, `Premium_LRS`, and `Premium_ZRS` values.

 `Standard_RAGZRS` and `Standard_GZRS` are new replication models that are meant to achieve even better durability of your data by replicating it geographically across zones. For common scenarios, you rarely require that level of availability.

We will take the following steps to manage the replication of Azure Storage accounts:

1. To change the replication model, you can use the following command:

```
$ az storage account update --name <account-name> --sku <new-sku>
```

2. Let's assume that we want to change the LRS model (which was just fine for the initial version of the application, but now new requirements appear and it has to be replicated geographically). To do so, we will execute the following command:

```
$ az storage account update --name <account-name> --sku
Standard_GRS
```

3. The same operation can be performed the other way round—we can stop geographical replication and replicate the data only inside a single data center:

```
$ az storage account update --name chapter08rep --sku Standard_LRS
```

However, it is not possible to switch from the Standard to the Premium version of Storage as this particular operation implies changing the underlying hardware. In that case, you will have to create a new Premium version of your account and migrate the data between those tiers. By changing the replication model, you are deciding whether you want to preserve your data in a single region or whether to also copy everything to a paired geographical location. Note that such an operation is not as simple as it looks:

- If you change from the local replication model (LRS or ZRS) to a geographical one (GRS or RA-GRS), you will have to pay the cost of transferring the data between two regions.

- You cannot always select the ZRS replication model as it is only available in those regions that support availability zones.
- Switching from GRS/RA-GRS to a local replication model can be dangerous if your application relies on high availability. If the destination region fails, you may render your application unresponsive and not working.
- Switching to ZRS is not possible, even if your region supports availability zones.

Remember that zone-redundant storage is quite special as is cannot be easy migrated to other models and is not available in every region. Nonetheless, you can always move data from one account to another, even if their replication models differ.

Choosing the correct replication model might by a tough decision depending on your understanding of the topic, yet remember that in many cases, you can do it after creating an account. The next section will describe how to work with file shares in Azure using Azure Files.

Setting up Azure file shares

Azure Files (or File Storage) is one of the extra offerings of the Azure Storage service. While Azure Blob storage allows you to store your files in a hierarchical manner and is designed for application development and integration, sometimes you need a file share, which can be integrated with your OS and act as additional storage for files and data. In this section, I will show you how you can set such a share up and configure it for use.

To perform this exercise, you will need a Storage account. You can use Azure PowerShell, the Azure portal, or the Azure CLI for that, depending on your expertise and what you are used to. If you want to learn what commands should you use, refer to the previous sections of this chapter.

 Note that you need a general-purpose account (either v1 or v2 as there are two types of accounts available) to use the file share feature. This functionality is not available for storage types created with a **Blob** type.

When a Storage account is created, by default, it has file shares enabled—all you need is to actually create one. This can be done by following these steps:

1. To create it, you need this simple command:

   ```
   $ az storage share create --name <share-name> --account-name
   <account-name>
   {
     "created": true
   }
   ```

 Note that a file share name has to be in lowercase.

2. To upload a file (which also can be performed in the batch manner), you can use the following command. You will have to provide the share name that you created, the actual Storage account name, and the source of the data uploaded:

   ```
   $ az storage file upload --share-name <share-name> --source
   C:\Users\MyUser\Desktop\myshare.txt --account-name <account-name>
   Finished[#################################################
   ###] 100.0000%
   ```

3. To list the uploaded files, you can run the following command:

   ```
   $ az storage file list --share-name myshare --account-name
   chapter08euw
   ```

Listing the files will result in a JSON array given as an output. As you can see, the output contains things such as the name of the file, its metadata, and even when it was modified:

```
[
  {
  "metadata": null,
  "name": "myshare.txt",
  "properties": {
  "contentLength": 17,
  "contentRange": null,
  "contentSettings": {
  . . .
  },
  "copy": {
  . . .
  },
  "etag": null,
```

```
"lastModified": null,
"serverEncrypted": null
},
"type": "file"
}
]
```

If you want, there is the possibility to list a specific file only (by using the `az storage file show` command and providing the correct path with the `--path` parameter); another possibility is to use Azure Storage Explorer to explore your Storage accounts and deployed services:

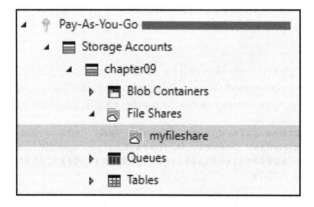

Figure 8.6 – The available file shares in Azure Storage Explorer

Besides managing file shares, you can also create and configure other Storage account features, such as blobs, tables, or queues. Each file storage can be attached to your local (or remote) computer by running a predefined command, which you can find in the Azure portal. When you go to your file share, you can find the **Connect** button:

Figure 8.7 – Connecting to a file share

When you click on it, you will see a new screen, where you will find commands for all supported OSes—Windows, Linux, and macOS:

Figure 8.8 – Connectivity options

By running these commands, you can map these shares to your computer. Thanks to that operation, you will be able to copy, delete, and read files directly from the mounted drive instead of using the Azure CLI. Once an Azure file share is mapped to your computer, it is visible as a network drive with a particular letter assigned to it (which can be, for example, `Z:` or `X:`). Under the hood, it uses SMB 3.0 protocol for all communication, so it can work with any OS that offers that kind of functionality (fortunately, it is supported by Windows, macOS, and Linux systems, so there is no such a thing as OS-locking, in that case).

The created share connects the following concepts:

- The Storage account
- File share
- Directories
- Files

That means that it abstracts away concepts such as the Azure Storage service and gives you seamless integration with the cloud by introducing a feature that looks like part of the OS. Azure Files also supports the concept of snapshots, which allow you to secure your environment against the corruption of files—either via application errors or the intended actions of malicious users. You can find more information about this feature at `https://docs.microsoft.com/en-us/azure/storage/files/storage-snapshots-files`.

Please proceed to the next sections, where you will learn how you can transfer large datasets from your local servers to Azure depending on the available network bandwidth.

Transferring large datasets with low or no network bandwidth

Sometimes, especially when migrating your workloads from on-premises environments to the cloud, you need to move large amounts of data that your systems have stored. For more advanced architectures, you may face a scenario where you have to transfer hundreds of gigabytes of data over the network. In cases when you do not have a dedicated connection between your local data center and Azure, transferring large datasets may not be efficient nor cost-effective. In this section, we will consider possible options for these scenarios and what options you have to succeed.

Understanding your case – low or no bandwidth

Before we get started, we have to understand your case. Take a moment to answer the following questions:

- Is a dedicated connection something you would consider? If so, is your ISP ready to provide one?
- Is the cost something you are considering? If not, implementing data transfer in an old-fashioned way may be a better option as it is something you already know and understand.
- How critical are your workloads? The more important the data is, the more reliable the way of migrating should be.
- How quickly do you want your workloads transferred to the cloud? Offline methods are not always the quickest ones as they require you to order hardware and copy data to it before transporting it to the data center of your choice.

Once the preceding questions are answered, we can focus on finding the right solution for your problem. As in this section, we are considering cases where you have no or very low network bandwidth; we will not consider things such as ExpressRoute for copying the data online over a dedicated network. Cases where you have no/low network bandwidth include the following scenarios:

- Systems hosted inside an internal network that cannot be connected to the internet
- Legal requirements that prevent you from sending the data over the public internet (although this can be addressed with ExpressRoute or VPN connections)
- All kind of systems that are temporarily online-only (such as systems installed on container ships or cruisers)

To understand how many times you would need to copy the data over the available network bandwidth, we can perform some simple calculations. Let's consider the following table:

Bandwidth/Data	100 Mbps	1 Gbps	10 Gbps
1 TB	22 hours	2 hours	13 minutes
10 TB	9 days	22 hours	2 hours
100 TB	92 days	9 days	22 hours
200 TB	185 days	18 days	2 days
500 TB	462 days	46 days	4 days
1 PB	925 days	92 days	9 days
5 PB	-	462 days	46 days
10 PB	-	925 days	92 days
20 PB	-	-	185 days

As you can see, the only competitive choice here is a bandwidth of 10 Gbps—at least when considering bigger workloads to copy. As in many cases, you may not have access to such a huge bandwidth, so copying the data over your internet connection may not be the case. This is where offline methods come into play.

Transferring data from on-premises to Azure

Microsoft offers a few ways of transferring data from your on-premises systems to their data centers. These choices include the following:

- The Data Box devices family, which offer dedicated hardware for offline transfers
- The **Import/Export** option, which allows you to ship your own disks to Azure Blob or the Azure Files service

When it comes to using Data Box, you will have to do two things:

- Deploy the Azure Data Box service inside your subscription.
- Order a preferred device.

Now, let's look at the step-by-step instructions for transferring large datasets with low or no network bandwidth:

1. To deploy the service, search for `Azure Data Box` in the marketplace and click on the **Create** button:

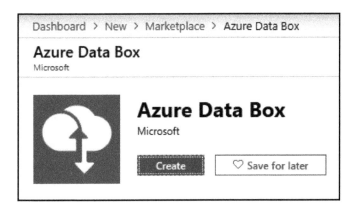

Figure 8.9 – Azure Data Box in Azure Marketplace

2. The next step is selecting the desired subscription, your region, and the data center you want to send your data to:

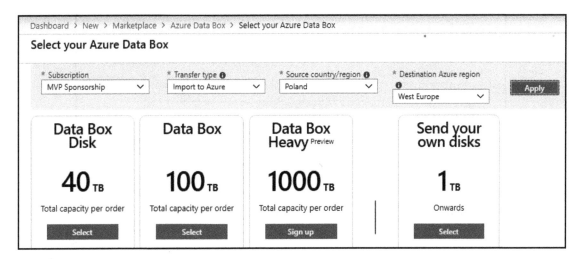

Figure 8.10 – The different Data Box options

3. From the preceding screen, you can also select the **Import/Export** option by selecting the **Send your own disk** option. The process of ordering a device will require you to also fill out the following form:

Figure 8.11 – The Data Box order details

You will have to provide information on the order name, what the destination data center is, how much data will be provided, and where it should be placed.

Once all the details are complete, you can confirm your order. Once the device is sent to you (or your disks are received from you and delivered to the data center), the process of importing data will start and your data will be available in the Storage account you selected during the process.

Depending on your choice, things may work a little bit differently. For the Data Box family, it is Microsoft's responsibility to deliver devices and migrate the data to the selected data center. If you are shipping your own hard disks, you will have to take care of things by yourself, including the following:

- Ensuring the proper disk types (SATA II/SATA III)
- Ensuring the proper OS version (64-bit Windows systems supporting **BitLocker Drive Encryption**)
- Ensuring .NET Framework availability

Remember that for the **Import/Export** functionality, your data will be secured with a 128-bit AES algorithm. If you are searching for a more advanced option, use the Data Box or Data Box Heavy options.

Depending on the choice, different features are available:

- If you intend on moving the data between region boundaries, you should use **Import/Export** as it is the only choice that gives you that option.
- If you want to export data from Azure, the **Import/Export** feature is the only option.
- If you want the easiest process, Data Box Disk is what you will be looking for as this is the fastest and the easiest option for most customers.
- If you do not want to manage the process of shipment, choose the Data Box family as this allows you to pass the responsibility to Microsoft.

For the Data Box family options, integration is much easier than managing your own disks. In many cases, all you need to do is buy a device and connect to your server racks. The process of creating an order is also simple as it can be performed from the Azure portal

Note that the Data Box service is not allowed for all types of subscriptions. Currently, only EA, CSP, Microsoft Partner Network, and Sponsorship offers can use that offer.

If you do not want to perform data migration by yourself, you can contact the Microsoft partners, which support data migration and will help achieve the best performance. Using the following link, you will find detailed instructions for performing the migration with Data Box Disk and the **Import/Export** option: `https://docs.microsoft.com/en-us/azure/databox/data-box-disk-deploy-copy-data`.

If low or no network bandwidth is not the case for you, take a look at the next section, where we are discussing medium and large dataset migration.

Transferring large datasets with medium or high network bandwidth

In the previous section, we covered transferring datasets when you have low or no network bandwidth available. However, there are still cases where your network connection is efficient enough to handle data transfer. In this section, we will cover some extra scenarios, including the ExpressRoute solution, which will help you understand how to copy your data to Azure without using Data Box family hardware or the **Import/Export** functionality.

Understanding your case – medium or high bandwidth

To get started, we have to understand what medium or high network bandwidth is. Refer to the previous section, where you can find a table presenting the time needed to send data over a network with a given bandwidth.

To find the best solution, we will go for the following assumptions:

- Medium network bandwidth can be declared as 100 Mbps–1 Gbps.
- High network bandwidth is everything over 1 Gbps.

By analyzing the table in the previous section, you can see that for medium bandwidth, the data transfer time can still be something that you're concerned with. For bigger workloads (such as hundreds of TBs or PBs), medium bandwidth will be rather problematic. You may wonder what options we have here. In general, there are two ways to handle the situation:

- If the estimated time is not reasonable, you should go to the previous section and check the solutions for handling low or no network bandwidth.
- If you can accept the data transfer time, you can proceed with the current section as we will consider tools allowing you to pass data to the data center over the internet.

When sending your data online, you should also consider one more option, which is ExpressRoute. This particular offering from Microsoft offers a private network connection, which can help you achieve better network performance, security, and reliability. On the other hand, it is designed to cover more advanced scenarios of connection, so ExpressRoute should never be your first choice when it comes to connecting and communicating with Azure. ExpressRoute scenarios include the following:

- Requirement not to send data over the public internet
- Azure connection redundancy
- Dynamic scaling of bandwidth
- National cloud connectivity

Take into consideration that ExpressRoute is not a free service and, depending on the tier and actual bandwidth, may cost you from hundreds to thousands of dollars.

 ExpressRoute requires you to ensure that your ISP supports giving you an option to connect to Azure using that particular solution. Not all locations provide that kind of functionality.

The following steps demonstrate the process of transferring data with medium or high network bandwidth:

1. To copy the data from the local source to Azure Storage, use the following command. In the following code, we are basically using the `azcopy` tool with the `cp` command, which will copy data from one location and upload it to a second one:

```
azcopy cp "C:\local\path"
"https://account.blob.core.windows.net/mycontainer1/?<sas-token>" -
-recursive=true
```

2. To obtains the SAS token required for authorization, you can use the following Azure CLI command. Here, we are basically generating a token for a specific container:

```
az storage blob generate-sas -c <container-name> -n <sas-name>
```

3. Once the command is executed, it may take a while to finish, depending on the size of the files to be moved and your network bandwidth. An alternative to azcopy, the REST API, will require using an HTTP protocol to push all the files. Here, you can find an example of a request—we are sending a PUT request to myblob in mycontainer with This is my blob! as the contents:

```
PUT https://myaccount.blob.core.windows.net/mycontainer/myblob
HTTP/1.1
x-ms-version: 2015-02-21
x-ms-date: <date>
Content-Type: text/plain; charset=UTF-8
x-ms-blob-content-disposition: attachment; filename="fname.ext"
x-ms-blob-type: BlockBlob
x-ms-meta-m1: v1
x-ms-meta-m2: v2
Authorization: SharedKey myaccount:key
Content-Length: 11
Request Body:
This is my blob!
```

Note that you will have to provide a proper method of authentication for a request. This includes using a pair account name as well as an account key or SAS token as in azcopy.

Using the REST API is significantly more complex compared to using azcopy as you will have to write your own tool that will send requests to the Azure Storage API.

When using azcopy, the typical syntax looks like this:

```
.\azcopy copy <source path> <destination path> --<flag-name>=<flag-value>
.\azcopy cp "C:\local\path"
"https://account.blob.core.windows.net/container" --recursive=true
```

As you can see, its usage is quite simple as the only thing that is required is to tell the application where the source and the destination are (see the parameters for the copy/cp command). We can also use the --recursive switch to allow azcopy to process all the files that are stored inside the source location.

Of course, azcopy supports authentication with SAS tokens, so you do not have to make your containers public to be able to copy the data.

When it comes to using the Data Box devices family, they can be ordered and configured via the portal:

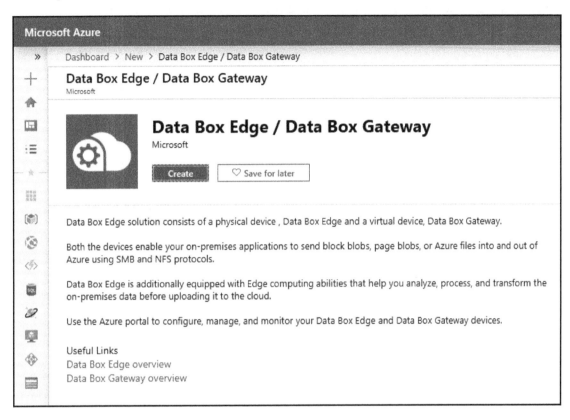

Figure 8.12 – Data Box Edge/Gateway in Azure Marketplace

The process of ordering devices is the same as with the other kinds of Data Box hardware. The benefits of using a dedicated device to transfer the data include things such as edge capability (the ability to perform preprocessing directly on a device) and simple configuration—you manage and configure the device using the Azure portal.

The available options

To sum up, for sending large amounts of data over the internet, you can consider the following tools:

- `azcopy`, which is a command-line tool for copying data to the Azure Storage service.
- **REST APIs of Azure Storage**: Instead of using additional tools, you can implement your own applications that will leverage available REST APIs and copy the data over HTTP.
- **Azure Data Factory**: If you need an orchestration, you can use Azure Data Factory to organize the work for you. It can be used in addition to the previous tools to ensure that everything happens in a controlled manner.

Whichever option you will choose, you should consider the following things:

- When copying data online, you will have to ensure that the connection is stable.
- In the case of any errors, which may happen during the copy operation, you will have to implement some kind of retry to avoid corrupted data.
- The ideal solution for online transfer is having a dedicated connection between your systems and the Azure data center. Failing to do so may result in the degraded performance of your own systems.

An alternative to the preceding may be using Data Box devices. While in the previous section we were considering them for offline data transfer, there are special devices in the family, such as Data Box Edge and Data Box Gateway, that can be used locally in your data center to pass the data online.

In general, there are two scenarios for transferring data to Azure—either during on-premises migration to cloud or as a defined process of gathering the data. While the former always requires you to move huge datasets, the latter is easier to handle as is considered before deploying the application to the cloud.

Ultimately, whether you face a low or high network bandwidth, the process can be similar by using the Data Box family devices. If you feel that the previous two sections do not address your scenario, take a look at the next one, where we will cover periodic data transfer.

Exploring periodic data transfer

In the previous two sections, we discussed the possibilities for data transfer when you have either high or low network bandwidth. However, there may still be cases where you need to copy your datasets from time to time. In such situations, you neither need to maintain a dedicated connection to Azure all the time nor want to implement a solution in a *do-and-forget* manner. In this section, we will cover periodic data transfer scenarios and address possible solutions for that kind of problem.

When considering periodic data transfer, you should consider the following factors:

- How often are you planning to perform copy operations?
- How much data will be moved to Azure each time?
- Is your network bandwidth going to be enough to end the operation before it is triggered once again?
- Can you perform copy operations over the public internet?
- Do you need your data immediately after copying it to the cloud?

Depending on your answer, the solution can be quite different. Let's consider some typical scenarios here:

- If you cannot provide a network bandwidth high enough and the frequency of uploads is quite high, you may face a problem where another copy operation is scheduled before the previous one has finished. This can lead to the general delay of your process and can sum up with each operation.
- If you cannot copy the data over the public internet, you will have to consider additional configuration options (ExpressRoute or a VPN connection) to be able to satisfy that requirement. In such cases, it may be beneficial to perform a continuous copy to avoid peaks in network connection and ensure a smaller amount of data is copied.
- If your data can be immediately accessible after a copy operation, you should not consider offline models of delivering data to Azure.
- If each time you are performing the data copy operation its amount is quite huge, an online transfer may not be the ideal method. In such cases, consider using Data Box devices to copy data onto them and send them to Azure data centers.

Once you know your requirements and your options, we will try to verify possible solutions. Note, that periodic data transfer may not necessarily mean that you copy data once a week or month—it can be any process that does not implement the continuous sending of data to the cloud.

For periodic data transfer, as for huge network bandwidth, you will have similar options when it comes to implementing a solution that will satisfy your requirements:

- For online data transfer, you can use `azcopy`, REST APIs, or Azure Data Factory as an orchestrator.
- For offline data transfer, you can use the Data Box family devices.
- You can also leverage the features of Data Box Edge/Gateway so that you can have a physical device that will be able to perform the copy operations to push the data to Azure Storage.

When considering maintenance, the easiest (and the most robust) way to implement periodic data transfer is with Azure Data Factory. With this Azure service, you can easily implement pipelines that move data from your on-premises environment to multiple Azure services. Now, follow these steps to implement periodic data transfer via **Azure Data Factory**:

1. Azure Data Factory can be easily created from the Azure portal—here, you can find detailed instructions on how to deploy the service from the Azure portal: `https://docs.microsoft.com/en-us/azure/data-factory/quickstart-create-data-factory-portal`.

2. Once it is deployed, you will able to implement pipelines, which allow you to take data from your on-premises storage and move them to Azure Storage, Azure SQL, or any other kind of Azure service (using custom scripts, which you can deploy and run in your pipelines). Here, you can find an example of possible linked services (see `https://docs.microsoft.com/en-us/rest/api/storageservices/Storage-Analytics-Metrics-Table-Schema`), which can be integrated using Azure Data Factory:

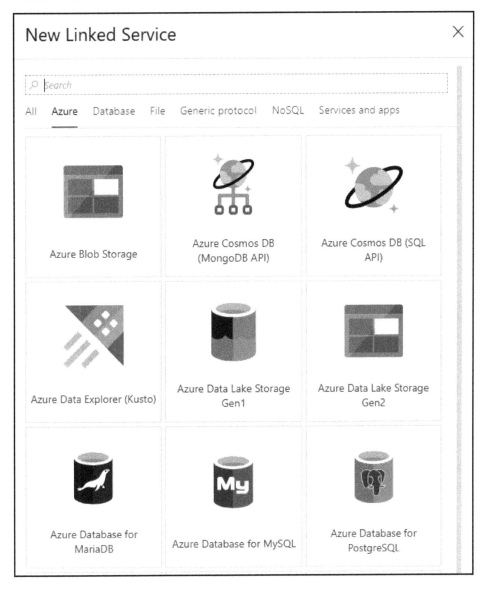

Figure 8.13 – Various linked services in Azure Data Factory

Note that Azure Data Factory can copy data from/to any source or destination that it can connect to via a custom protocol, so you can easily set schedules for data operations and modify them whenever you need to do so.

For periodic data transfer, your implementation will rely mostly on your requirements. When using `azcopy` or REST APIs, you will have to write your own applications, which will take care of either running `azcopy` with proper parameters or calling proper endpoints for data digestion and upload. Things are a little bit different with Azure Data Factory—this particular tool allows you to implement data transfer pipelines using a graphical interface, which greatly simplifies delivering a production-ready solution.

With the last three sections, we have covered a problem that you may face when migrating from on-premises to the Azure cloud or when implementing hybrid solutions where you have to administer some parts of your workloads in your own data center, but simultaneously, you aim at having the data stored in one place (for example, for machine learning purposes).

The last section of this chapter will discuss the problem of security when using Azure Storage as your storage component.

Enabling security for Azure Storage

As Azure Storage will be the backbone of many of your services, proper security management and ensuring that you follow all the best practices will be crucial for your workload's safety. In this section, we will cover additional security features for Azure Storage so that you can learn what should be verified or turned on before going into production with your infrastructure.

To perform this exercise, you will need a Storage account. You can use Azure PowerShell, the Azure portal, or the Azure CLI for that, depending on your expertise and what you are used to. If you want to learn what commands should you use, refer to the previous sections of this chapter.

Once your Storage account is created, we can focus on delivering proper security functionalities. By taking the following steps, we will enable security for your Azure Storage account:

1. When you go to the Azure portal and find your Storage account, you can find a blade that is called **Advanced security**:

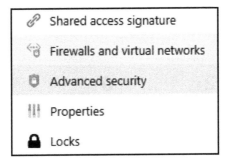

Figure 8.14 – The Advanced security blade

2. When you click on it, you will see a new screen where you can find a feature called **Advanced security**, which is disabled by default:

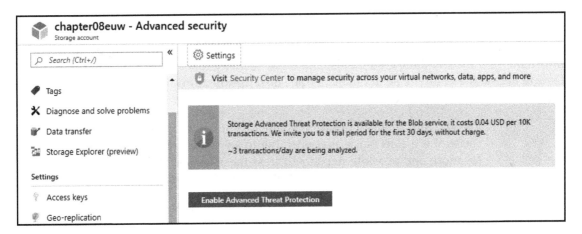

Figure 8.15 – Enabling Advanced security

3. By clicking on the **Enable Advanced Threat Protection** button, you will see that the screen changes a little and now, each transaction that is performed on the account is being analyzed against malicious activities:

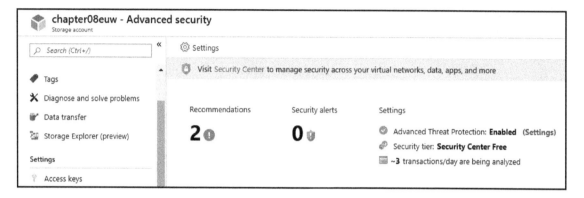

Figure 8.16 – View of the enabled Advanced security feature

The **Advanced security** option that is featured is connected to the Security Center service. The higher the tier of Security Center that you have, the more advanced the analytics are that are performed against the transactions.

The **Advanced security** feature works by analyzing the diagnostics logs of the Storage account and searching for known malicious patterns, which aim at digesting personal information, company data, credentials, and other security tokens. Another important feature here is the ability to send emails to the subscription administrators about malicious activities.

Emails from Security Center contain additional information about the cause of the alert (such as connecting to an account from an unusual location) and possible steps to address these issues. Make sure you are listed as a subscription administrator to receive these emails.

For now, the following alerts are raised for Azure Storage accounts:

- **Access from an unusual location**: For example, you normally access your account from the USA and after 1 hour, somebody from Italy tries to access the account.
- **Application anomaly**: Your application, which normally reads a few hundred rows per minute, starts to do the same, but per second.

- **Anonymous access**: It is rarely a good practice to allow anonymous access for production systems.
- **Data exfiltration**: Your data is being queried with a specific pattern, which may imply data theft.
- **Unexpected delete**: The data deleted does not seem to be related to any previous operations performed on the account.
- **Access permission change**: Somebody or something changed the **Role-Based Access Control (RBAC)** settings or data availability levels.
- **Access inspection**: Somebody or something queries your Storage account to learn the RBAC rules.
- **Data exploration**: Somebody or something uses a wide range filter, which may imply unauthorized access, to learn what is stored in your Storage account.

Of course, this list may change as new alerts are added to Security Center. When securing Storage accounts, always consider enabling this functionality, as it can detect unauthorized access and notify you when an unexpected situation happens. As an administrator, you may find it beneficial to be able to learn about all the unexpected behavior or set alerts to an operations group that is responsible for data breaches. The value of the data gathered becomes more and more important for many people and companies, so it quickly becomes an important resource requiring special attention.

Summary

This chapter covered many aspects of working with Storage accounts as a common solution for data storage. We discussed different features that can help you achieve better performance, security, and durability of data. One of the most important topics is importing and exporting data between datacenters or your on-premises servers. With the skills gained in this chapter, you will be able to migrate loads of data with ease, as well as maintain its security. If you feel that you somehow need more information regarding this topic, feel free to explore the Azure documentation (see `https://docs.microsoft.com/en-us/azure/storage/common/storage-import-export-service`) for more verbose examples.

In the next chapter, you will find information relating to high-availability and disaster-recovery scenarios.

9
High Availability and Disaster Recovery Scenarios

When working as an Azure administrator, you often have to understand and even implement multiple policies that ensure your applications are available in case of an outage and can quickly recover from a disaster. This chapter focuses on reviewing monitoring solutions and backup plans for multiple services and using components such as Azure Front Door to manage your infrastructure globally and from a single point.

In this chapter, we will cover the following topics:

- Monitoring Azure VMs
- Monitoring Azure Storage services
- Monitoring Azure App Service
- Implementing Azure SQL backup
- Implementing Azure Storage backup
- Implementing Availability Zones for VMs and high availability
- Monitoring and managing global routing for web traffic with Azure Front Door
- Designing backup plans for VMs

Let's get started!

Technical requirements

To complete the exercises in this chapter, you will need the following:

- Access to an Azure subscription (created in `Chapter 1`, *Getting Started with Azure Subscriptions*)
- Azure PowerShell installed on your computer: `https://docs.microsoft.com/en-us/powershell/azure/azurerm/other-install?view=azurermps-6.13.0`
- The Azure CLI: `https://docs.microsoft.com/en-us/cli/azure/install-azure-cli?view=azure-cli-latest`
- ArmClient: `https://github.com/projectkudu/ARMClient`

Monitoring Azure VMs

When your systems are deployed, the most important thing is to keep them running and easily investigate the issues they are facing. In this section, we will cover proper Azure VM monitoring scenarios and correct implementations. This will give you insights into the current capabilities of the Azure cloud and the different solutions available, all of which can be used for different infrastructures.

Creating a VM

To get started, you will need a working VM. If you do not have one, you can quickly deploy one. To do so, use the following Azure CLI command (you can find the command reference in `Chapter 3`, *Configuring and Managing Virtual Networks*):

```
az vm create
```

The same functionality is available via the following PowerShell cmdlet:

```
New-AzureRmVM
```

 Remember to pass all the required parameters, enter the expected VM size, and wait a few minutes for the process to complete.

If you want, you can also use the Azure portal and create a machine using a step-by-step wizard, as shown in the following screenshot:

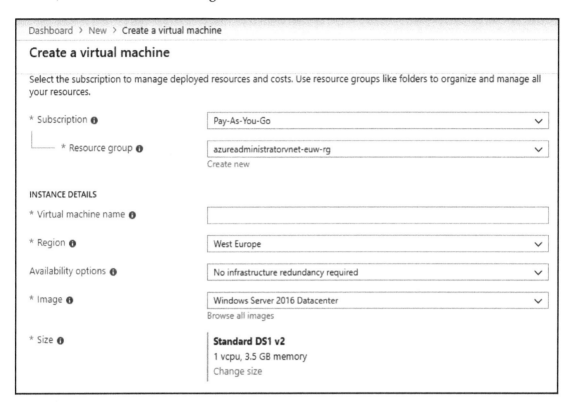

Figure 9.1 – Creating a VM

This wizard allows you to set the following parameters for a new VM:

- Basic settings such as its name, the image used, or the size of your machine
- Disks used by your VM (with one required parameter, which is OS disk type – HDD or SSD)
- Networking settings (VNet, open ports, and load balancing solutions)
- Management options (auto-shutdown, backup, monitoring of a VM)
- Advanced topics (proximity placement groups, Azure Dedicated Host, and more)

To create a VM, you only need to enter parameters for the **Basic** tab – the rest will be automatically propagated once you go to the **Review + create** page. The feature described in this section works for both Windows and Linux machines. Therefore, do not worry and select what you prefer to work with.

Enabling monitoring

To enable monitoring while creating a VM, follow these steps:

1. The two basic types of VM diagnostics and monitoring are boot diagnostics and OS guest diagnostics, which can be set during a VM's creation:

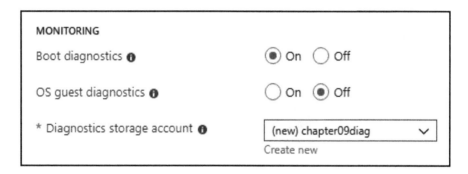

Figure 9.2 – Configuring VM monitoring settings

They give you the following features:

- The ability to understand what is happening when a machine is starting. Some updates or modifications may affect how your VM boots, so it is important to know that you can analyze what is happening and introduce proper adjustments.
- Information about the status of the OSes that have been deployed to a machine.

2. The same can be set after a VM is provisioned. To do so, go to the **Diagnostics settings** blade and search for agent and boot diagnostic settings, as shown in the following screenshot:

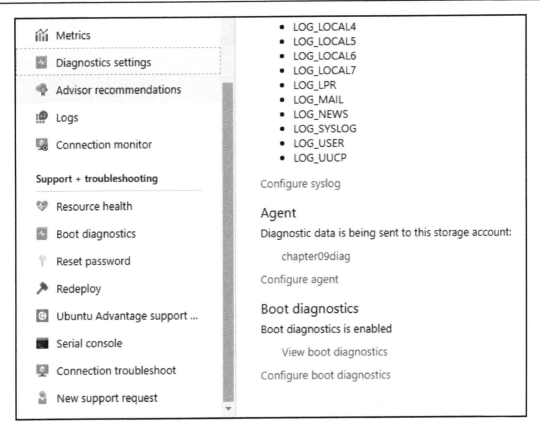

Figure 9.3 – Diagnostics settings blade

3. Here, when you click on the **Configure boot diagnostics/Configure agent** link, you will gain access to the feature's configuration, where you can turn it on or off. Once your logs have been configured, you can browse them by accessing the storage account you selected for the logging purpose. Depending on the OS running on your machine, available tables may differ a little, but in general, most of the logged things are stored in tables named **WADMetrics**.

Logs that are stored can be digested by any tool that can connect to your storage account. Use that to your advantage when implementing your own monitoring solutions.

4. When it comes to availability, you can use one of the newer features, called **Insights**:

Figure 9.4 – Insights blade

It will allow you to connect your VM to an Azure Monitor workspace, which will gather all the necessary information about your machine's health.

 Once enabled, getting all the necessary information about a machine can take several minutes. Be patient as Azure Monitor does so.

From this screen, you will able to access detailed information about the current status of your machine. For example, we can check the generic resource health to understand recent or past issues. In the following screenshot, you can see, for example, on what day an event (**Machine crashed**) happened, the description of the issue, and the possible steps to proceed:

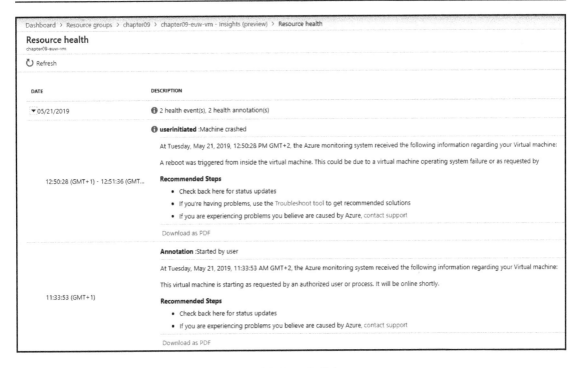

Figure 9.5 – Resource health view

For this particular feature, everything is managed by Azure Monitor, which seamlessly integrates with your resource. If you want to check the details, you can go directly to your workspace and check the information gathered there.

Understanding the details

You must be wondering how Azure Monitor manages to do this. In fact, under the hood, Azure Monitor uses a set of extensions that are installed on your machine once Insights has been enabled:

NAME	TYPE	VERSION
DependencyAgentLinux	Microsoft.Azure.Monitoring.DependencyAgent.DependencyAgentLinux	9.*
LinuxDiagnostic	Microsoft.Azure.Diagnostics.LinuxDiagnostic	3.*
OMSExtension	Microsoft.EnterpriseCloud.Monitoring.OmsAgentForLinux	1.*

Figure 9.6 – Extensions installed by Azure Monitor

They allow for different monitoring capabilities such as network monitoring, forwarding OS events and logs, and crash dumps collection. If you go to the network map of your machine, you will see that there are plenty of different connections being established from your machine that pass information to Azure Storage and Azure Monitor:

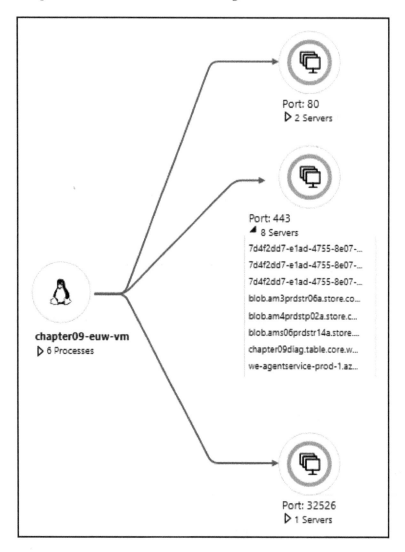

Figure 9.7 – Diagram based on data gathered by Azure Monitor

Azure Monitor is one of the most important services available on Azure and allows you to monitor your IaaS workloads. It combines monitoring VMs, VNets, and the OS itself to give you a bigger picture of your system. Using Azure Monitor and its workspaces require some experience as this feature does not give you all the information you require immediately.

 To find out more about health monitoring in Azure and all the available capabilities of this particular tool, go to `https://docs.microsoft.com/en-us/azure/virtual-machines/windows/monitor`.

In this section, we discussed the topic of monitoring Azure VMs using various features available for this service. Please proceed to the next topic, which is monitoring Azure Storage, to learn more about monitoring features available for other Azure services.

Monitoring Azure Storage services

As Azure Storage is one of the most important services in Azure, proper monitoring and understanding of issues surrounding it may be crucial for your system to be stable and efficient. In this section, we will cover the best way to monitor storage accounts (and SaaS in general) so that you can implement the solution suited to your requirements. This solution should be one that performs well in terms of maintenance and complexity.

To perform this exercise, you will need a storage account. You can use Azure PowerShell, the Azure portal, or the Azure CLI for that, depending on your expertise and what you are used to. To create an account with the Azure CLI, run the following command:

```
$ az storage account create --resource-group "<rg-name>" --name "<account-name>"
```

The same can be done with Azure PowerShell:

```
New-AzureRmStorageAccount -Location <location> -Name <name> -ResourceGroupName <rg-name> -SkuName <selected-sku> -AccessTier <selected-tier>
```

Once your account has been created, we can focus on enabling the monitoring features on it. For storage accounts, the easiest way when it comes to monitoring is using Azure Monitor (which was also described in the previous section). When it comes to Azure Storage, some part of the functionality is already available on the storage account. Follow these steps to access it:

1. Go to the **Metrics** blade:

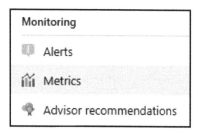

Figure 9.8 – Metrics blade

2. On the new screen, you will see a chart that displays a selected metric (such as egress, ingress, or the number of transactions). In this particular case, we are interested in the general availability of the service. To display the value, use the following filter – we want to check the availability metrics for the account:

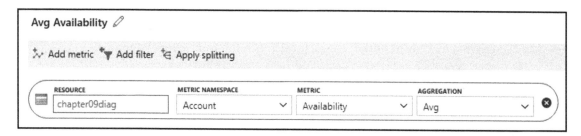

Figure 9.9 – Filtering values

3. This will give you a detailed view of the general availability of your instance of Azure Storage and information about when it faced certain issues. In fact, the same can be achieved using the REST API, which each storage account exposes. To ease things a little bit, we will use a tool named `armclient`. With the following two commands, you will get information about the availability of your account in terms of the last available hourly interval:

```
armclient login

armclient GET
"/subscriptions/<subscriptionId>/resourceGroups/<resourceGroup>/pro
viders/Microsoft.Storage/storageAccounts/<accountName>/providers/mi
crosoft.insights/metrics?metricnames=Availability&api-
version=2018-01-01&aggregation=Average&interval=PT1H"
```

The preceding code block performs the following operations:

- Authenticates further requests in Azure
- Sends a GET request to a specific endpoint with all the required parameters and headers

The result of running the preceding command may look like this. It displays information on the metric that was gathered for the specific time interval, aggregated as an average value:

```
{
  "cost": 0,
  "timespan": "2019-05-22T11:01:44Z/2019-05-22T12:01:44Z",
  "interval": "PT1H",
  "value": [
    {
      "type": "Microsoft.Insights/metrics",
      "name": {
        "value": "Availability",
        "localizedValue": "Availability"
      },
      "unit": "Percent",
      "timeseries": [
        {
          "metadatavalues": [],
          "data": [
            {
              "timeStamp": "2019-05-22T11:01:00Z",
              "average": 100.0
            ...
    }
  ],
```

```
    . . .
}
```

Using the REST API, you can quickly build a solution that will monitor your storage accounts on your behalf.

 `armclient` supports logging with a username and password, as well as a service principal. Use those kinds of authentication to leverage the tool in applications that work in the background and should not interact with a user.

Under the hood, everything that is displayed in the Azure portal or on Azure Monitor charts is based on the data returned by the REST API. With `armclient`, you can quickly get all the metrics available for your storage account. These can be used for further queries (see the previous code blocks for clarification):

```
armclient GET
/subscriptions/<subscriptionId>/resourceGroups/<resourceGroup>/providers/Mi
crosoft.Storage/storageAccounts/<storageAccount>/providers/microsoft.insigh
ts/metricdefinitions?api-version=2018-01-01
```

The result of the preceding command is as follows. Since the endpoint being used is different than the one used previously, here, we got the available metrics rather than aggregated values:

```
{
  "value": [
    {
      "id":
"/subscriptions/5.../resourceGroups/.../providers/Microsoft.Storage/storage
Accounts/.../providers/microsoft.insights/metricdefinitions/UsedCapacity",
      . . .
      "category": "Capacity",
      "name": {
        "value": "UsedCapacity",
        "localizedValue": "Used capacity"
      },
      . . .
    . . .
  }]
}
```

Each metric can be queried with a proper interval and aggregation type so that you can get the data you are interested in, in the form you are looking for.

As you can see, Azure Storage monitoring can be seamlessly enabled and integrated with the service without any prior knowledge of monitoring tools. Now, let's proceed to another Azure service – Azure App Service – to learn how to work with monitoring using **Platform-as-a-Service (PaaS)** components.

Monitoring Azure App Service

When it comes to PaaS, one of the most popular services from Azure is Azure App Service, also known as Web Apps. They allow you to quickly get started with a server for hosting your web applications, which can be easily configured and adjusted to your needs. Besides purely development experience, Azure App Service also includes a set of features that make monitoring and diagnosis a piece of cake. In this section, I will show you how to monitor your web application and find the root cause of issues you may face.

To get started, we will need an instance of a Web App in Azure. You can deploy it really quickly using the Azure CLI:

```
$ az appservice plan create -g <rg-name> -n "<plan-name>" --sku <sku>
$ az webapp create -g <rg-name> -n "<webapp-name>" -p "<plan-name>"
```

To create an instance of Azure App Service, you need two commands:

- The first one will create an Azure App Service Plan that gives you resources (CPU, memory, and storage) that can be used by your applications.
- The second one creates the actual Web App, which will host the files of your application.

 Remember that you can attach multiple Web Apps to a single App Service Plan.

Once your Web App has been created, we can focus on implementing various monitoring features and validating their availability. When it comes to monitoring PaaS services, especially Azure App Service, one of the best services is Azure **Application Insights**. In fact, they are available as one of the settings of your application:

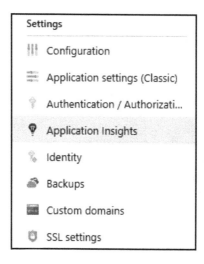

Figure 9.10 – Applications Insights blade

Initially, this feature is disabled and requires you to install an extension to get things working. So, let's begin:

1. Install the extension directly from the Azure portal using the **Turn on site extension** button:

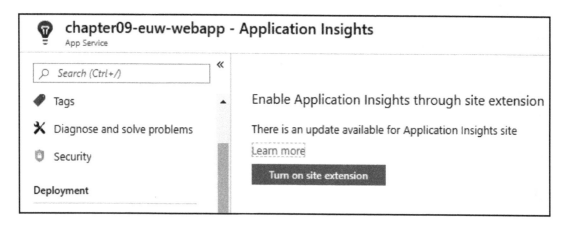

Figure 9.11 – Enabling the extension

The extension can also be installed during a deployment (for example, using ARM templates). In this section, we are covering a scenario where redeployment is not possible/requires many additional actions before it can be performed.

2. Once you click the button, you will have to configure the plugin by providing additional information about Azure Application Insights such as resource name, the technology stack you are aiming at (.NET, .NET Core, Node.js, or Java), and enabled features (**Profiler**, **Snapshot debugger**, and so on):

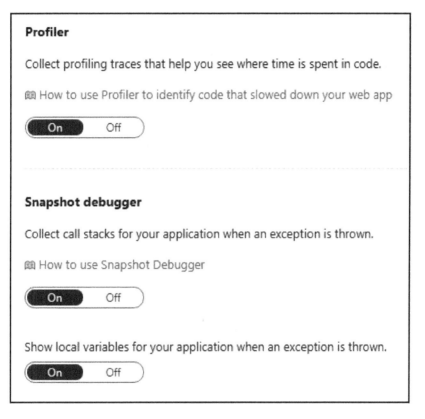

Figure 9.12 – Additional features such as Snapshot debugger and Profiler

3. The last thing required here is clicking on the **Apply** button and confirming that you want to apply the changes:

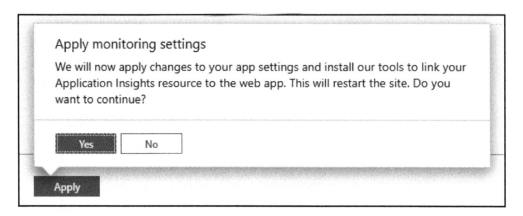

Figure 9.13 – Confirming the changes

Now, the process of provisioning the extension will start. This can take several minutes to complete.

Note that this will restart your website, so ensure you are not performing this action during the peak traffic hours of your application!

Now, let's check the actual capabilities of the feature.

Exploring capabilities of Azure Application Insights

Once your Azure Application Insights instance is ready, you can go to it and start browsing its capabilities. Let's check it out:

1. The thing we are interested in the most here is the **Availability** blade. You can find it in the **Investigate** section:

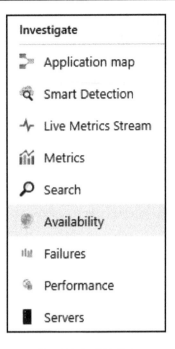

Figure 9.14 – Availability blade

2. From this screen, you will be able to perform two important actions:
   - Verify the availability of your application.
   - Create a test that periodically checks the status of your website.
3. To create a test, click on the **+ Create Test** button:

Figure 9.15 – Creating an availability test

4. From the new screen, you will be able to configure a test where you can decide how you want to access an application and specify the criteria that will mark the test as failing:

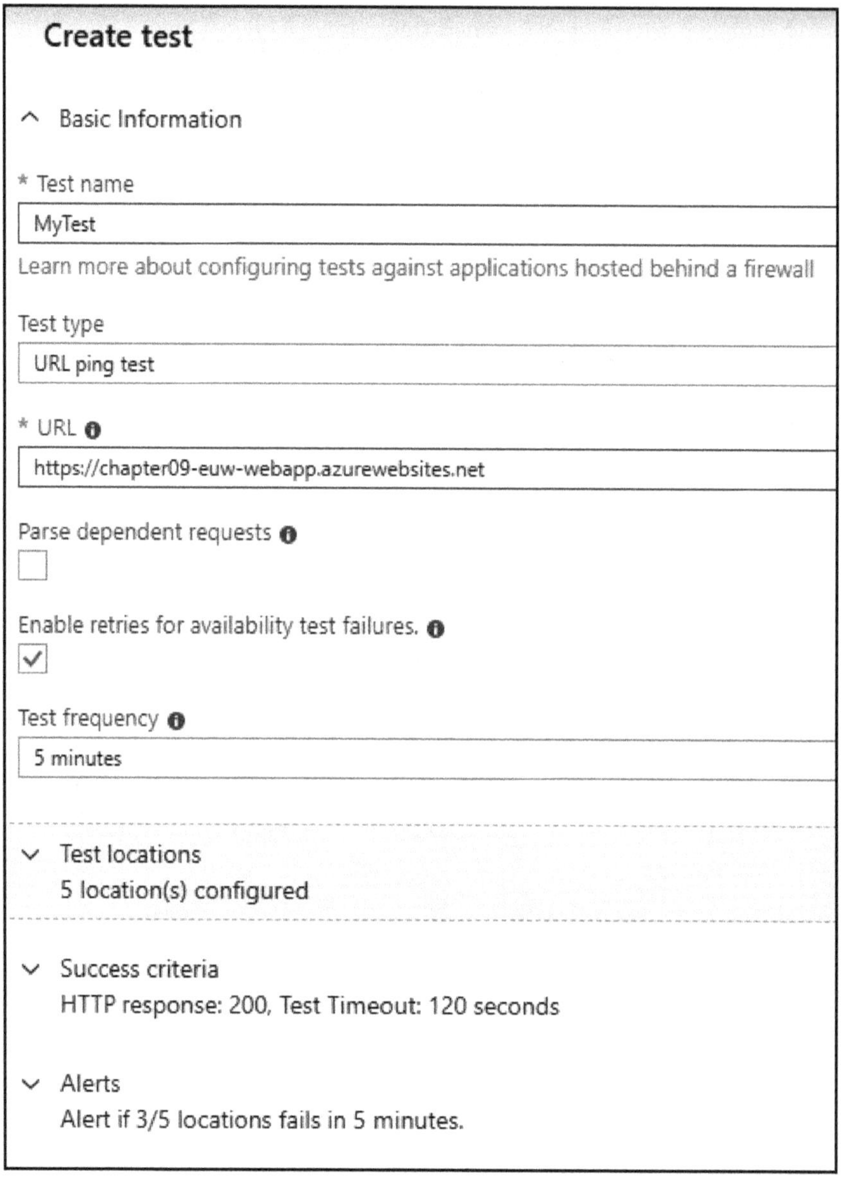

Create test

∧ Basic Information

* Test name

MyTest

Learn more about configuring tests against applications hosted behind a firewall

Test type

URL ping test

* URL ❶

https://chapter09-euw-webapp.azurewebsites.net

Parse dependent requests ❶

☐

Enable retries for availability test failures. ❶

☑

Test frequency ❶

5 minutes

∨ Test locations
   5 location(s) configured

∨ Success criteria
   HTTP response: 200, Test Timeout: 120 seconds

∨ Alerts
   Alert if 3/5 locations fails in 5 minutes.

Figure 9.16 – Availability test settings

Once your availability tests have run, you will be able to see their results, as shown in the following screenshot:

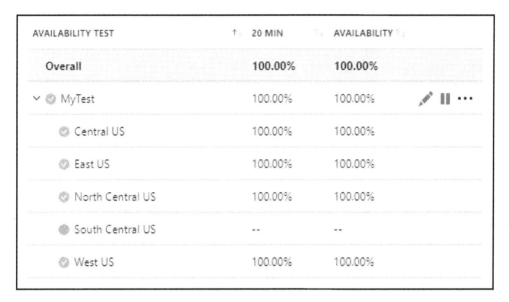

Figure 9.17 – Working availability test

Note the following things:

- Tests can be executed from different locations, which will ensure that your problem is or is not related to a region.
- You can have multiple tests covering different scenarios.
- For more advanced scenarios, upload the WEBTEST files (go to `https://docs.`
  `microsoft.com/en-us/visualstudio/test/quickstart-create-a-load-test-`
  `project?view=vs-2019`), which cover multi-step scenarios of testing web applications.
- When availability tests are failing, you can add email recipients who will be notified when things are not working at that moment in time.

Azure Application Insights is a powerful service that is not limited to availability tests only. In the *Further reading* section, you will find additional information about using additional tools such as alerts, Smart Detection, and API access. Depending on your use case, you can leverage this Azure resource as either a sink for metrics or a complex solution and a dashboard, which will cover most of your requirements when it comes to web application monitoring.

For now, we have covered monitoring features for various Azure services such as Azure VMs, storage accounts, and Azure App Service. The next topic will help you understand Azure SQL backup capabilities.

Implementing Azure SQL backup

Backing up is one of the most important features when it comes to implementing disaster recovery and proper business continuity scenarios. If you are using a relational database such as Azure SQL, it is really important to ensure that you can roll back from any situation you may face (planned or unplanned). In this section, you will learn how to implement backups for Azure SQL databases, as well as the backup capabilities of this service.

Creating our SQL server and database

To get started, we will need an instance of an Azure SQL server and a database. You can do this really quickly using the Azure CLI and the following commands. What we are doing here is creating an Azure SQL Server with the `az sql server create` command and then creating a SQL database with the `az sql db create` command:

```
$ az sql server create -g <rg-name> -n <server-name> -l westeurope -u
<admin-username> -p <admin-password>
$ az sql db create -n c<db-name> -g <rg-name> -s <server-name>
```

 Make sure your password does not contain your admin login – Azure will prevent you from creating an Azure SQL server that does not satisfy that policy.

Once your server and database have been created, we can focus on understanding and implementing proper backup policies.

Backing up your databases

When you go to the Azure portal and access your Azure SQL server, you will see that there is a **Manage Backups** blade:

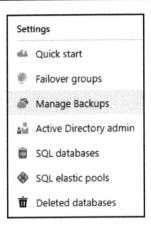

Figure 9.18 – Manage Backups blade

This feature allows you to configure how (and which) backups are made. Before we dig into this, I would like you to understand some Azure SQL backup rules and functionalities:

- Azure SQL backups are stored on RA-GRS storage accounts, which guarantee that, even in the case of catastrophic failure, you will be able to recover. This is the default built-in position of Azure SQL and works right after your Azure SQL server has been created.
- You do not pay for those built-in backups as they are automatic and included in the service's price.
- Those automatic backups are kept for between 7 and 35 days.

As shown in the following screenshot, the default value is **35 days**:

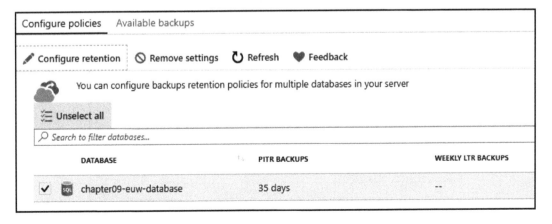

Figure 9.19 – Backup configuration

The default backup is called a Point-in-Time backup and its default retention value is set to 35 days.

 Note that backups are set for each database separately. This makes sense, especially if you have more and less important databases (such as logs and transaction details).

If you click on the **Configure retention** button, you will be able to configure additional backup types, such as the following:

- Weekly backups
- Monthly backups
- Yearly backups

The **Configure policies** screen for backups allows you to configure each time interval separately, as shown here:

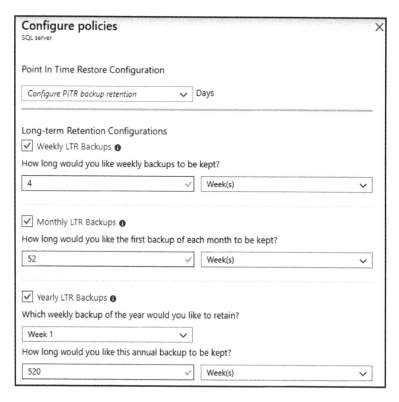

Figure 9.20 – Configure policies screen

On this screen, you can decide how long you want to keep backups (weekly, monthly, or yearly).

Note that the maximum time you can store a backup is 520 weeks (10 years). After that period, you will have to implement your own storage solution (such as Blob Storage with an Archive tier for blobs) to keep the backups for even longer.

Once your backup has been created, it is stored in the internal Azure storage account. Point-in-Time backups are created with the following policies in mind:

- A full database backup is created weekly.
- A differential database backup is created every 12 hours.
- A transaction log backup is created every 5-10 minutes.

Automatic Point-in-Time backups cannot be disabled.

What's more is that the retention period for a Point-in-Time backup can be changed using Azure PowerShell:

```
Set-AzSqlDatabaseBackupShortTermRetentionPolicy -ResourceGroupName <rg-
name> -ServerName <server-name> -DatabaseName <db-name> -RetentionDays
<7-35>
```

The preceding command requires passing a server name, database name, and a number defining how many days backups should be kept.

In the *Further reading* section, you will be able to find some extra information about backups in Azure SQL services. When using it, take into consideration that it is a managed version of SQL Server. This means that it abstracts away most of the administration concepts you may be familiar with for configuring and managing standalone versions of this product. The advantages of Azure SQL are more frequent updates and ease of configuration. There is no longer a need to RDP to a machine and tweak all the settings manually. Here, you can just script most of the settings (using the Azure CLI, ARM templates, or other tools) and easily move a database or recreate it in another region.

Understanding how backups work for managed services such as Azure SQL is crucial to be able to use them proficiently and effectively. To compare different Azure components, let's check how backups work for Azure Storage.

Implementing Azure Storage backup

I have mentioned a few times that Azure Storage is the backbone of many Azure services. Because it is so important, sooner or later, you will face a need to back up the data stored in storage accounts. The problem here is that there is no automatic backup for this service. What's more is that it does not offer any kind of backup at all! In this section, we will find a proper solution to this issue and learn how to implement it properly.

To complete this exercise, you will need a storage account. To do so, please refer to the *Monitoring Azure Storage services* section of this chapter, where you can find detailed instructions on how to create your own storage account.

Backing up your storage account data

The easiest way to back up Azure Storage is to copy the data from one account to another. Let's consider the following scenarios:

- Do you want to immediately restore your account in any region? If so, this section is for you.
- Do you only want to secure your data in case of catastrophic failure? If so, use GRS models for Azure storage accounts.
- Is it acceptable to only have access to a read-only copy of your primary data? If so, RA-GRS is something you'll want, without the need for additional backup.
- Do you want to secure your LRS accounts in case of accidental deletion or malicious activity? If so, continue reading.

Once you understand your scenario, we can focus on implementing a proper backup strategy. This is something you will have to implement on your own, so decide on the following:

- How often a backup should be made
- What data should be copied
- How to ensure backup correctness

The preceding questions are quite difficult to both answer and implement (as they introduce quite a different level of complexity to a system). The ideal solution should take various factors into account, such as the following:

- How important the data that's been gathered is for your company
- How much data can be lost in case of failure
- How much time you have for performing a restore operation

 Remember that a lack of backup support for Azure Storage may be a reason not to select this service as a storage solution. It is always worth mentioning this fact and that you may have to redesign your architecture if this becomes cumbersome.

In this section, we'll only focus on the proper implementation of a backup operation – we will not consider things such as triggering it and validating backups. To get started, you will need an additional account (you can find instructions for this at the very beginning of this section). Consider whether it is okay to have it in the same region or whether you need another data center for it. Now, let's check our capabilities when it comes to data copying:

- As backups are made periodically, one of the best options to achieve the best results is using Azure Data Factory.
- There are two additional options that may be interesting to you – `azcopy` and the REST API, each of which the storage account exposes.

The backup scenario details for Azure Storage were covered in the *Periodic data transfer* section of `Chapter 8`, *Implementing Storage and Backup*. Take a look at it to find out more about how to use `azcopy`, the REST API, or **Azure Data Factory** (**ADF**).

Whether you use REST APIs, `azcopy`, or ADF, the functionality will mostly depend on your concrete implementation. Since Azure Storage is a service, which itself acts as a backup solution for many Azure services, there was never a real need to implement a backup strategy for it. In fact, it is quite easy to introduce such a feature by yourself – if you use ADF, it does not require that you have any programmatic skills. However, remember the following things when creating backups for Azure Storage:

- If you are copying data between different Azure regions, there will be an additional charge for egress.
- Consider what will happen if your data transfer is interrupted.
- Think about proper backup validation and ensuring its correctness.
- Make sure you know the time needed to recover from a disaster. You may have a backup, but switching to it or recovering from it may be unacceptable in terms of time.

In the *Further reading* section, you will find two very practical articles that describe two different scenarios:

- Azure Block Blob backup
- Using ADF to copy the data between tables

I believe that they should give you great insights into your problems and inspire you to build your own pipelines and solutions for Azure Storage backup. Remember that Azure Storage may not be the ideal fit for your systems, especially if a backup is something you do not want to focus on when managing a solution. There are other storage solutions in Azure (Azure SQL, Cosmos DB, Maria DB, and MySQL, to name a few) that may satisfy your requirements better.

In this section, we discussed how to back up Azure Storage and what always has to be considered when using that service on production environments. Now, let's discuss how to ensure **high availability** (**HA**) for VMs.

Implementing Availability Zones for VMs and HA

As an administrator, you have to take care of VMs that host different workloads and applications. In the easiest scenario, you do not have to take care of HA in terms of geo-redundancy. In other words, as long as you do not have to replicate the machines across regions, the easiest way to ensure everything works is using Availability Sets. However, Availability Sets only give you the option to secure against failed updates. When it comes to a data center failure, you need a more sophisticated feature. This is where **Availability Zones** (**AZs**) come into play. In this section, we will implement an AZ for our VMs to make sure they can survive even a region-wide disaster.

Availability Sets versus Availability Zones

Before we get started, I would like to remind you of a difference between Availability Sets and AZs:

- **Availability Set**: This ensures that each VM is provisioned in a separate update/fault domain. However, this works in fives. This means that the first five machines will be deployed to five different domains, then each additional machine is assigned to one of the already created ones.

- **AZ**: This is a way to achieve geographical reliability. This means that your machines will be provisioned across different zones for a single region (let's assume the West Europe region has three different zones – if you provision three VMs across them, each one will be hosted inside a different data center building).

When it comes to availability, you need the following:

- An Availability Set, in order to reach the guaranteed 99.95% SLA for VMs (assuming you have at least two machines)
- An AZ, in order to ensure your system can survive a region going down

 Remember that not all Azure regions support AZs. The full list can be found in the *Further reading* section.

Now, let's learn how to implement AZs for machines hosted in Azure.

Implementing AZs

To implement AZs, follow these steps:

1. Select an AZ during VM creation, as shown in the following screenshot:

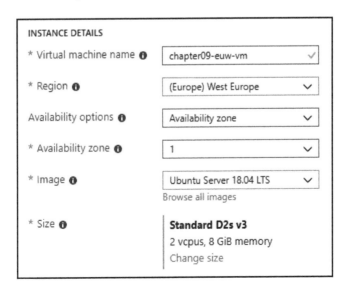

Figure 9.21 – Configuring availability for a VM

Note that you will have to select a proper region (if a region of your choice does not support AZs, the **Availability zone** option will be grayed out).

2. Once the proper option is selected, you will see a new dropdown where you can select the ID of a zone. In most cases, you will have to select one of three different options. At some point in the future, there may be regions that offer more than three zones.

The same can be achieved using the Azure CLI – we can use the `az vm create` command with the `--zone` switch to denote the zone in which a machine will be created:

```
$ az vm create -n <vm-name> -g <rg-name> --location <location> --zone <1,2,3>
```

The preceding scenario works for a single VM. Note that a single machine will not give you any guarantees (if a single zone goes down, so does your VM). This is why in that setup, you should deploy two or three different machines that host the same workload and can work separately.

Implementing redundancy in terms of AZs requires deploying either stateless workloads or achieving some way of communicating between machines. Those concepts come from distributed computing and will not be addressed in this book.

AZs can be also used for VM scale sets, as shown in the following screenshot:

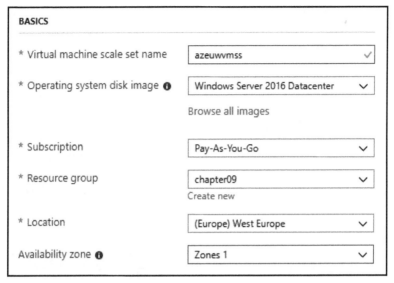

The concept itself is the same as with individual VMs – when a VMSS uses AZs, machines are deployed one by one to a separate zone. Of course, in a scenario where you have five or seven machines, there will be zones that host more than a single machine. This is, of course, perfectly fine as long as your application does not implement some kind of placement constraint that may affect its availability. Now, let's learn how AZs actually work.

Understanding how AZs work

The concept of AZs is really easy – in the case of a zone failure, your workload should still be intact. This means that AZs can secure you from a single data center failure (network outage, power outage), but still cannot protect you from an entire region disaster. If we assume that a region contains three zones and you deploy seven machines, the placement will look like this:

- **Zone 1**: VM1, VM4, VM7
- **Zone 2**: VM2, VM5
- **Zone 3**: VM3, VM6

If Zone 1 fails, you still have four machines able to work on your workloads. This does not mean that an application will not be intact (it will require some load balancing of the current services and possibly that you rerun some of the processes), but it can survive a possible outage.

On the other hand, AZs are meant to protect you only against a local failure – they do not guarantee durability when a disaster occurs that affects all the zones at once. To secure against that kind of failure, you will have to implement some kind of geo-redundancy.

The topic of availability becomes quite complicated when you consider what may happen if some part of your system fails but you want to continue with an ongoing process. Hence, it is important to understand the implications of provisioning machines across zones. To find out more, you can visit the links in the *Further reading* section. We will now switch topics a little bit and learn how to define global routing using the Azure Front Door service.

Monitoring and managing global routing for web traffic with Azure Front Door

In Azure, you have access to many different services when it comes to routing your web traffic in your applications. You can choose Azure Application Gateway, Azure Load Balancer, or Azure Traffic Manager. You can also implement your very own solution or combine available options and create a custom system. In fact, the perfect choice depends on the OSI level you are aiming at. The downside of all of these services is the lack of global traffic support. The only option that is close to achieving that kind of functionality is Azure Traffic Manager, but it works on the DNS level, which is not ideal for many scenarios. In this section, you will learn what Azure Front Door is and how to use it to manage and monitor global routing and traffic across regions.

Understanding Azure Front Door

Before we dive into this topic, you have to understand what Azure Front Door really is. When it comes to supported OSI levels, we can separate Azure services like this:

- Level 4 (Azure Load Balancer)
- Level 7 (Azure Application Gateway, Azure Front Door, Azure Traffic Manager)

Now, depending on your needs, you may require a different set of functionalities:

- If you need SSL offloading, you have to operate at the application level (level 7). Load Balancer will not offer you this kind of feature.
- If you need to be as close to the network layer as possible, you will have to choose level 4 services (so in the case of Azure, Azure Load Balancer).
- If you want to perform URL routing, once again, you will have to address this problem with level 7 services. Use Azure Application Gateway or Azure Front Door to achieve what you need.

> Sometimes, the best solution to a problem is using multiple services at once – you may want to initially route requests to a particular VMSS with Azure Application Gateway and then load balance the traffic between machines with Azure Load Balancer. Do not focus on using only one service.

As there are many different solutions in Azure when it comes to traffic routing, you may wonder what the purpose of another similar service such as Front Door is. To understand this better, consider its following traits:

- Azure Front Door uses the Azure backbone network to route traffic. This ensures that packets are transferred over reliable and optimized network paths, thus reducing latency and improving performance.
- Azure Front Door shares the reliability model of Azure Traffic Manager. This means it survives even entire Azure region failures.
- It offers health probes, URL routing, WAF integration, and custom forwarding paths, making it a really flexible and robust solution for global applications.

To get a better understanding of this, we will create a new instance of Front Door.

Creating an Azure Front Door instance

Now, we will create an instance of Front Door and check how we can route and monitor traffic. In order to monitor and manage the global routing for web traffic with Azure Front Door, follow these instructions. You can create an Azure Front Door instance from the Azure portal by searching for it in the Marketplace, as follows:

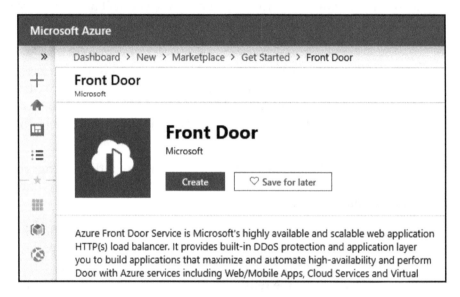

Figure 9.23 – Azure Front Door in the Azure portal

The routing model of Azure Front Door consists of three levels:

- **Frontend hosts**
- **Backend pools**
- **Routing rules**

They can all be configured either during the Front Door instance's creation or once it has been provisioned and is ready. Here, you can find an example configuration of Front Door, which allows me to connect to my blog through it:

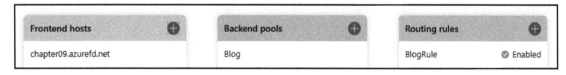

Figure 9.24 – Configuring Front Door

The preceding feature is accessible via the **Front Door designer** blade in your Azure Front Door instance. Once routing has been configured, I will see that by going to `https://chapter09.azurefd.net/`, I will be able to see the main page of my blog, which is hosted under `https://thecloudtheory.com`:

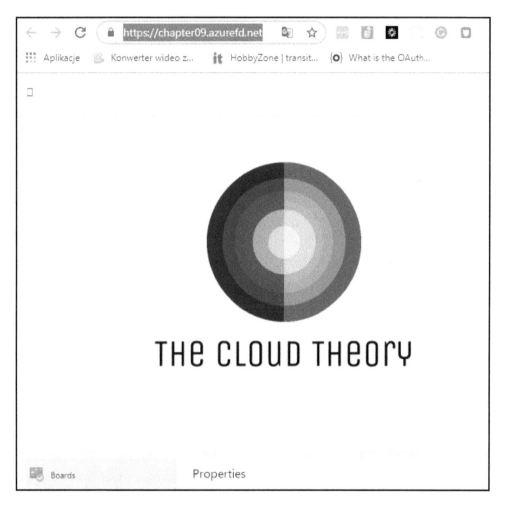

Figure 9.25 – My blog available via Azure Front Door

Since the frontend pool is connected to the backend pool, I have access to the following features:

- Azure Front Door sends health probes to each backend defined in the pool. From here, I can set weights that determine in which order they should be accessed.

- I can configure how a healthy backend is defined (in other words, how many successful probes should be returned to mark it as healthy).
- I can define routing rules (which URLs should be matched, whether it is a forward or a redirect route, whether it should match the only HTTP or also HTTPS).

When users access your backend through the frontend pool, each request is monitored and diagnosed by Azure Front Door. You can view all the available statistics by accessing the **Metrics** blade:

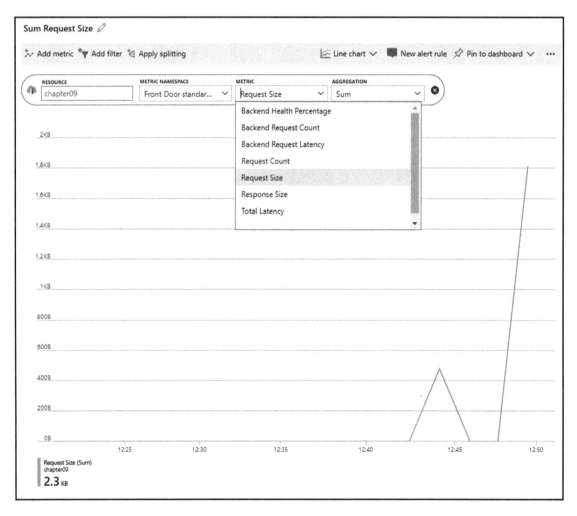

Figure 9.26 – Metrics view

However, some of the features such as **Web Application Firewall** (**WAF**) are not accessible directly from the Azure Front Door instance – they have to be configured separately by creating additional instances and connecting them to your Front Door service. In the *Further reading* section, you will find many articles on additional configuration features and advanced scenarios of using this Azure product. Under the hood, when your users access your backends via Azure Front Door, they are routed through an internal Azure network infrastructure. This greatly improves the stability of the connection, lowers latency, and offers greater reliability. If you have had a chance to use Azure Traffic Manager, you are probably aware of its global deployment status. This means that even if multiple regions fail, routing configured via such a service still works.

In the *Further reading* section, you will find additional articles that describe how more advanced features of Azure Front Door work. As this is quite a new service, there are still things that are not that obvious in many situations (such as WAF configuration, which happens outside of an Azure Front Door instance). When considering the routing services, try to answer the question *What features are really important to me?* If you need routing on level 4 of the OSI model, only Azure Load Balancer will satisfy your requirements. Otherwise, you have to choose an option depending on the features of the service. For example, if you want a global routing service that can route across subscriptions, is not tied to a single region, offers URL rewriting and SSL offloading, and gives you caching capabilities, Azure Front Door is something you should use.

The last topic of this chapter is how we can design backups for VMs in Azure. Let's get started!

Designing backup plans for VMs

If your system is based on VMs, making sure they are backed up and secure is one of the most important things to do as an administrator. Considering a proper backup plan – when to perform it, how and what to store in it, and so on – will be crucial for ensuring that your disaster recovery/business continuity plans work. In this section, we will try to investigate what is possible when it comes to backing Azure VMs up and how to implement proper backup policies. When it comes to backing up a VM in Azure, you have to understand the reason you need to do so. Let's take a look at the workloads that can be run on VMs:

- Stateless services, which can be easily migrated to another machine.
- Stateful services, which store their state directly on a machine. In the case of failure, you may lose data.

Unless you are running stateful services, implementing sophisticated backup plans for your machines may not necessarily be something you want to spend your energy on. Here are the reasons why:

- Stateless services do not store anything important on the machines they run. If they do so, they are no longer stateless.
- In the modern computing solution, it is much more important to be able to quickly recover via proper automation scripts than performing and validating backups.
- The desired state of machines before deployment can be achieved via multiple different tools (DSC, Ansible, and custom extensions for VMs) without the need to get it from a backup.

However, there still are cases where you just have to implement a proper backup. Let's understand the available options. Each VM in Azure has a blade called **Backup**:

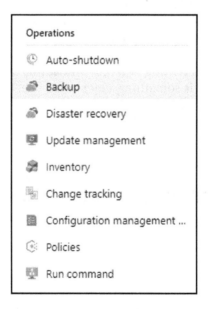

Figure 9.27 – Backup blade

From here, you will be able to configure a backup policy for your machine. Note that the backup functionality is not a direct feature of Azure VMs – in fact, it is a separate service called Azure Backup. Before a backup is enabled, you have to create a Recovery Service vault that will be responsible for managing and storing backups:

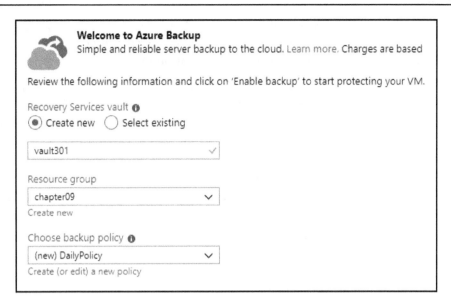

Figure 9.28 – Configuring a backup

Depending on your needs, you may need to configure the backup so that it's performed either daily or weekly. Of course, the retention policy for different time periods can also be configured:

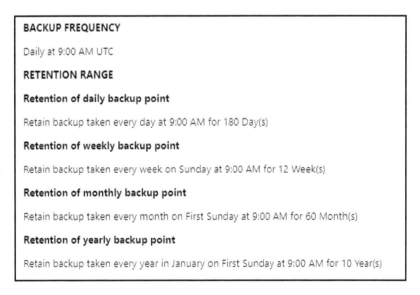

Figure 9.29 – Various options for backup retention

Once the backup is enabled, Azure will create snapshots of your machine on a defined basis. Azure Backup stores each backup in a storage account that gives you an option to select whether you wish to use an LRS or GRS replication model.

Azure Backup for Azure VMs simplifies the backup process by moving the responsibility for it to the cloud. Still, it is your responsibility to ensure that the whole process and created backups really satisfy your requirements. Note that having a backup does not mean that you will be able to recover from a disaster – if a whole region experiences problems, you may not be able to move your workloads without an implemented process for that. Once the backup for a VM is enabled, the **Backup** blade will change its appearance a little bit:

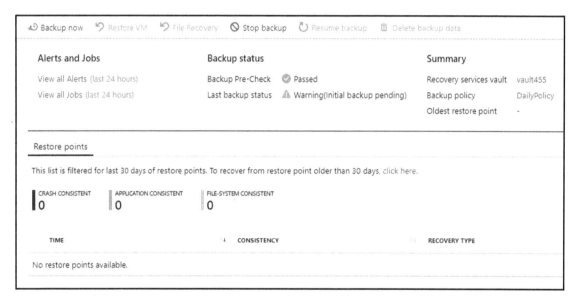

Figure 9.30 – Backup blade with a backup configured

From here, you can steer the backups (by initializing them manually) and recover them in case of any issues with a VM.

In the *Further reading* section, you will find an article that mentions a more advanced scenario with an encrypted VM. Nonetheless, the most important thing when it comes to backups is the scenario you are facing. If your machine does not hold any application state, backing it up does not give you much of an advantage. In such cases, it is much more important to have a proper automation tool that will allow you to script your infrastructure and quickly recover it in a new place.

Summary

In this chapter, we discussed various topics such as monitoring, backups for various services, and HA. As an Azure administrator, you will often face challenges regarding those things as you will be responsible for production systems that need maintenance and ensuring that they follow all the rules and best practices.

In the next and final chapter, we will cover automation topics to complete the path we took in this book.

Further reading

Monitoring Azure App Service:

- Availability tests with firewalls: `https://docs.microsoft.com/en-us/azure/azure-monitor/app/ip-addresses#availability-tests`
- Smart Detection: `https://docs.microsoft.com/en-us/azure/azure-monitor/app/proactive-diagnostics`
- The Application Insights API: `https://dev.applicationinsights.io/quickstart/`

Implementing Azure Backups:

- Automated backups: `https://docs.microsoft.com/en-us/azure/sql-database/sql-database-automated-backups`
- LTR backups: `https://docs.microsoft.com/en-us/azure/sql-database/sql-database-long-term-retention`

Implementing AZs for VMs and HA:

- Managing the availability of VMs in Azure: `https://docs.microsoft.com/en-us/azure/virtual-machines/windows/manage-availability`
- Replication and consistency in distributed systems: `https://www.cs.helsinki.fi/webfm_send/1256`

Implementing Azure Storage backup:

- Azure Block Blob Storage backup: `https://azure.microsoft.com/pl-pl/blog/microsoft-azure-block-blob-storage-backup/`
- ADF (copying data to and from a table): `https://docs.microsoft.com/en-us/azure/data-factory/connector-azure-table-storage`

Monitoring and managing global routing for web traffic with Azure Front Door:

- **Azure Front Door caching:** `https://docs.microsoft.com/en-us/azure/frontdoor/front-door-caching`
- **Configuring WAF:** `https://docs.microsoft.com/en-us/azure/frontdoor/waf-front-door-custom-rules-powershell`
- **URL rewriting:** `https://docs.microsoft.com/en-us/azure/frontdoor/front-door-url-rewrite`

Designing backup plans for VMs:

- **Backing up encrypted VMs:** `https://docs.microsoft.com/en-in/azure/backup/backup-azure-vms-encryption`

Automating Administration in Azure

10

The bigger the system, the more time required to manage and verify changes made to it. This is why administrators often try to automate common activities that allow them to focus on things that really require their attention.

In this chapter, we will focus on integrating different services with Azure Event Grid, Azure Automation, and Azure Logic Apps so that readers can learn additional capabilities of Azure when it comes to monitoring, auditing, and managing multiple system components.

The following main topics are covered in the chapter:

- Starting/stopping Azure **virtual machines** (**VMs**) during off-hours
- Monitoring Blob storage with Azure Event Grid
- Monitoring **Azure Container Registry** (**ACR**) with Azure Event Grid
- Integrating **File Transfer Protocol/Secure File Transfer Protocol** (**FTP/SFTP**) servers with Azure Logic Apps
- Integrating Office 365 with Azure Logic Apps
- Integrating Azure SQL Server with Azure Logic Apps
- Managing updates for VMs
- Tracking changes in VMs

Technical requirements

To perform exercises from this chapter, you will need the following:

- Access to an Azure subscription (created in `Chapter 1`, *Getting Started with Azure Subscriptions*)
- Azure PowerShell installed on your computer. To install it, please check the guide available at `https://docs.microsoft.com/en-us/powershell/azure/azurerm/other-install?view=azurermps-6.13.0`.
- The Azure **command-line interface** (**CLI**): `https://docs.microsoft.com/en-us/cli/azure/install-azure-cli?view=azure-cli-latest`

Starting/stopping Azure VMs during off-hours

In many cases, services you are administering do not have to be enabled once developers and testers finish their workday. In on-premises systems, whether your system is running or not does not affect its cost—you have already paid for the hardware, so it should be on to utilize its resources. Fortunately, in Azure, you may use out-of-the-box features that can help you achieve the expected level of VM automation and governance. Let's check how this can be done with just a few steps.

Getting started with a VM

In cloud environments, things are quite different—once a machine is not needed, it should be deallocated to save money. In this section, you will learn how to create a schedule for starting and stopping an Azure VM so that it reflects the team's workday. To get started, you will need a working VM. If you do not have one, you can quickly deploy one. To do so, use the following Azure CLI command (you can reference `Chapter 3`, *Configuring and Managing Virtual Networks*, for complete instructions on how to use the command line or PowerShell for VM creation):

```
az vm create
```

The same functionality is available via a PowerShell cmdlet:

```
New-AzureRmVM
```

Remember to pass all the required parameters (name of the machine, resource group) and enter the expected VM size (by providing the `--size` parameter), then wait a few minutes for the process to complete. If you want, you can also use the Azure portal and create a machine using the step-by-step wizard:

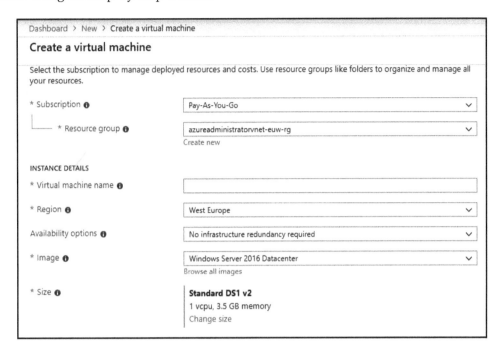

Fig. 10.1 – Creating a VM in the Azure portal

Currently, when a VM is created through the portal, you can also select an **AUTO-SHUTDOWN** option:

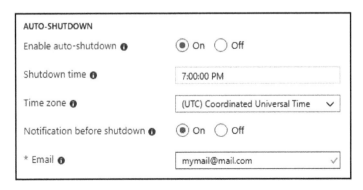

Fig. 10.2 – Configuring auto-shutdown

This will allow you to automatically shut down a VM on a specific schedule. However, take into consideration that this feature will not turn a VM on. To do so, you will need either an automation script or to do it each time manually. To automatically shut down a machine during off-hours, we will use an Azure Automation account, which we will be creating in the next section.

Creating an Automation account

To create an Azure Automation account, follow these steps:

1. To create an Azure Automation account, you can use the marketplace (by clicking on the plus (+) button on the left) and search for `Automation`:

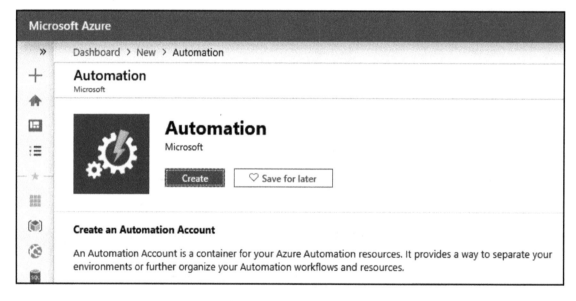

Fig. 10.3 – Automation account in Azure Marketplace

2. For account creation, you can stick with the default values. The only things needed here will be the account name, subscription, resource group, and the desired location:

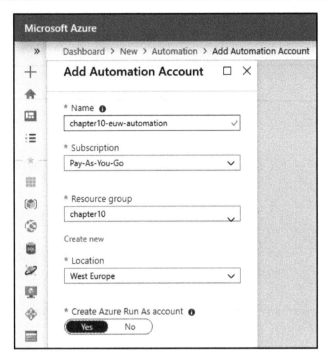

Fig. 10.4 – Automation account form

3. Once your account is created, go to it (you can either use a search box in the middle of the top bar of the portal or just go to your resource group and click on the machine you created) and find the **Start/Stop VM** blade, which looks like this:

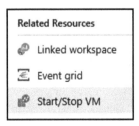

Fig. 10.5 – Start/Stop VM blade

From this place, you will have access to a configurable solution that allows you to quickly decide how a VM should be stopped, and when.

4. Because there is no solution assigned to your account, click on the **Manage the solution** link and then on the **Create solution** button:

Fig. 10.6 – Creating a solution

5. In the search box, enter Start/Stop VM and select the **Start/Stop VM during off-hours** solution. Once you see the panel with the solution description, click on the **Create** button:

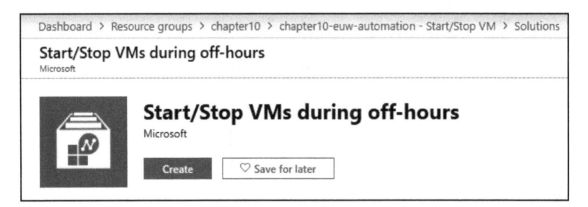

Fig. 10.7 – Start/Stop VMs during off-hours solution

You will have to provide two separate things:

- An **Operations Management Suite** (**OMS**) workspace, which is connected to an Automation account and is responsible for running and monitoring your solution. OMS is, in fact, a deprecated Azure service.
- The actual parameters for a solution so that you can select the schedule of how it works.

An example solution may be configured like this:

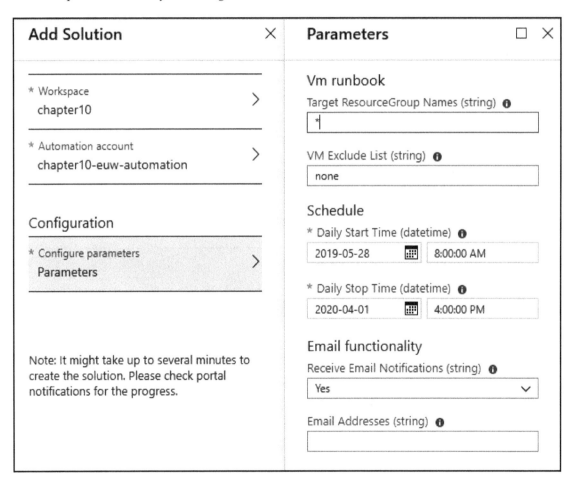

Fig. 10.8 – Solution configuration

Once you are ready with the configuration, you can click the **Create** button.

After several minutes, your solution should be ready—you can go to the selected resource group and click on the **Deployments** blade:

Fig. 10.9 – Deployments blade

Once the solution is ready, it will ensure that your VM is turned on and off according to the defined schedule. Under the hood, the solution you deployed creates PowerShell runbooks, which are responsible for turning a VM on and off. You can find them in the **Runbooks** blade in your Automation account:

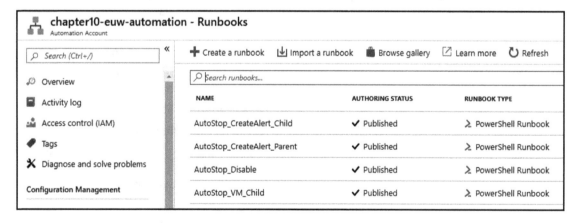

Fig. 10.10 – Runbooks view

Each of the runbooks can be reviewed and modified if you need to do so.

 Using an Automation account is not necessarily required to achieve this particular set of functionalities—if you want, you can try to leverage Azure Functions written in PowerShell (`https://docs.microsoft.com/en-us/azure/azure-functions/functions-reference-powershell`) or **representational state transfer** (**REST**)/CLI commands. These are run using any kind of orchestrator that can authenticate in Azure.

Detailed instructions on the topic in this section, including information regarding how solutions and Automation accounts work, can be found in the *Further reading* section. I strongly advise you to take a look at this particular Azure service, as it is full of powerful features such as change tracking, update management (which will be covered in this chapter), and other VM management features that are really important from an administrator's perspective.

We will now proceed with the next automation solution, which is monitoring Blob storage using the Azure Event Grid service.

Monitoring Blob storage with Azure Event Grid

When it comes to native ways of monitoring what is stored inside an Azure Blob storage, there is no tool that allows you to do this. However, you may still want to implement that kind of functionality—either to introduce some way of validating what is actually stored or to understand the actual data volume and inflow.

In this section, we will use Azure Event Grid with Azure Functions, written in PowerShell, to discuss the possibilities and show you the easiest way to achieve this functionality. To get started, we will need the following services deployed to a resource group:

- Azure storage with a selected kind of Blob storage
- Azure Event Grid integrated with the Storage account (see `Chapter 2`, *Managing Azure Resources*, for reference)

To deploy the Blob storage, use the following command:

```
az storage account create -g <rg-name>-n <account-name> --kind BlobStorage
--access-tier <Hot|Cold>
```

It is important to select `--kind` as `BlobStorage` as Azure Event Grid integration does not work with general-purpose accounts.

Once the account is created, you can go to the portal so that we can proceed with the topic. To configure the integration between a Storage account and Azure Event Grid, follow these steps, which describe the process in detail:

1. In the Azure portal, search for your Storage account and click on the **Events** blade:

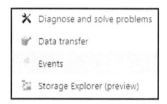

Fig. 10.11 – Events blade

2. On the screen that will be displayed, you will be able to select a recipe that you can use to get started. As we want to monitor uploaded blobs and logic apps, select the first recipe, and ensure **Logic Apps** is selected:

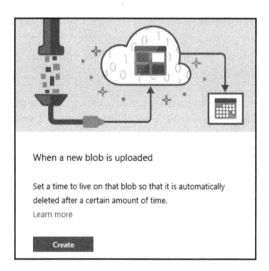

Fig. 10.12 – Recipe view

3. Once a recipe is selected, you will see a designer that will help you create your application. The very first step is connecting a Storage account with Azure Event Grid:

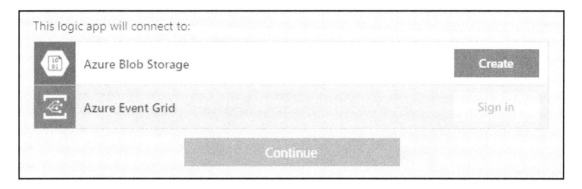

Fig. 10.13 – Connecting Storage account with Azure Event Grid

When you click on the **Create** button, you will be asked to provide two things:

- The name of the connection
- The Storage account you would like to connect

Once you are ready to proceed, click on the **Continue** button once more:

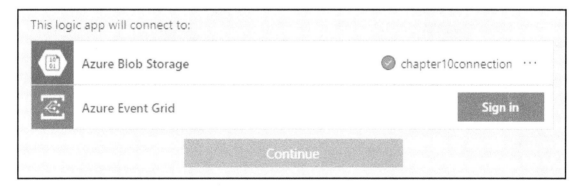

Fig. 10.14 – Proceeding with the recipe

 Sometimes, you may not see your Storage account (for example, it is deployed to a subscription you do not have access to). In such cases, use the **Manually enter connection information** option to provide the values manually.

4. To provide the Event Grid connection, click on the **Sign in** button, which will display a new step:

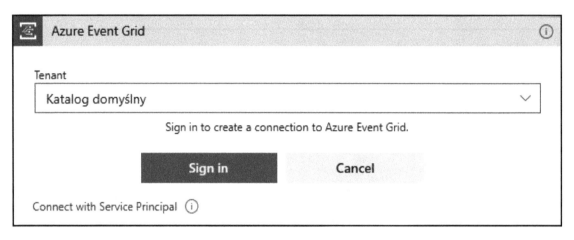

Fig. 10.15 – Signing in to Azure Event Grid

 On the preceding screen, there is a **Tenant** field, which declares in which Azure **Active Directory** (**AD**) tenant an instance of Event Grid should be created. The Katalog domyślny value was not translated in my case, but it mentions the default tenant for my account.

5. Once you select the value of the tenant you want, click once more on the **Sign in** button. You will be asked to sign in once more, and once the authentication is completed, you will see that the integration is ready to be created:

Fig. 10.16 – Integration connected to services

6. Click on the **Continue** button and you will see a logic app generated, which can be modified to fulfill your expectations:

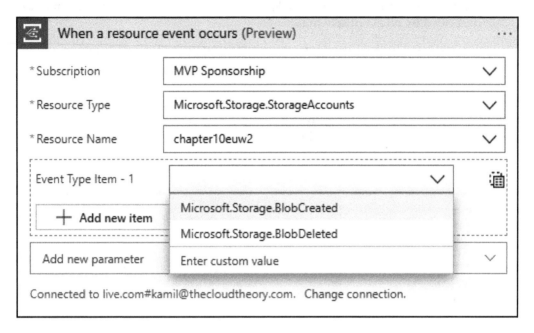

Fig. 10.17 – Configuring logic app with Azure Event Grid connector

7. Once you are satisfied with your application, click on the **Save As** button on the left of the screen to create the application inside your subscription.

Once we have the initial setup ready, we can continue with more advanced topics.

Extending your setup

A really nice feature of Azure Logic Apps and Azure Event Grid integration is their ability to use predefined events without a need to know what they are (as displayed in the preceding screenshot—you immediately have access to `BlobCreated` and `BlobDeleted` events). Now, each time an event is sent to Azure Event Grid, it will be handled by your logic app. The flow can be described as follows:

1. A blob is uploaded to your Storage account.
2. An event is generated by the account (`BlobCreated` or `BlobDeleted`, in the case of a blob deletion).

3. An event is picked up by Azure Event Grid and forwarded to all interested subscribers.

4. A subscriber receives an event, which contains the metadata and information described by an event schema.

As Azure Event Grid calls the receiver (as opposed to other models, where you have to pool the broker), it offers improved performance (reactive architecture) and easy integration with any **HyperText Transfer Protocol** (**HTTP**) endpoint (without the need to implement additional protocols such as **Message Queuing Telemetry Transport** (**MQTT**) or the **Advanced Message Queuing Protocol** (**AMQP**). You can quickly test the behavior of the application by uploading a blob using the Azure portal. Follow these steps to do so:

1. Go to your Storage account, and click on the **Blobs** service:

Fig. 10.18 – Blobs service

2. If you do not have a container, you will have to create it (with the **+ Container** button):

Fig. 10.19 – Creating a container

3. Then, select the container and click on the **Upload** button:

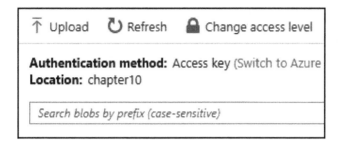

Fig. 10.20 – Upload button

 Another option is using the Microsoft Azure storage Explorer application to access a container and upload a file of your choice.

4. Once a blob is uploaded, go back to your logic app and check the execution status:

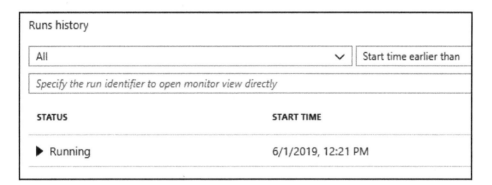

Fig. 10.21 – Logic app in the Running state

Depending on your flow, the execution will end quickly or you will have to wait for several seconds or a few minutes (for example, because you are making external calls that are waiting for the **application programming interfaces** (**APIs**) to respond). Nonetheless, each execution will handle an event similar to this one:

```
{
  "topic":
"/subscriptions/.../resourceGroups/chapter10/providers/Microsoft.Storage/st
orageAccounts/chapter10euw2",
```

```
    "subject":
"/blobServices/default/containers/chapter10/blobs/B13634_10_17.PNG",
    "eventType": "Microsoft.Storage.BlobCreated",
    "eventTime": "2019-06-01T10:21:36.8740173Z",
    "id": "629372c5-601e-007b-3563-1894e106e3f2",
    "data": {
      <data-object>
    },
    "dataVersion": "",
    "metadataVersion": "1"
}
```

Inside, you will see a `data` object containing the most important information:

```
"api": "PutBlockList",
"clientRequestId": "1b3c334f-c3b8-4dd8-835b-efe148c4f064",
"requestId": "629372c5-601e-007b-3563-1894e1000000",
"eTag": "0x8D6E67AEDC0AE36",
"contentType": "image/png",
"contentLength": 5851,
"blobType": "BlockBlob",
"url":
"https://chapter10euw2.blob.core.windows.net/chapter10/B13634_10_17.PNG",
"sequencer": "00000000000000000000000000000AED000000000026c7a3",
"storageDiagnostics": {
  "batchId": "262f554d-1404-4e78-9b3d-171153620e04"
}
```

Depending on your requirements, you may want to use different fields (`contentType`, `url`, `contentLength`) to implement a proper flow and decide what to do with a file.

Azure Event Grid integration is a great way of building both simple and advanced flows that may help you manage applications. Those scenarios include the following:

- Diagnosis of the load on your Storage accounts
- Ensuring only proper (in terms of content type/size) content is uploaded
- Validating the content

In the *Further reading* section, you will find more articles describing the service and possible scenarios that may help you understand Azure Event Grid better. Proceed to the next section to learn more about monitoring ACR, once again using the Event Grid service.

Monitoring ACR with Azure Event Grid

As containers become more and more popular, proper management of their hubs and monitoring actions is required to ensure your systems are working flawlessly. In Azure, you can very easily create your own registry for storing your images using ACR.

In this section, we will try to implement seamless integration between ACR and Azure Event Grid to see what kind of functionalities it offers.

We are covering ACR in response to the growing popularity of containerized applications and systems backed by Docker and Kubernetes. In the simplest scenarios, you could host your container images using shared galleries such as Docker Hub. The downside of such a solution is a third-party dependency, no performance guarantees, and integration options. This is why many companies decide to host their own container registries. An option would be also to use a registry offered by your cloud provider (such as ACR from Microsoft).

When working with modern systems that leverage containers, you will quickly realize that the number of containers hosted and used grows rapidly and that you need some means of control over them. This is where Azure Event Grid comes in handy.

Integrating ACR with Azure Event Grid

To get started, we will need an instance of ACR. To create it via the command line, run the following command:

```
az acr create -n <name> -g <rg-name> --sku <Classic|Basic|Standard|Premium>
```

Once the ACR instance is created, find the instance you want in the portal and go to it. The integration with Azure Event Grid is very similar to what you can find in the previous section.

Let's get started with the integration:

1. Click on the **Events** blade and then on the **+ Event Subscription** button:

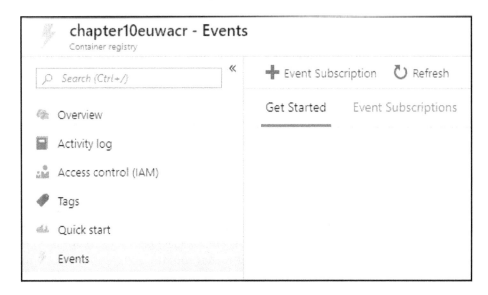

Fig. 10.22 – Events blade

2. On the next screen, besides providing the name of the subscription and the schema (we will go for the **Event Grid** schema), you will have to decide which events you are interested in and select them:

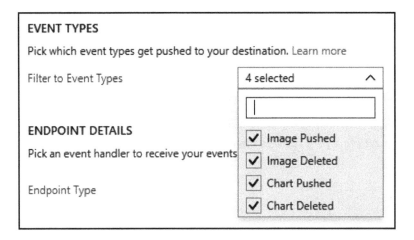

Fig. 10.23 – Available events for ACR

The last thing required here will be the endpoint type. While you can choose between many different positions (**Event Hub**, **Storage Queue**, **Hybrid Connection**), we will go for the **Webhook** position. In case you are not familiar with what a webhook is, let me describe the concept briefly. Webhooks are simple HTTP endpoints that act as a point of contact between external services and your services. They can be used to receive a message, start a process, or send an event.

3. As you may currently not have an endpoint that can be used by you, you can quickly create a web application using the following command, which will create a new deployment inside a resource group, using a template passed via the `--template-uri` parameter:

    ```
    az group deployment create --resource-group <rg-name> --template-
    uri
    "https://raw.githubusercontent.com/Azure-Samples/azure-event-grid-v
    iewer/master/azuredeploy.json" --parameters siteName=<site-name>
    hostingPlanName=<hosting-plan-name>-plan
    ```

    This will deploy an example web application inside the selected resource group.

4. Once the application is deployed, obtain its endpoint using the `az webapp show` command, which displays all the information related to this specific web app. We are using the `--query` parameter to limit the data returned to `defaultHostName` only:

    ```
    az webapp show --resource-group <rg-name> --name <webapp-name> --
    query defaultHostName
    ```

5. Once the hostname is returned, prepend `https://` and append `/api/updates` to the hostname, and use this endpoint as the webhook:

Fig. 10.24 – Passing an endpoint

6. Click on the **Confirm Selection** button and then on the **Create** button.

Congratulations! You have just connected ACR with an application that can handle all the events.

 The deployed application handles the endpoint validation by properly responding to the validation event. If you want to provide your custom solution, you will have to implement the logic on your own (see the *Further reading* section for details).

When the integration is on, each event sent to Azure Event Grid will be handled by the integrated application. As mentioned in the previous sections, ACR generates four different events for now:

- **Image pulled**
- **Image pushed**
- **Chart pushed**
- **Chart deleted**

The idea of the functionality is simple—once an image is pushed to/pulled from the registry, an event is raised that is picked up by Azure Event Grid and routed to subscribers. The same goes for charts deployed to ACR. Azure Event Grid calls the configured endpoints and passes the metadata of an event so that a subscriber can decide what to do with it.

 It is important to remember that not all events that might be generated by ACR are integrated with Azure Event Grid (so you will receive events related to images and charts pushed to the service, but other things such as management actions, **Identity and Access Management** (**IAM**) changes, and repositories will not be handled by this particular topic).

You can check the statistics of the Azure Event Grid integration by going to the **Events** blade and then clicking on the **Event Subscriptions** tab:

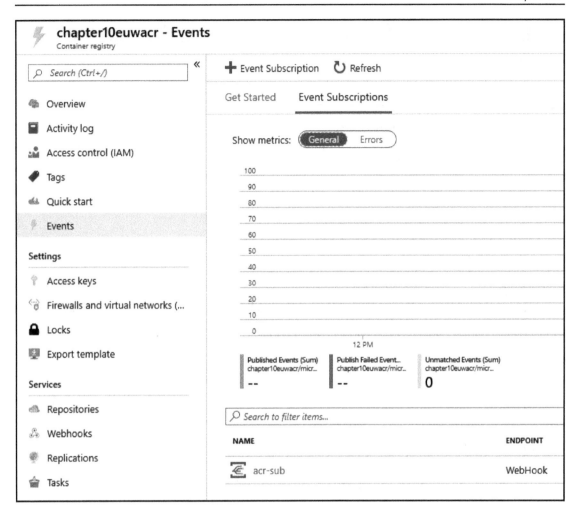

Fig. 10.25 – Events blade with the Event Subscription button

In the *Further reading* section, you will find a link about validating Event Grid endpoints. Reading the article is really important if you want to introduce custom webhooks and the endpoints of Event Grid topics, as Azure Event Grid requires a specific way to authenticate them.

In the next section, you will learn more about one of the serverless offerings of Azure—Azure Logic Apps—to integrate FTP/SFTP servers.

Integrating FTP/SFTP servers with Azure Logic Apps

When it comes to hosting files, FTP servers are still popular as simple and well-known environments for file sharing. When working as an administrator, you probably have at least one FTP server under your control. You may wonder if there is any way to integrate such a service with Azure. Fortunately, you can very easily create a logic app that will handle changes on your server and let you integrate with other Azure services.

For this exercise, we will need two components:

- An FTP server
- An Azure Logic Apps instance

If you do not have an FTP server, you can quickly deploy one using recipes from the marketplace:

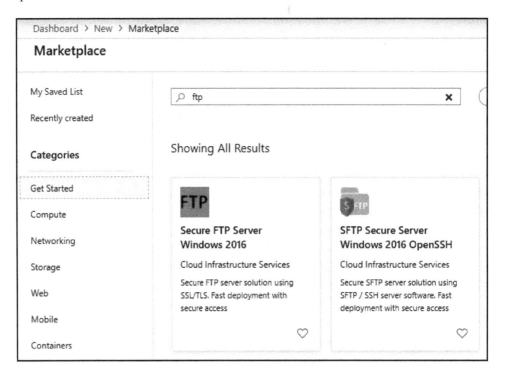

Fig. 10.26 – Available FTP servers in Azure

Let's now check how to use it.

Creating an Azure Logic App instance

To create a logic app instance, go to the marketplace and search for `logic app`:

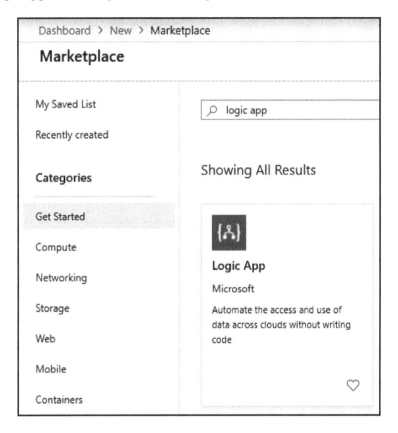

Fig. 10.27 – Logic App in Azure Marketplace

You will have to enter all the required fields:

- **Name**
- **Location**
- **Resource group**
- **Subscription**

Once you have all the details, click on the **Create** button to initialize the process of deploying your application. With your application deployed, we can start adding the FTP server integration:

1. Go to your logic app and click on the following recipe:

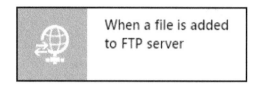

Fig. 10.28 – Recipe for logic app triggered by file added

This will start a wizard that will guide you through the process of integrating the server with Azure. You will start with creating the connection to your FTP server:

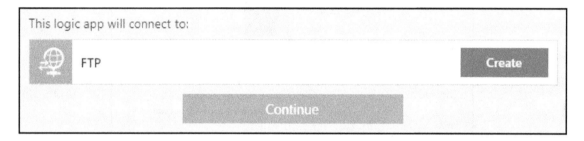

Fig. 10.29 – Creating a connection

2. Click on the **Create** button to provide the required values. You will see the following form, which you will have to fill in to proceed:

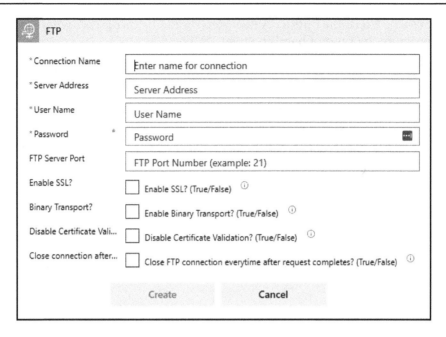

Fig. 10.30 – Configuring a connection

Of course, not all of the fields are required—in fact, the only values you are expected to provide are as follows:

- **Connection name**
- **Server address**
- **Username**
- **Password**

Once you click on the **Create** button, the process of validating the connection will start. If everything is correct, you will see that the connection is green:

Fig. 10.31 – logic app connected to an FTP server

3. Press the **Continue** button. A new step should be displayed, where you can configure the rules of handling the FTP files:

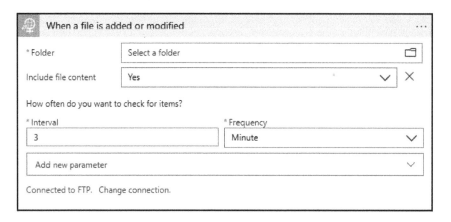

Fig. 10.32 – Configuring the rules of a trigger

You can add other steps to extend your application.

4. Once you are ready, click on the **Save** button to finish the changes and let the application do its job.

 If you are using an Azure VM, make sure that port 21 is open. Failing to do so will result in errors in your connection.

Congratulations! Your Azure Logic App should now be ready and running. Let's now discuss how the setup works in detail.

Understanding the setup

Depending on the frequency of your checks defined in the application, Azure will start analyzing your FTP server sooner or later. Now, when the evaluation takes place, two things may happen:

- The application is not triggered because there was no change in the files or directories.
- The evaluation is positive and your application is triggered.

The Azure Logic Apps connector handles the state of your FTP server, so you do not have to worry about notifying it about any changes. However, make sure your FTP server does not become too big as it may affect the performance of the logic app. You can very easily extend your logic app with other steps offered in the FTP section, such as the following:

- **Copy file**—for copying files between servers
- **Create file**—so that you can create a file on the FTP server
- **Delete file**—for deleting files from the FTP server
- **Get file content**—for fetching information about a file
- **List files**—for browsing files
- **Get file metadata**—for fetching the metadata of a file

All those steps can be integrated with each other to build a complex solution covering everything needed to work with files stored on FTP servers. In the following screenshot, you can find an example of a very simple pipeline that gets a file's content once it is added or modified on a server:

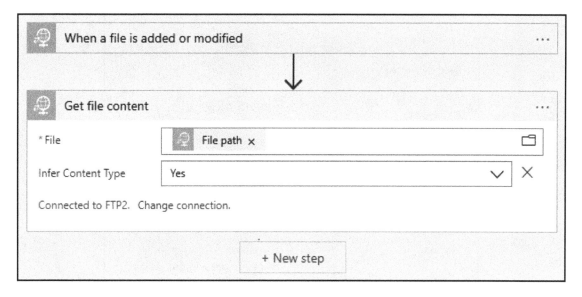

Fig. 10.33 – Example logic app

Once the file is fetched by Azure logic apps, you can pass it wherever you want (including Office 365 applications, Azure Functions, or other Azure services that you have integrated). Let's now continue with another exercise to see how Azure logic apps may integrate with Office 365 connectors.

Integrating Office 365 with Azure Logic Apps

If you have access to Office 365, you probably see the value of integrating things such as meetings, emails, and OneDrive files with Azure services. This can greatly enhance the capabilities of your company, as you can implement extra functionalities that may help in either managing the applications or monitoring them by closing the gap between a deployed application and a developer.

In this section, we will see the capabilities of Azure Logic Apps when it comes to Office 365, and what can be achieved with this service. To get started, you will need an instance of Azure Logic App. To get it, follow these steps:

1. Search for `logic app` in the marketplace:

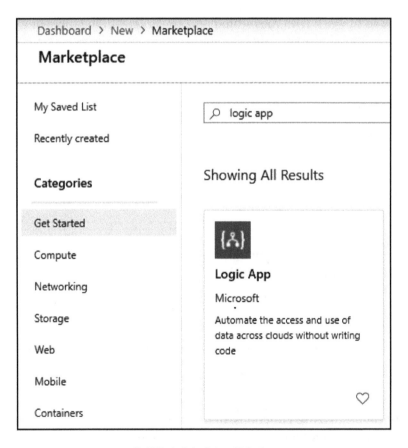

Fig. 10.34 – Logic App in Azure Marketplace

2. Then, you will have to provide all the required values for your instance, including the following:

   - **Name**
   - **Location**
   - **Resource group**
   - **Subscription**

3. The last step is clicking on the **Create** button. After a few seconds, your application should be up and running.

Now, let's start integrating Office 365 with Azure Logic Apps, with the help of the following steps:

1. When you access your brand new Azure Logic App, you will be offered a bunch of different recipes to get started. We can, for example, get started with emails received by your Outlook account:

Fig. 10.35 – Recipe for connecting to Outlook

2. Traditionally, you will have to sign in to integrate the external service with your application in Azure:

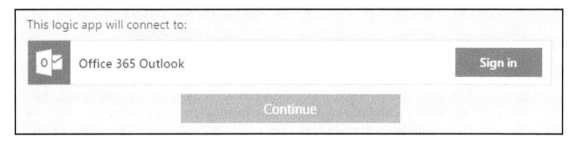

Fig. 10.36 - Connecting to Office 365

3. When you click on the **Sign in** button, you will be able to provide the credentials for your Office 365 account. Once the credentials are provided and your account is connected, you will be able to configure the feature:

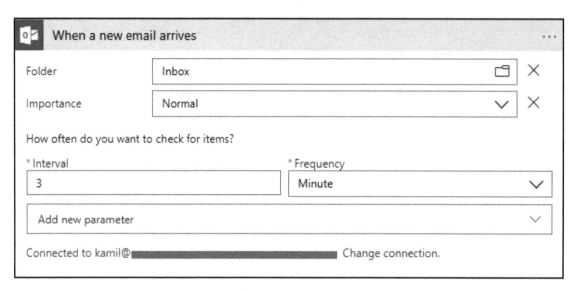

Fig. 10.37 – Configuring the application

Of course, you are not limited to Outlook only—you can integrate other Office 365 applications such as Forms, Excel, or OneDrive (see this link for a services description: https://docs.microsoft.com/en-us/office365/servicedescriptions/office-365-service-descriptions-technet-library). By selecting the desired Office 365 service and integrating it with an Azure logic app, you are making a connection between those two cloud components. In this section, we selected Outlook as the ingredient of the application so that we can easily introduce a logic based on incoming email messages.

The integration is based on the credentials you provided, which means that if you want to avoid connecting your account with Azure Logic Apps, you will have to enter a username and a password for an artificial user account. Depending on the service you selected, the way your logic app works will differ slightly. In my case, when I get a message sent to my Outlook account, this will be noticed and the flow of my application will start. This opens multiple interesting possibilities:

- I can initiate a process depending on the mail subject or content.
- I can automatically delete or move an email.
- I can approve something somebody is asking me in a message.

There are multiple options available that you can use:

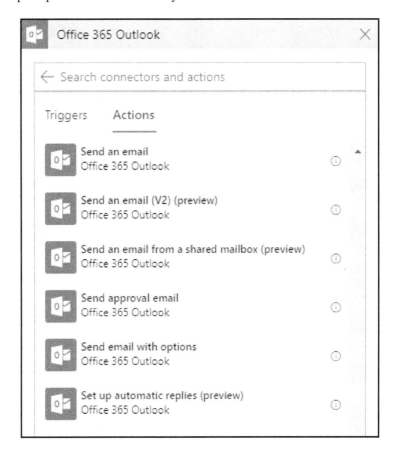

Fig. 10.38 – Available options for Outlook

 Integrating Office 365 with logic apps may require additional permissions. If your connection works but you cannot add any action to your application, make sure your Azure AD account can manage email messages. See the following connector reference for more information: https://docs.microsoft.com/en-us/connectors/outlook/.

In the *Further reading* section, you can find the details of the connector for Office 365. Take a look at that article so that you can build better applications based on this particular logic apps connection. It will give you deeper insights into the structure of the connector and the properties that it offers. Let's now do the last exercise using Azure Logic Apps, where you will see how to integrate with Azure SQL Server.

Integrating Azure SQL Server with Azure Logic Apps

With Azure Logic Apps, you can very easily integrate with cloud-based SQL Server instances, which gives you interesting integration options. You can quickly build a solution that can access data stored inside the **Structured Query Language** (**SQL**) tables and read it for further analysis, data validation, or integration with other services. In this section, we will learn how to connect to Azure SQL Server from your application so that you can integrate with a database without the need to configure and manage it.

Note that this section focuses on integrating the **Platform as a Service** (**PaaS**) offering of SQL Server in Azure, called Azure SQL Server. While the instructions can be still applied to an on-premises version of this database, the primary goal is to integrate with the managed version of it.

All we need now is an Azure Logic App instance.

Getting started with Azure Logic Apps

To get started, we will need two separate components:

- An Azure Logic Apps instance
- An Azure SQL database

To create a logic app instance, go to the marketplace and search for `logic app`:

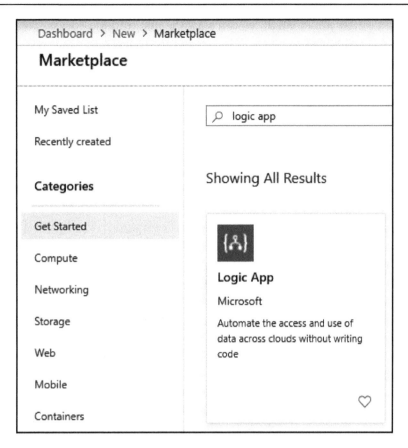

Fig. 10.39 – Logic App in Azure Marketplace

You will have to enter all the required fields:

- The name of your application
- Location
- Resource group
- Subscription

Azure SQL can be created using the Azure CLI, using two commands—`az sql server create` for SQL Server creation and `az sql db create` for creating a SQL database:

```
$ az sql server create -g <rg-name> -n <server-name> -l westeurope -u
<admin-username> -p <admin-password>
$ az sql db create -n c<db-name> -g <rg-name> -s <server-name>
```

Once those two services are created, we can start the integration process. To integrate SQL Server with an Azure logic app, you will have to perform a few simple steps, which are described here:

1. Click on the **Create Blank Template** button, as for now, we are not interested in the default recipes:

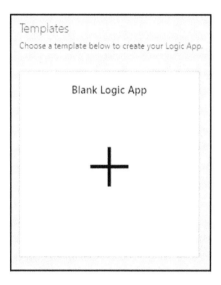

Fig. 10.40 – Getting started with blank logic app

2. The next step is searching for the connector. On the next screen, enter `sql` and click on **SQL Server**:

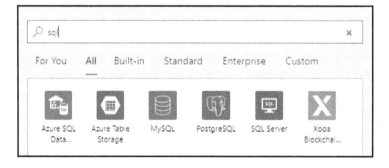

Fig. 10.41 – Searching for SQL Server

3. You will have to decide whether you need a trigger or an action. Triggers allow you to react to an event, while an action works by performing an operation and is often the result of a trigger. If this is the very first step of your application, go to **Triggers** and select the one you want:

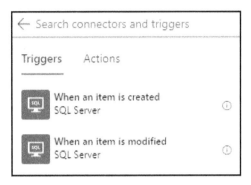

Fig. 10.42 – Selecting a trigger

4. Provide the details of the connection, select the right SQL database, and provide the credentials that should be used for this particular connection with SQL Server:

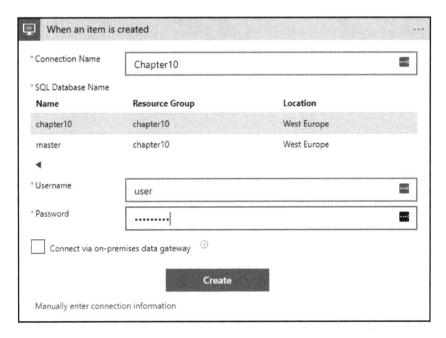

Fig. 10.43 – Configuring the connection

5. Once the connection is created and validated, you can start developing your application, starting with the SQL Server trigger:

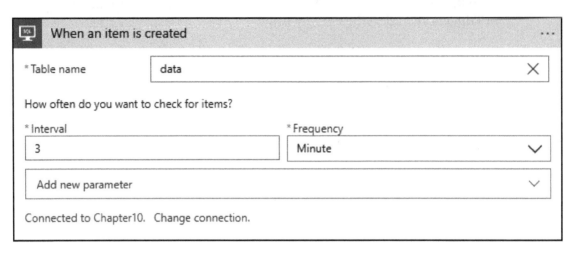

Fig. 10.44 – Configuring the trigger

When the application is configured, it will be evaluated with the defined interval (in my case, it was 3 minutes). This does not mean that the application will be triggered—the flow of the application only starts if the condition is satisfied (an item is created). By connecting your logic app with Azure SQL Server, you are allowing the application to pool your database and check whether a new record has been added.

This should not be implemented on tables that run on production and are used by other applications.

If you want to monitor records, it's a better option to implement a way to copy records from one table to another and only use the secondary ones for your administration tasks. Thanks to this approach, you are not affecting the performance of a single table by less important operations and can extract only the columns you are interested in.

In the *Further reading* section, you will find extra articles on the topic we have just described. An especially interesting one defines the approach to implement a bulk data transfer with Azure Logic Apps. If you are searching for a simple solution for transferring the data, this may be something you are looking for. Please proceed to the next exercise, where we will discuss ways to manage updates for VMs in Azure.

Managing updates for VMs

The topic of update management is really important for every IT administrator. Failed updates may seriously affect the workloads you are working on by affecting the performance of machines or causing operating system crashes. Automatic updates are not something you are aiming for in each and every situation, and proper update monitoring is really difficult to achieve.

Getting started with the Update Management feature

In this section, we will see the Update Management feature that helps in controlling updates and controlling the compliance of VMs. To get started, you will need a working VM. If you do not have one, you can quickly deploy one. To do so, use the following Azure CLI command:

```
az vm create
```

The same functionality is available via a PowerShell cmdlet:

```
New-AzureRmVM
```

Remember to pass all the required parameters and enter the expected VM size, then wait a few minutes for the process to complete. If you want, you can also use the Azure portal and create a VM using the step-by-step wizard:

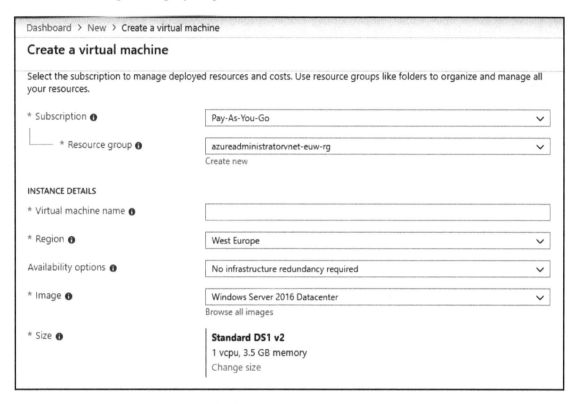

Fig. 10.45 – Creating a VM

Once your VM is created, search for it in the Azure portal and open the main screen so that you can proceed with the instruction. Now, let's walk through the following instructions to learn how to manage updates on VMs:

1. Update management for Azure VMs is done via the **Update management** blade:

Fig. 10.46 – Update management blade

By default, this feature is not enabled on VMs as it requires a Log Analytics workspace to work with.

2. To enable it, select the **Enable for this VM** option and click on the **Enable** button:

Fig. 10.47 – Enabling Update Management for a VM

If you have a workspace created (as well as an Automation account), you do not have to create them in this step. Instead, select the instances you want to connect with the Update Management feature.

The process of enabling the feature on a machine can take several minutes, so be patient. Once the feature is deployed, it should look more or less like this:

Fig. 10.48 – Updates view

3. To create a new deployment of updates, click on the **Schedule update deployment** button. This will take you to the following screen:

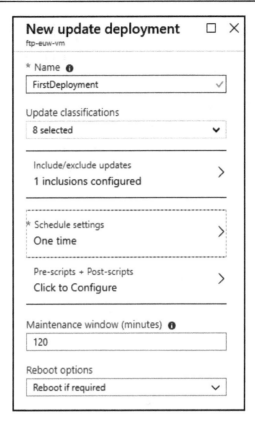

Fig. 10.49 – Configuring a deployment

4. From this screen, you will be able to configure the following features:
   - Which updates should be included (both in terms of their identifiers and classification)
   - What is the schedule
   - How long the maintenance should last
5. Click on the **Create** button after the deployment is configured.

Once the deployment is scheduled, the Update Management feature will try to ensure that your machine is compliant with the requirements and that it is not missing any security fixes and new functionalities. The Update Management feature is an optional feature that you may enable. In this example, we enabled it for a single VM so that we can track how updates are introduced to it.

Enabling the feature for multiple machines

The previous step described involved defining a single deployment of changes. With that approach, we were able to configure how changes are introduced and decide what is important for us. While in that example we considered only a single machine, update management can also work with multiple machines at once. This can be achieved via your Automation account in the **Update management** blade:

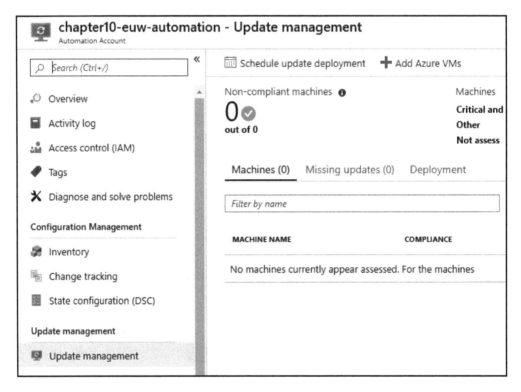

Fig. 10.50 – + Add Azure VMs button

In the preceding screenshot, you can see the **+ Add Azure VMs** button, which is a quick way to configure more than a single VM to be covered by the Update Management feature.

In the *Further reading* section, you will find an article that describes this particular feature in detail. If you seek to know how update management works in terms of different operating systems, more advanced scenarios, and ensuring compliance, it's not to be missed. The last exercise from this book will guide you through tracking changes in VMs.

Tracking changes in VMs

When managing VMs, it is important to know what was changed, and when. If you are leveraging an immutable infrastructure and never perform changes manually (instead, you are using Automation scripts and custom VM images), you may already have a solution for tracking changes that suits your needs. However, there are still cases where the process you are working in does not guarantee the right management of changes, and it is hard to audit them.

In this section, we will discuss the **Change tracking** feature and see how it works for our purpose. To get started, you will need a VM with which you can work. If you do not have one, take a look at the previous sections from this chapter, where the process is discussed in detail.

Continuing our discussion forward, let's track changes in a VM with the help of the following instructions:

1. To enable the **Change tracking** feature, go to your VM and find the **Change tracking** blade:

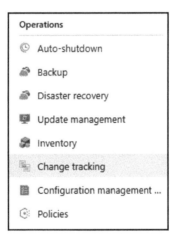

Fig. 10.51 – Change tracking blade

2. The screen that you see here allows you to configure the Log Analytics workspace and Automation account that steer the feature:

Change Tracking

Enable consistent control and compliance of this VM with Change

This service is included with Azure virtual machines. You only pay for logs

This service requires a Log Analytics workspace and an Automation us configure the nearest workspace and account for use.

(●) Enable for this VM   ( ) Enable for VMs in this subscription

Location ❶

| West Europe | ∨ |

Log Analytics workspace ❶

| chapter10 | ∨ |

Automation account subscription ❶

| MVP Sponsorship | ∨ |

Automation account ❶

| chapter10-euw-automation | ∨ |

[Enable]

Fig. 10.52 – Enabling the feature

In the preceding example, my machine had already been linked to Log Analytics. In your case, you will be able to either select a workspace or create a new one.

3. The deployment of the feature may take a while, so be patient. Once the feature has been deployed, you will see no changes noticed by it:

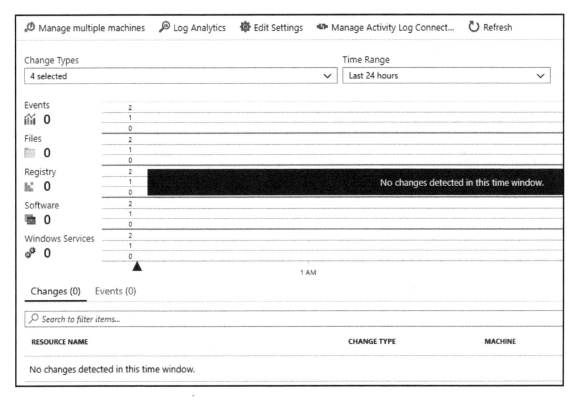

Fig. 10.53 – Update tracking view

Note that it watches the following things on your machine:

- Events related to it
- File modifications
- Registry changes
- Software installations
- Windows services operations

4. If you click on the **Edit Settings** button, you will be able to configure each of the filters in detail:

Workspace Configuration
Change Tracking

+ Add   🔗 Documentation

Windows Registry	Windows Files	Linux Files	File Content	Windows Services

GROUP	ENABLED	REGISTRY KEY
Recommended	false	HKEY_LOCAL_MACHINE\Software\Classes\Directory\Background\ShellEx\ContextMenuHandlers
Recommended	false	HKEY_LOCAL_MACHINE\Software\Classes\Directory\ShellEx\ContextMenuHandlers
Recommended	false	HKEY_LOCAL_MACHINE\Software\Classes\Directory\Shellex\CopyHookHandlers

Fig. 10.54 – Configuring the feature

 By default, the **Change tracking** feature does not monitor all the recommended things. To make it work, ensure that it is configured by you and that it covers all the factors you want to monitor.

Using the **Change tracking** feature is similar to the usage of update management, described in the previous section. It also uses the Log Analytics workspace so that everything is automated and integrated with each other in a seamless way.

In this exercise, we have discovered possibilities for changes and modifications that may be tracked (such as new values of registry entries). The important thing here is remembering that everything is disabled by default—you have to mark things that you want to monitor. **Change tracking** can be very easily configured by adding the registry keys or files you want to monitor:

Fig. 10.55 – Adding a file for tracking

Make sure you have configured it properly (by adding all the files to monitor or enabling monitoring of particular registry entries). In the *Further reading* section, you will find extra information on this topic—including limitations of the feature and known issues—that may help you troubleshoot this functionality.

Summary

This was the last chapter of this book. We covered aspects connected to other parts of it, but with a focus on automating your actions and duties. You learned about things such as tracking changes of VMs and keeping them running only during working hours. We also extended your knowledge regarding Azure Logic Apps, which is a common tool of many Azure administrators. I hope that the book helped you in getting started with Azure and that it pointed to all the places you can go to keep building your skills in relation to the Azure cloud.

Further reading

Starting/stopping Azure VMs during off-hours:

- Start/Stop VMs during off-hours: https://docs.microsoft.com/en-us/azure/
  automation/automation-solution-vm-management

Monitoring Blob storage with Azure Event Grid:

- Event delivery monitoring: https://docs.microsoft.com/en-us/event-
  grid/monitor-event-delivery
- Dead letter and retry policies: https://docs.microsoft.com/en-us/azure/
  event-grid/manage-event-delivery
- Event Grid scenarios: https://docs.microsoft.com/en-us/dotnet/standard/
  serverless-architecture/event-grid

Monitoring ACR with Azure Event Grid:

- Azure Event Grid—security and authentication: https://docs.microsoft.com/
  en-us/azure/event-grid/security-authentication

Integrating Office 365 with Azure Logic Apps:

- Office 365 connector details: https://docs.microsoft.com/en-us/connectors/
  office365connector/

Integrating Azure SQL Server with Azure Logic Apps:

- Managing Azure SQL logins: https://docs.microsoft.com/en-us/azure/sql-
  database/sql-database-manage-logins
- Bulk data transfer with logic apps: https://social.technet.microsoft.com/
  wiki/contents/articles/40060.sql-pagination-for-bulk-data-transfer-
  with-logic-apps.aspx

Managing updates for VMs:

- Update Management feature description: https://docs.microsoft.com/en-us/
  azure/automation/automation-update-management

Tracking changes in VMs:

- Change tracking description: https://docs.microsoft.com/en-us/azure/
  automation/change-tracking

Other Books You May Enjoy

If you enjoyed this book, you may be interested in these other books by Packt:

Hands-On Data Science and Python Machine Learning
Frank Kane

ISBN: 978-1-78728-074-8

- Learn how to clean your data and ready it for analysis
- Implement the popular clustering and regression methods in Python
- Train efficient machine learning models using decision trees and random forests
- Visualize the results of your analysis using Python's Matplotlib library
- Use Apache Spark's MLlib package to perform machine learning on large datasets

Kali Linux Cookbook - Second Edition
Corey P. Schultz, Bob Perciaccante

ISBN: 978-1-78439-030-3

- Acquire the key skills of ethical hacking to perform penetration testing
- Learn how to perform network reconnaissance
- Discover vulnerabilities in hosts
- Attack vulnerabilities to take control of workstations and servers
- Understand password cracking to bypass security
- Learn how to hack into wireless networks
- Attack web and database servers to exfiltrate data
- Obfuscate your command and control connections to avoid firewall and IPS detection

Leave a review - let other readers know what you think

Please share your thoughts on this book with others by leaving a review on the site that you bought it from. If you purchased the book from Amazon, please leave us an honest review on this book's Amazon page. This is vital so that other potential readers can see and use your unbiased opinion to make purchasing decisions, we can understand what our customers think about our products, and our authors can see your feedback on the title that they have worked with Packt to create. It will only take a few minutes of your time, but is valuable to other potential customers, our authors, and Packt. Thank you!

Index

A

Active Directory (AD) 392
ad hoc SAS 214
Advanced Message Queuing Protocol (AMQP) 394
application programming interfaces (APIs) 395
Availability Set
  versus Availability Zones (AZs) 366
Availability Zones (AZs)
  about 250, 366, 367
  implementing 367, 368, 369
  implementing, for high availability 366
  implementing, for virtual machines 366
  versus Availability Set 366
  working with 369, 370
Azure Active Directory tenant
  creating 153
  user, creating 150, 151, 152
Azure AD B2B
  reference link 156
Azure AD, user
  role, assigning 157, 158, 159, 160
Azure AD
  application, creating 162, 163, 164, 165
  application, registering 161
  directory roles, managing 175, 176, 177, 178, 179
  groups, creating 165, 166, 167, 168, 169, 170
  groups, managing 170, 171, 172, 173, 174, 175
  guest user, creating 153, 154
  user creation process, describing 155, 156
  users, creating 148, 149, 150
  users, monitoring and auditing 179, 180, 181, 182, 183, 184
Azure App Service
  monitoring 353, 354, 355, 356

Azure App Services
  securing, with MSI 208, 209, 210, 211, 212, 214
Azure Application Insights
  capabilities, exploring 356, 357, 358, 359, 360
Azure Blueprints
  about 22
  artifacts 28
  assigning 26, 27, 28, 29, 30, 31, 32
  assignment, using 23, 24, 26
  using, for repeatable deploy and update operations 22
Azure CLI
  peering, creating 108, 109, 111, 112, 113
Azure Container Instances (ACI)
  about 269
  VNet, enabling in 295, 296, 297
Azure Container Registry (ACR)
  about 381
  integrating, with Azure Event Grid 397, 398, 399, 400, 401
  monitoring, with Azure Event Grid 397
Azure Data Factory (ADF) 365
Azure Event Grid
  ACR, integrating with 397, 398, 399, 400, 401
  ACR, monitoring with 397
  Blob storage, monitoring with 389, 390, 391, 392, 393
  used, for automating resource group management 86
Azure file shares
  creating, concepts 322
  setting up 318, 319, 320, 321, 322
Azure Fluent 76
Azure Front Door
  about 370, 371
  instance, creating 372, 373, 374, 375

used, for managing global routing for web traffic 370

used, for monitoring global routing for web traffic 370

Azure Kubernetes Service (AKS)
  about 269
  VNet, enabling in 289, 290, 291, 292, 293, 294

Azure Logic Apps
  Azure SQL Server, integrating with 412
  FTP/SFTP servers, integrating with 402
  instance, creating 403, 404, 405, 406
  Office 365, integrating with 408, 409, 410, 411, 412
  working with 412, 413, 414, 415, 416, 417

Azure Policy
  examples 21, 22
  validation results 20, 21
  working with 17, 18, 19

Azure portal
  peering, creating 105, 106, 107, 108

Azure Resource Manager (ARM) templates, tools
  Azure Fluent 76
  Pulumi 76
  Terraform 76

Azure Resource Manager (ARM) templates
  about 71
  automation scripts 74, 75
  reference link 72
  tools 76, 77
  used, for performing deployments 70, 71, 72
  writing 72, 73

Azure resources
  access, configuring 202, 203, 204, 206

Azure Service Fabric cluster
  features, reference link 195
  securing 190, 191, 192, 193, 194, 195

Azure services
  securing, with service endpoints 125

Azure SQL Server
  integrating, with Azure Logic Apps 412

Azure SQL
  backup, implementing 360
  databases, backing up 360, 361, 362, 363
  server and database, creating 360

Azure Storage accounts
  alerts 338
  creating 125, 126
  finding logs, enabling 310, 311, 312, 313, 314, 315
  monitoring logs, enabling 310, 311, 312, 313, 314, 315
  network access, configuring 306, 307, 308, 309, 310
  reference link 315
  replication mode, selecting 316, 317, 318
  replication, managing 315, 316
  security, enabling 336, 337, 338, 339

Azure Storage services
  monitoring 349, 350, 351, 352, 353

Azure Storage
  account data, backing up 364, 365, 366
  backup, implementing 364

Azure subscription, types
  Microsoft sponsorship subscriptions 16
  Visual Studio subscriptions 16

Azure subscription
  Cloud Solution Provider (CSP) 11, 12, 13
  Enterprise Agreement (EA) 13
  obtaining 8, 9
  Pay-As-You-Go (PAYG) 9, 10, 11
  subscription models 14, 15, 16
  types 16

Azure Virtual Machines
  about 347, 348, 349
  automation account, creating 384, 385, 386, 387, 388, 389
  creating 342, 343, 344
  monitoring 342
  monitoring, enabling 344, 345, 346, 347
  starting, in off-hours 382
  stopping, in off-hours 382
  working with 382, 383, 384

Azure
  data, transferring from on-premises to 324, 325, 326, 327, 328

B

Blob storage, monitoring with Azure Event Grid
  setup, extending 393, 394, 395, 396, 397

Blob storage
  monitoring, with Azure Event Grid 389, 390,

391, 392, 393

C

Cloud Solution Provider (CSP)
about 8, 11, 12, 13
reference link 12
Container Networking Interface (CNI) 289
Core Infrastructure Suite (CIS) 15
cost management
analyzing 36, 37, 38, 39
Azure Advisor 43, 44
budgets 40, 41, 42, 43
cost analysis 39
monitoring 36, 37, 38, 39
Cross-Origin Resource Sharing (CORS) 21
custom role
creating 198, 199, 200, 201, 202

D

data disks
adding 230
creating 231, 232, 233
DDoS protection
configuring 285, 286, 287, 288
Desired State Configuration (DSC)
using 236, 237, 238, 239, 240, 241, 242
DNS zone
creating 132, 133, 134
DNS
configuring, within VNet 134, 135, 136

E

Enterprise Agreement (EA) 8, 13
Enterprise Enrollment 15
ephemeral disks
reference link 230
Event Grid schema
reference link 87

F

File Transfer Protocol/Secure File Transfer Protocol
(FTP/SFTP) 381
FTP/SFTP servers, integrating with Azure Logic
App

Azure Logic App instance, creating 403, 404,
405, 406
setup 406, 407
FTP/SFTP servers
integrating, with Azure Logic Apps 402

G

General Availability (GA) 22, 257
Geographically Redundant Storage (GRS) 315
global routing
managing, for web traffic with Azure Front Door
370
monitoring, for web traffic with Azure Front Door
370
guest user features
reference link 156

H

high availability (HA)
configuring 250, 251, 252
HyperText Transfer Protocol (HTTP) 394

I

Identity and Access Management (IAM) 202, 400
Infrastructure as Code (IaC) 70, 236
Internet Information Services (IIS) 238

J

jumpbox 260

L

load balancing
capabilities 270
implementing 270, 271, 272, 273, 274, 275,
276, 277
methods 271
Locally Redundant Storage (LRS) 315
Logic App
creating, reference link 90
low or no network bandwidth
about 323, 324
data, transferring from on-premises to Azure
324, 325, 326, 327, 328
large datasets, transferring with 322

M

Managed Identity (MI) 206
Managed Service Identity (MSI)
  configuring 206, 207, 208
  identities, types 207
  used, for securing Azure App Services 208, 209,
  210, 211, 212, 214
management automation
  implementing 44, 45, 46, 47, 48, 49, 50, 51, 52,
  53, 54
medium or high network bandwidth
  about 328, 329, 330, 331
  available options 332
  large datasets, transferring with 328
Message Queuing Telemetry Transport (MQTT)
  394
MFA authentication
  enabling 184, 185, 186, 187, 188, 189, 190
  reference link 190
Microsoft sponsorship subscriptions 16
Multi-Factor Authentication (MFA) 184

N

naming resolutions
  configuring 132
Network Address Translation (NAT) 291
network interface (NIC)
  about 234
  adding 234, 235, 236
Network Security Groups (NSGs)
  about 101, 234
  adding, to subnet 137, 138, 139, 140
  configuring 136
  creating 136
Network Watcher, features
  Connection troubleshoot 282, 283, 284
  Effective security rules 281
  IP flow verify 280, 281
  Next hop 281
  Packet capture 282, 283, 284
  VPN troubleshoot 282, 283, 284
Network Watcher
  monitoring and diagnosing 277, 278, 279
NSG rules

adding 142, 143, 144
reviewing 140, 141, 142

O

Office 365
  integrating, with Azure Logic Apps 408, 409,
  410, 411, 412
Operations Management Suite (OMS) 387

P

Partition Key (PK) 220
Pay-As-You-Go (PAYG)
  about 8, 9, 10, 11
  reference link 10
periodic data transfer
  exploring 333, 334, 335, 336
Platform-as-a-Service (PaaS) 353, 412
pricing calculator
  about 37
  reference link 37
Pulumi 76

Q

quotas
  usage and management, checking 33, 34, 35,
  36

R

RDP
  used, for connecting to VMs 262, 263, 264
Redis Cache
  VNet, enabling in 298, 299, 300, 301, 302, 303
representational state transfer (REST)
  reference link 389
resource group locks 82, 83, 84, 85
resource group management, automating with
  Azure Event Grid
  event subscription, creating 86, 87, 88, 89
  gathered data, analyzing 89, 91, 92, 93, 94
resource group management
  automating, with Azure Event Grid 86
resource groups
  available resources, listing 66, 67
  browsing 64, 65, 66

managing 62, 63, 64
resources, moving 67, 68, 69
resource locks
    delete 78
    implementing 78, 79
    read-only 78
    resource group locks 78, 82, 83, 84, 85
    subscription locks 78, 79, 80, 81
resource naming conventions
    implementing 94, 95
    resource group 96, 97
    resources 97, 98
    subscription 95, 96
resource provider (RP)
    about 69, 70
    managing 58, 59, 60, 61, 62
Role-Based Access Control (RBAC) 132, 202, 339
Row Key (RK) 220

S

SAS tokens
    generating, for different services 218, 219, 220, 222, 223, 224, 225, 226, 227
Server and Cloud Enrollment (SCE)
    about 15
    components 15
Server-Side Request Forgery (SSRF) 211
service endpoints
    configuring 128, 129, 130, 131
    creating 127, 128
    used, for securing Azure services 125
Service Level Agreement (SLA) 300
Shared Access Policies
    creating 215, 216, 217, 218
    managing 215, 216, 217, 218
    revoking 214, 215
    using 214, 215
Shared Access Signature (SAS) 214
SSH
    used, for connecting to VMs 262, 263, 264
Structured Query Language (SQL) 412
subnets
    configuring 119, 120, 122, 123, 124, 125
    creating 119, 120, 121, 122

network security group (NSG), adding to 137
    used, for creating VNet 136, 137
Subscription Enrollment 15
subscription locks 79, 80, 81
subscription models 14, 15, 16
subscription policies
    implementing 16

T

Terraform 76
Total Cost of Ownership (TCO) calculator
    about 37
    reference link 37

V

Virtual Hard Disks (VHDs) 233
Virtual Machine Scale Set (VMSS) 242, 272
Virtual Machines (VMs), monitoring
    capabilities, extending 246, 247, 248
    configuring 244
    connection monitor, enabling 248, 249
    guest-level monitoring, configuring 244, 245
Virtual Machines (VMs)
    about 270, 381
    access, securing to 258, 259, 260
    Availability Zones, implementing for 366
    backup plans, designing 375, 376, 377, 378
    changes, tracking 423, 424, 425, 426, 427
    connecting to 260, 261, 262
    feature, enabling for multiple machines 422
    scaling caveats 243
    scaling out 242, 243
    scaling up 242, 243
    Update Management feature, using 417, 418, 419, 420, 421
    updates, managing 417
Virtual Network (VNet), connecting
    about 114
    different resource groups 117, 118, 119
    same resource group 115, 116, 117
Virtual Network (VNet)
    about 234, 271, 306
    creating 120, 125, 126
    creating, with subnet 136, 137
    DNS, configuring within 134, 135, 136

enabling, in Azure Container Instances (ACI) 295, 296, 297

enabling, in Azure Kubernetes Service (AKS) 289, 290, 291, 292, 293, 294

enabling, in Redis Cache 298, 299, 300, 301, 302, 303

in multiple regions 114

in single region 113, 114

Visual Studio subscriptions 16

VM deployment
  about 252
  resources, deploying with tools 256, 257, 258
  solutions, browsing 253, 254, 255

VNet peering
  configuring 102, 103, 104, 105

creating 102, 103, 104, 105

VNet-to-VNet connection
  configuring 113
  creating 113

W

Web Application Firewall (WAF) 277, 375

web traffic
  global routing, managing with Azure Front Door 370
  global routing, monitoring with Azure Front Door 370

Z

Zone Redundant Storage (ZRS) 315